# When the
# Moon Set
# Over Haifa

# When the Moon Set Over Haifa

**ANGELINA DILIBERTO ALLEN**

BAHÁ'Í
PUBLISHING
WILMETTE, ILLINOIS

Bahá'í Publishing, Wilmette, Illinois

401 Greenleaf Ave, Wilmette, Illinois 60091
Copyright © 2021 by the National Spiritual Assembly
of the Bahá'ís of the United States
All rights reserved. Published 2021
Printed in the United States of America ∞

25   24   23   22     3   4   5

Library of Congress Cataloging-in-Publication Data

Names: Allen, Angelina Diliberto, author.
Title: When the moon set over Haifa / Angelina Diliberto Allen.
Description: Wilmette, Illinois : Bahá'í Publishing, [2021] |
    Includes bibliographical references.
Identifiers: LCCN 2021025056 (print) | LCCN 2021025057
    (ebook) | ISBN 9781618512048 (paperback) | ISBN
    9781618512055 (epub)
Subjects: LCSH: Bahais—Biography. | 'Abdu'l-Bahá, 1844–
    1921—Death and burial.
Classification: LCC BP390 .A435 2021  (print) | LCC BP390
    (ebook) | DDC 297.9/3092—dc23
LC record available at https://lccn.loc.gov/2021025056
LC ebook record available at https://lccn.loc.gov/2021025057

Cover design by Carlos Esparza
Cover photo by Farzam Sabetian
Book design by Patrick Falso

He is, and should for all time be regarded, first and foremost, as the Center and Pivot of Bahá'u'lláh's peerless and all-enfolding Covenant, His most exalted handiwork, the stainless Mirror of His light, the perfect Exemplar of His teachings, the unerring Interpreter of His Word, the embodiment of every Bahá'í ideal, the incarnation of every Bahá'í virtue, the Most Mighty Branch sprung from the Ancient Root, the Limb of the Law of God, the Being *"round Whom all names revolve,"* the Mainspring of the Oneness of Humanity, the Ensign of the Most Great Peace, the Moon of the Central Orb of this most holy Dispensation—styles and titles that are implicit and find their truest, their highest and fairest expression in the magic name 'Abdu'l-Bahá.

—Shoghi Effendi, *The World Order of Bahá'u'lláh,* p. 134

# Acknowledgments

The completion of this work involved the help of many members of my family. Thanks go to my husband, Andrew Allen; his parents, John Kenton and Mary Allen; my father, Edward N. Diliberto; and two of my sisters, Dawn Diliberto Shelley and Marguerite Diliberto Bulkin, for the hours of conversations we shared about the significance of the centenary of the passing of 'Abdu'l-Bahá and the public reading of His Will and Testament.

Much gratitude is owed to friends near and far who took an interest in reading early drafts of this work and who helped me piece together important information: Sheila Wolcott Banani, Kit Bigelow, Heidi Davis, Omid Ghaemmaghami, Kathryn Jewett Hogenson, Larry Hosack, Shirin Fozi, Joel S. Nizin, Brent Poirier, Bette Roberts, Robert Stockman, and Sonjel Vreeland.

Some of the research for this book led me to find new friendships in Germany, and I would like to give particular thanks to the German National Bahá'í Archive and Library Committee.

The research for this project could not have been accomplished without the help of the U.S. National Spiritual Assembly's archivist, Edward Sevcik. My deepest thanks go to Nat Yogachandra and Bahhaj Taherzadeh at the U.S. Bahá'í Publishing Trust for their encouragement and to Christopher Martin for his keen insights, clarity of thought, fine editing, and most important of all, his joyful spirit.

Finally, a very special expression of gratitude to Carol Kelsey Rutstein, daughter of Curtis Kelsey, whose life is a reminder that the events commemorated in this book were not so long ago.

# Contents

# Note to the Reader

The Tablets from 'Abdu'l-Bahá to individual believers cited in this book are obtained from the U.S. Bahá'í Archives. While some of the translations of the Tablets may have been revised in later years, in most cases throughout this book, the original translation of the Tablets has been used. This is for historical purposes and for the purpose of understanding the events in the lives of the people mentioned in this book. The English translations made at the time of the original Tablet and sent to the recipient with the original are published here as historical documents, not as authorized translations.

Furthermore, Shoghi Effendi on numerous occasions cautioned against attributing too great an importance to pilgrims' notes—or the personal impression of 'Abdu'l-Bahá's words from an individual believer: "It was chiefly in view of the misleading nature of the reports of the informal conversations of 'Abdu'l-Bahá with visiting pilgrims, that I have insistently urged the believers of the West to regard such statements as merely personal impressions of the sayings of their Master, and to quote and consider as authentic only such translations as are based upon the authenticated text of His recorded utterances in the original tongue."\*

Further guidance regarding the use of pilgrims' notes can be found in a letter dated October 2, 1935, written on behalf of Shoghi Effendi to the National Spiritual Assembly of the United States and Canada: "He would also urge you to attach no importance to the stories told about 'Abdu'l-Bahá or to those attributed to Him by the Friends. These should be regarded in the same light as the notes and impressions of visiting pilgrims. They need not be suppressed, but they also should not be given prominence or official recognition."\*\*

The Universal House of Justice has made clear that the Bahá'í Faith has two sources of authoritative interpretation: 'Abdu'l-Bahá, Whose authority is derived from His appointment in the Kitáb-i-Aqdas and the Kitáb-i-'Ahd (Book of the Covenant) as the Center of Bahá'u'lláh's Covenant; and the Guardian, whose authority is derived from 'Abdu'l-Bahá's Will and Testament:

> A clear distinction is made in our Faith between authoritative interpretation and the interpretation or understanding that each individual arrives at for himself from his study of its teachings. While the former is confined to the Guardian, the latter, according to the guidance given to us by the Guardian himself, should by no means be suppressed. In fact such individual interpretation is considered the fruit of man's rational power and conducive to a better understanding of the teach-

---

\* Shoghi Effendi, *The World Order of Bahá'u'lláh*, p. 5.
\*\* Shoghi Effendi, *Directives from the Guardian*, p. 1.

ings, provided that no disputes or arguments arise among the friends and the individual himself understands and makes it clear that his views are merely his own. Individual interpretations continually change as one grows in comprehension of the teachings. As Shoghi Effendi explained: "To deepen in the Cause means to read the writings of Bahá'u'lláh and the Master so thoroughly as to be able to give it to others in its pure form. There are many who have some superficial idea of what the Cause stands for. They, therefore, present it together with all sorts of ideas that are their own. As the Cause is still in its early days we must be most careful lest we fall under this error and injure the Movement we so much adore. There is no limit to the study of the Cause. The more we read the Writings the more truths we can find in them and the more we will see that our previous notions were erroneous." So, although individual insights can be enlightening and helpful, they can also be misleading. The friends must therefore learn to listen to the views of others without being over-awed or allowing their faith to be shaken, and to express their own views without pressing them on their fellow Bahá'ís.*

A final note should be added about the transliteration of Bahá'í terms and the names Bahá'u'lláh, 'Abdu'l-Bahá, and spellings of the salutation Alláh-u-Abhá. In a letter dated April 8, 1923, the Guardian established a universal standard for transliteration of Bahá'í terms: "[The Guardian] has given the list of the best known

---

* The Universal House of Justice, letter dated May 27, 1966, cited in *Messages from the Universal House of Justice, 1965–1986*, no. 35.13.

and most current Bahá'í terms, and other Oriental names and expressions, all properly and accurately transliterated, the faithful spelling of which by all the Western friends will avoid confusion in [the] future, and insure in the matter a uniformity which is greatly needed in all Bahá'í literature."*

For historical purposes in this book, the majority of Bahá'í terms and names mentioned in documents prior to 1923 have been kept in their original transliterated form; nevertheless, some of these spellings have been changed to the spelling outlined by the Guardian in order to avoid confusion.

---

* Shoghi Effendi, *Bahá'í Administration*, p. 43.

# Introduction

This publication has been prepared to commemorate the one hundredth anniversary of the ascension of 'Abdu'l-Bahá and the one hundredth anniversary of the public reading of the Will and Testament of 'Abdu'l-Bahá. Contained in these pages are the recollections of the six Western Bahá'ís who were present in Haifa at the time of the passing of 'Abdu'l-Bahá and who were also present at the public reading of His Will and Testament, a document so potent that "it needs a century of actual working before the treasures of wisdom hidden in it can be revealed. . . ."[1]

The distance of one hundred years does not diminish our historical proximity to these events, yet the depth of a century gives us a more comprehensive realization of the unrivalled uniqueness of the person of 'Abdu'l-Bahá. Never in religious history has there been such a figure as 'Abdu'l-Bahá. He was the son of Bahá'u'lláh, the Prophet-Founder of the Bahá'í Faith—a Faith destined to usher in a new cycle in religious history. Bahá'u'lláh enjoined His followers to turn to 'Abdu'l-Bahá as the "perfect exemplar" of His teachings.[2] In His Book of the Covenant, Bahá'u'lláh established a Covenant between Himself and His followers where He made clear that, after His passing, His followers must turn to His son 'Abdu'l-Bahá as the Center of the Covenant and appointed head of His Cause.

In a ministry that lasted twenty-nine years, from 1892 to 1921, 'Abdu'l-Bahá advanced the Cause of Bahá'u'lláh by developing a worldwide teaching campaign to spread His Father's spiritual principles to every corner of the globe, united the followers of Bahá'u'lláh in the East and established the Cause of Bahá'u'lláh in the West, and left a Will and Testament in which He specified the administrative and institutional framework through which the World Order of Bahá'u'lláh will be realized.

'Abdu'l-Bahá was born on May 23, 1844—the very night in which this new religious cycle was born. It was the night in which the Báb declared Himself as the Herald of "Him Whom God shall make manifest" Who was no other than Bahá'u'lláh, the "Glory of God," the Promised One of all ages.[3] The Báb proclaimed that He was a Messenger of God and that humanity stood at the threshold of the beginning of a new religious cycle in which the Promised One, Bahá'u'lláh, would fulfill the religious prophecies of the last five thousand years and initiate a new religious cycle in which humanity would advance toward the next stage of its development, which is the "unification of all the peoples of the world into one universal family."[4]

This "Bahá'í cycle," wrote 'Abdu'l-Bahá, is "a cycle that must extend over a period of at least five hundred thousand years."[5] It is a cycle born out of the completion of the Adamic cycle, a cycle that began with Adam and concluded with Muḥammad, a cycle in which the succession of religious teaching was progressive, a cycle in which God guided His creation through a progression of spiritual teachers, each with laws and precepts that advanced civilization through each of its successive stages.

If we scan the history of religion over the past five thousand years, one can see how Divine Revelation has been progressive in nature.[6] We know that five thousand years ago, Krishna advanced the understanding that all existence is one reality, and that all parts or divisions are, in essence, part of one whole existence.[7]

Commensurate with the teachings of Krishna, the Prophet Abraham advanced the concept of monotheism—the concept that there was only one God.[8]

Following Abraham was Moses, the Law-Giver. He made clear the distinction between God-given laws and man-made laws, so that the peoples of the world would come to trust in the idea of the infallibility of God's guidance for His creation.[9]

Following Moses was Zoroaster, Who lived three thousand years ago. At the center of His teachings was the exercise of one's free will to choose between good and evil, truth and falsehood.[10]

Buddha advanced the idea that a human being has the capacity to develop spiritually through a meditative process that leads to harmony between both body and soul in perfect equanimity and awareness.[11]

Over two thousand years ago, Jesus Christ introduced the concept that God's Word was not only taught through His divine Messengers but was manifested in the Divine Messenger Himself.[12]

This succession of divine prophecy from Krishna, Abraham, Moses, Zoroaster, Buddha, and Jesus Christ was concluded by Muhammad, the "Seal of the Prophets," Who taught there is only one God and through Whom the divine lineage of more than five thousand years of the prophetic cycle was sealed and divine prophecy complete.[13]

From our point of view today, it is clear that humanity has matured toward higher stations of spiritual and societal development by way of the religious teachings of these Divine Teachers. Each of these Divine Messengers suffered persecution, banishment, and degradation for the sake of God's Will. The result of such suffering was the lasting transformation of the civilization in which that divine Teacher appeared.

The purpose of the Báb's mission was to prepare humanity for the advent of Bahá'u'lláh, the "Promised One of all Ages," Whose divinely ordained laws and ordinances would break from the religious traditions of the past and usher in a new civilization on earth. The Báb was the Herald of the Dispensation of Bahá'u'lláh—a Dispensation characterized by the vision and promise that the human race will become one and that a global civilization of peace and justice, and of prosperity and well-being, will be established on earth.

The Báb did not come to reform the religions of the past. He came to usher in the fulfillment of the religious prophecies of the past five thousand years, from Abraham to Muḥammad. The Báb explained that humankind is created with the God-given capacity to accept those very teachings that will guide humanity to the next stage of human development.[14] It is no surprise then that the word "Báb" means "Gate"—a door, an entryway, a portal—through which humanity may enter the next stage of its development.[15]

That is not to say that the Báb's message was readily accepted in nineteenth-century Persia. In fact, the Báb was not only opposed by Persia's government and its Islamic clerics, He was eventually put to death by their malevolent efforts to quell the spread of the Báb's teachings—teachings that were revolutionary at the time and only a precursor to the world-unifying teachings of Bahá'u'lláh.

The Báb upheld the importance of science and praised the cultural and scientific developments of the West. He called for the setting aside of animosity between religions, and summoned humanity to embrace the independent investigation of truth. The most progressive of His teachings was His call for the advancement of women and the need for universal education.[16] One of the Báb's most prominent followers was the Persian poetess Ṭáhirih, who, in a dramatic gesture inspired by the teachings of the Báb, appeared unveiled in public. Her bold, courageous and outspoken support of the teachings of the Báb eventually led to her arrest and murder by the Islamic authorities. To her executioner she said, "You may kill me as soon as you like but you cannot stop the emancipation of women."[17]

The Báb's ministry—a ministry focused on preparing His followers for the advent of "Him Whom God shall make manifest," Who was none other than Bahá'u'lláh, the Promised One, the Glory of God, the Prince of Peace, the Desire of the World—lasted six years. The prophetic fulfillment expected by the Hindus, the Buddhists, the Zoroastrians, the Christians, the Muslims, and the Jews is manifest in Bahá'u'lláh:

> To Israel He [Bahá'u'lláh] was neither more nor less than the incarnation of the "Everlasting Father," the "Lord of Hosts" come down "with ten thousands of saints"; to Christendom Christ returned "in the glory of the Father"; to Shí'ah Islám the return of the Imám Ḥusayn; to Sunní Islám the descent of the "Spirit of God" (Jesus Christ); to the Zoroastrians the promised Sháh-Bahrám; to the Hindus the reincarnation of Krishna; to the Buddhists the fifth Buddha.[18]

Bahá'u'lláh's teachings and laws promise a significant advancement in the way we live on earth. A study of the writings of Bahá'u'lláh will persuade the fair-minded observer that such laws and teachings must originate from God, for the power to advance civilization is given to God alone to actualize through His chosen Manifestation for this Day. Therefore, Bahá'u'lláh proclaimed the will of God when He announced that this is the day of the independent investigation of truth, the reconciliation of science and religion, and the recognition that all the divinely ordained religions are the members of one common Faith. This is the day for the elimination of extremes of wealth and poverty, the elimination of religious and social prejudices, and the equality of women and men. This is the day of racial harmony, of the application of spiritual solutions to social and economic problems, and of the emergence of world citizenship. This is the day of the unity of nations and the selection of a universal language by which all the peoples of the earth shall converse together. This is the day for the refinement of the human brain, the extension of human inventions, and the raising of the standard of physical health. This is the day for humanity to be liberated from the curse of war. In short, this is the day for the furtherance of the intellectual, moral, and spiritual life of the human race.[19]

The uniqueness of the day in which we live is that we bear witness to the rapid disintegration of the religious doctrines of the past and the slow and steady implementation of new religious teachings arising gradually through stages of crisis and victory. These twin processes move civilization closer and closer to its distant yet glorious destiny. Rapid transformation would only result in transient change; therefore, the civilization envisaged by Bahá'u'lláh will take root gradually, thereby giving it permanence. It is as if the world passes through spring—when the Manifestation of God declares His mission—into the summer, when the heat of His divine teachings illuminate humanity. During the darkest and most perilous days of 'Abdu'l-Bahá's ministry—when opposition to the revolutionary teachings of Bahá'u'lláh seemed at its height—'Abdu'l-Bahá wrote, "'Whatsoever is latent in the innermost of this holy cycle shall gradually appear and be made manifest, for now is but the beginning of its growth and the dayspring of the revelation of its signs.'"[20]

This new religious cycle can be imagined as a banner unfurling before our eyes. Emblazoned on this banner is the name of the Báb—the Herald of this new cycle—and the name of Bahá'u'lláh—the Glory of God—crowning its unfurled edges. If the Revelation of Bahá'ulláh can be imagined as such an emblem upon which is written God's commandments for this day, then it was 'Abdu'l-Bahá who would carry this emblem from its origin in the East to the far reaches of the West. Indeed, 'Abdu'l-Bahá did more than carry the message of Bahá'u'lláh to the West; He established it in the very heart of the North American continent. Of this achievement, Shoghi Effendi wrote:

'Abdu'l-Bahá's historic journeys to the West, and in particular His eight-month tour of the United States of America, may be said to have marked the culmination of His ministry, a ministry whose untold blessings and stupendous achievements only future generations can adequately estimate. As the day-star of Bahá'u'lláh's Revelation had shone forth in its meridian splendor at the hour of the proclamation of His Message to the rulers of the earth in the city of Adrianople, so did the Orb of His Covenant mount its zenith and shed its brightest rays when He Who was its appointed Center arose to blazon the glory and greatness of His Father's Faith among the peoples of the West.[21]

The passing of 'Abdu'l-Bahá marked the close of an historical period known as the Heroic Age of the Bahá'í Faith. The Heroic Age was a period that began with the Declaration of the Báb on the evening of May 22, 1844 and concluded with the ascension of 'Abdu'l-Bahá on November 28, 1921. It was in the Heroic Age that "the life of the Cause had been generated," and "in which its greatest heroes had struggled and quaffed the cup of martyrdom" and "whose splendors no victories in this or any future age, however brilliant, can rival."[22] This period of heroism was followed by the "Formative Age" of the Cause of Bahá'u'lláh—an age that shall stretch "over a vast period of time" and witness the rise and establishment of the divinely ordained Administrative Order of the Cause, until it reaches the fringes of the "Golden Age" of the Cause which will ultimately lead to "the establishment of the Most Great Peace, to the World Bahá'í Commonwealth" and to the "birth and efflorescence of a world civilization."[23] Therefore, this commemoration marking the hundredth anniversary of the passing of 'Abdu'l-Bahá is also a commemoration marking the hundredth anniversary of the Formative Age of the Revelation of Bahá'u'lláh.

If Bahá'u'lláh can be likened to the sun that manifests God's "most divine essence," then 'Abdu'l-Bahá can be likened to the moon, which reflects the light of the sun, mirroring the divine light of Bahá'u'lláh's teachings.[24] Shoghi Effendi wrote that 'Abdu'l-Bahá was "the Moon of the Central Orb of this most holy Dispensation."[25] The night of 'Abdu'l-Bahá's ascension was a night of the waning moon, which illustrates the profound darkness that was felt

8

by those who were present at the time of the passing of 'Abdu'l-Bahá. The darkness would be only temporary, for the passing of 'Abdu'l-Bahá marked the dramatic opening of the Formative Age, a period in the history of humanity that will witness the unfoldment of a religious cycle that will last half a million years.[26]

There were six Western believers in Haifa on the night of the ascension of 'Abdu'l-Bahá: Mr. John Bosch and Mrs. Louise Stapfer Bosch from Geyserville, California; Dr. Florian Krug and Mrs. Grace Krug from New York, and Fraulein Johanna Hauff from Stuttgart. All of them were there as pilgrims. The only other Western believer present in Haifa was Mr. Curtis Kelsey from New York, who was in Haifa to install electrical power plants to light the shrines of the Báb and Bahá'u'lláh. Because of the profound significance of the events that unfolded before, during, and after the passing of 'Abdu'l-Bahá, it is important to understand something about the lives of these six Western believers who were present at the time of His ascension.

This book tells the story of these believers, how they became Bahá'ís, the circumstances that led them to Haifa, and how their experience at the time of the ascension of 'Abdu'l-Bahá shaped their path of service to the Cause of God. The intent is to give the reader the feeling of being in the holy land, one hundred years ago, when the moon of 'Abdu'l-Bahá set over Haifa.

# 1 / John and Louise Bosch

This is the story of the Western believers who were in Haifa on the night of the passing of 'Abdu'l-Bahá. They were Mr. Curtis Kelsey, Fräulein Johanna Hauff, Dr. Florian Krug, Mrs. Grace Krug, Mr. John D. Bosch, and Mrs. Louise Bosch.

Mr. Curtis Kelsey of New York was staying in a small room in the back of the Western Pilgrim House at 4 Haparsim Street. He was called to Haifa to install an electrical system to illuminate the shrines of the Báb and Bahá'u'lláh.

Fräulein Johanna Hauff from Stuttgart, Germany, was there as a pilgrim and stayed at the Western Pilgrim House. On the night of the ascension, she was given permission to stay in the house of 'Abdu'l-Bahá.

Dr. Florian Krug and his wife Mrs. Grace Crossman Krug were staying in the house of 'Abdu'l-Bahá at 7 Haparsim Street. The Krugs were from New York, and although they were in Haifa as pilgrims, they had plans to live in Haifa indefinitely. Dr. Florian Krug hoped to serve as physician to the family of 'Abdu'l-Bahá.

Mr. John D. Bosch and his wife Mrs. Louise Stapfer Bosch stayed in the Western Pilgrim House. They had recently completed a successful short-term pioneering trip to the island of Tahiti, and upon their return to California, they had asked 'Abdu'l-Bahá for permission to come on pilgrimage. 'Abdu'l-Bahá responded on April 8, 1921 in a telegram that read "Bosches permitted, Abbas."[1] By the end of April, 1921, they set out on a journey to Haifa, which was preceded by a modest teaching trip through Europe, where they visited the regions of their childhood. They traveled through France, Switzerland, Germany, and Italy, and they reached Haifa on November 14, 1921. For Louise, it was her second pilgrimage. For John, it was his first. They would be among the last pilgrims to be in the physical presence of the Master.

John David Bosch was born in St. Gallen, Switzerland in 1855 and apprenticed in the wine-making industry. He immigrated to the United States in 1879 where he lived with his sister in Nebraska. In 1887 he moved to California, became a United Stated citizen, and in 1901 bought forty-five acres of land in Geyserville, California. Although he worked in the wine industry in Sonoma County, his own property was used for producing nonalcoholic grape juice.

He learned of the Bahá'í Faith in 1903 when he was on a train from San Francisco to Cloverdale, California. One of the passengers was reading a book about 'Abdu'l-Bahá. Upon inquiring about the book, John was cautioned by the passenger that to hear of this Cause was the greatest privilege but that it would be followed up by the greatest obligations, and it would be better for John if he did not know of the Cause if he could not follow its principles.[2] Such a serious caution increased John's interest, and he asked how he might learn more. He was told that he would have to contact Mrs. Helen Goodall in Oakland. Of that first encounter, John explained, "I called on Mrs. Goodall early in 1904 on Jackson Street in Oakland (California) and she gave me the first inspiring words and explanations of the Báb, Bahá'u'lláh, and 'Abdu'l-Bahá."[3]

After studying the teachings for a year, John asked Mrs. Goodall how he might write to 'Abdu'l-Bahá and declare his belief in the teachings of Bahá'u'lláh. At that time, new believers wishing to declare their Faith communicated directly with 'Abdu'l-Bahá. Therefore, writing such a communication to 'Abdu'l-Bahá meant learning how to convey one's feelings in a manner worthy of such a declaration of Faith while at the same time allowing for a freedom of expression removed from ritual and unfettered by sanctimony and pretense. Mrs. Goodall explained there was no prescribed form in which to express himself to 'Abdu'l-Bahá and suggested to John that he write to 'Abdu'l-Bahá in his own way. Bahá'u'lláh taught that every human being is endowed with a soul capable of recognizing God. He wrote, "I have perfected in every one of you My creation, so that the excellence of My handiwork may be fully revealed unto men. It follows, therefore, that every man hath been, and will continue to be, able of himself to appreciate the Beauty of God, the Glorified." Therefore, Bahá'u'lláh concludes in this passage, "the faith of no man can be conditioned by anyone except himself."[4]

Over the next week, John prepared himself to write to 'Abdu'l-Bahá and declare himself a believer. Shoghi Effendi, Guardian of the Bahá'í Faith, has explained that "when a person becomes a Bahá'í, he gives up the past only in the sense that he is a part of this new and living Faith of God, and must seek to pattern himself, in act and thought, along the lines laid down by Bahá'u'lláh."[5] Upon becoming a Bahá'í, John would try to pattern himself in accordance with the high standards of the Bahá'í teachings.

In the morning hours of May 29, 1905, a holy day marking the eighteenth year since the passing of Bahá'u'lláh, John wrote to 'Abdu'l-Bahá. The letter was handwritten in John's elegant penstrokes. Each letter was shaped like a mistral leaning eastward, and each word bore the appearance of a light breeze flowing over a landscape. John's words were characteristically unpretentious yet fully expressive of his soul's desire:

Geyserville, California
Allah'o Abha
In God's Name,
To the Greatest Branch:
   I believe in the existence of an Almighty Power, of which we all are created and descendants.
   By degree and choices we had manifestations and I sincerely believe that Thou art one of this higher exalted manifestations of the Universal Power.
   Thy teachings are proof of the continuance of the spiritual evolution and may my name be entered in the Great Book of this Universal Life is my earnest request.
   My watchword will be "Justice."
Humbly Thy servant,
John D. Bosch
May 29, 1905[6]

In less than a fortnight, 'Abdu'l-Bahá replied to John in a Tablet written in Persian. Both the Persian Tablet and its English translation were sent to John in the care of Helen Goodall:

Convey longing greetings from me to Mr. John D. Bosch and say:
"O thou John D. Bosch!
Raise the Call of the Kingdom and give the glad tidings to

the people. Guide them to the Tree of Life, so that they may
gather the fruits from that Tree and attain the great Bounty."
Signed: Abdul-Baha Abbas
Acca June 11, 1905
Translated by Mirzá Ameen Ullah Fareed,
Chicago, December 23, 1906[7]

John David Bosch and Louise Stapfer Bosch were both from
Switzerland, but they did not meet there. Instead, they met in the
United States at the suggestion of their mutual Bahá'í friends, Mr.
Edward and Mrs. Lua Getsinger. Louise was born in Zurich on July
11, 1870. She said that when she was nineteen years old, she came
to New York in 1889 and "full of Swiss determination and industry,
and brimming with hope and the idealism of youth. Homeopathy
was my field of interest and I longed to be a source of healing and
comfort to the distressed."[8]

Louise became a Bahá'í through the teaching efforts of Miss
Fanny S. Montague of Dobbs Ferry, New York. Louise explained
that Miss Montague was "the first who spoke to me of the Cause
of God. May my soul be a ransom to her! She connected me with
Miss Sarah Farmer, the founder of Green Acre, whom I followed to
Green Acre where a new life opened for me."[9] In addition to Miss
Sarah Farmer, Louise had the good fortune of meeting several other
Bahá'ís who helped her study the teachings, particularly Mrs. Lua
Getsinger.

Of all the Bahá'ís with whom Lua kept close contact, Lua
claimed that there were five special friends with whom she felt the
deepest spiritual connection, and she referred to them as "a glorious collection of souls": Mary Lucas, Juliet Thompson, Mariam
Haney, May Maxwell, and Louise Stapfer (Bosch).[10] Many years

later, Louise reflected on that moment of becoming a Bahá'í and wrote, "How fortunate I was to find the Faith of Bahá'u'lláh in 1901, just as I entered my 30's. It filled me with a zeal to serve and a recognition of how privileged one is to be part of the beginning of a New Order."[11] Louise wrote to 'Abdu'l-Bahá to declare herself a believer and received the following Tablet from the Master, dated 1904:

The Maid Servant of God, Louise

O thou who art advancing towards God!

Verily the Cause is great and the Lord is Merciful and Clement. Trust in the Grace of Thy Lord, and be firm in love for Him who has created thee and made thee. The veils shall be removed, the shining lamp shall beam, the clouds shall be dispelled, the lights of the Sun of love shall appear on the horizons and God shall grant thy wishes and give thee the power of deeds.

It is incumbent upon thee to depend wholly upon the Center of Lights, and call out for love, universal peace and harmony amongst the people in the East of the earth and its West, so that the foundation of rancor may be destroyed and the edifice of love and faithfulness be set up, and that the heavenly powers may govern the mortal sentiments and the merciful feelings may become manifest in the human realities.

This is becoming of those maidservants of God, who are attracted to that Beauty which is shining from the Horizon of the Kingdom of God upon the world.

Upon thee be greeting and praise.[12]

In 1909, Louise Stapfer made a pilgrimage to the holy shrines in 'Akká and Haifa, and while she was there, she had the bounty of meeting 'Abdu'l-Bahá. She made the journey with the newly-wed couple Mrs. May Bolles Maxwell and Mr. William Sutherland Maxwell. Louise and May had become close friends when May Bolles (Maxwell) spent time deepening the believers in New York between 1903 and 1905. Their friendship was the most meaningful of Louise's early Bahá'í life, and it was a friendship that defied words, as noted by Louise herself when she wrote, "I cannot speak of the great benefits to my life and the transformation I experienced through the association of May Maxwell."[13] In another instance, Louise wrote, "I was a young believer in New York and not yet understanding very well the Message that I had received. In my love and friendship for May Maxwell I found a complete transformation and a wholly new existence."[14]

After receiving encouragement from Edward and Lua Getsinger, John and Louise began corresponding in 1913—he from his home in Geyserville, California, and she from her place of work at a girl's school called Briarcliff Manor in New York. Naturally, the subject of their letters centered on the Bahá'í Cause and its laws and teachings. Although both John and Louise spoke English fluently, Louise wrote the following letter in German, perhaps in order to be more familiar. Louise wrote of her concern that John's profession as a wine-maker conflicted with Bahá'í teachings. She raised the issue with delicacy but directness:[15]

October 22, 1913
Dear Friend,

I will try to also write a few words in German to you; yesterday I quickly responded to your last letter which contained the newspaper extract of Oct. 1899. Yes, that is a very interesting article. I read it through twice on the way home from

New York to Briarcliff. Naturally the question occurred to me immediately what you were going to do, or what you will have done since the Revelation of Baha Ullah cast a new light on wine-making for you. I also thought of the conversation we had with Abdul Baha at table in Acca one day. Mr. and Mrs. Maxwell took me along to Acca five years ago, and we were there for six days. Abdul Baha told us how it had come about that Muhammad had forbidden the drinking of wine. He said that one day the disciples of Muhammad at table (or in any case while eating) had started quarreling over an argument, and finally one of them took the bone of a leg of mutton that they had just eaten and hit his opponent with it. In the end Muhammad had to be called to come and separate the quarrelling men and restore peace. As they had all drunk wine with their food, they had got rather heated. That day Muhammad forbade the drinking of wine in the future and made it into a law. And so it is customary among the Muslims to this day to drink no wine, although in these days of breaking away from all prophetic laws, that law has long since been broken. But Abdul Baha added that the law of Muhammad has been renewed by Baha Ullah, Who had explained or revealed that it is not good to drink (or eat) anything which has fermented outside the stomach: all food or drink should be fermented inside the stomach and by the stomach.

I have little doubt that you will have talked to Abdul Baha about your business of wine-making and that He will have given you an explanation. Also, Abdul Baha said to a friend in New York that one should give up the habit of drinking only gradually, and this will at any rate apply also to the human race, and so it would take at least two or three generations to change the habits of one's ancestors.

I had previously thought that you were dealing only with unfermented wine, or grape juice. I had thought so because of what is printed on your letters or envelopes, but these are minor matters.

You must have worked very hard all your life to achieve all that you have achieved, and you must have genius. That pleases Abdul Baha, as it does others.

The newspaper extract talks about your travels and your studies abroad in Germany, France, and Spain, yet you wrote to me in your first letter that you had already come to Nebraska in 1876, and now I would like to know how old you are. I think that you must be 1000 years old! In the picture you look terribly young, but one cannot tell anything from this kind of picture. I would prefer a photograph, if you have had time to make an appointment with a photographer.

What you are telling me about a journey to the old home-land to explain the truth to the people there, yes, that would certainly be ideal. I cannot at all imagine my doing so, but as for you I can imagine it very well, you appear to have been called to do this and will probably do it. You may believe me when I say that I would like to be part of it, since it is also my people, yet there would have to be considerable changes in me to achieve this.

Do you still have relatives in Switzerland? I still have an old aunt there who has a noble soul, but until the present day it has been impossible for me to inspire her with belief in the truth of Baha Ullah. She is old (but spiritually young), and I know that God will not hold it against her that she cannot see or recognize the light of her Lord Jesus in the words of the Holy Spirit for this day. Perhaps we may meet once more in this life, then we may be able to discuss the matter, which would be better than letters. I shall now write to her that I have found a Bahai compatriot in you, and that will please and interest her very much: a compatriot from the Toggenburg—that really sounds quite romantic, do you not think so?

In your last letter, you did not tell me whether the Toggenburg is in fact real farm country; please do not fail to make that clear to me when next you write to me. Since I have never been in farm country, I have only vague conceptions of it, but it seems to me nevertheless that I must have been in real farm country once—perhaps as a child with my so greatly loved grandfather, which is entirely possible since he had a brother in the Toggenburg. Undoubtedly there must be such a place somewhere that I have in mind. Other than that, I feel as you do. It is very strange, but in fact I would not like to end my life anywhere but in <u>America</u>, in the United States. My aunt does not find that strange, since I, as she wrote, have spent the greater part of my life here and have gathered all my experiences here. That obviously ties one to the land, as you must also have felt. I also like the spirit of this country and the mainly newness that comprises it. My artistic friends, of whom I have a few, tell me that only those who have no feeling or genius for art or antiquities can prefer this country to Europe. Then I always tell them that I belong to the farm country.

I am ending this at last—the bell of the last class of the day is just sounding, and they will now come running in order to inform me of their various ailments!

With best wishes, hoping that our Lord may visit your apartment in Geyserville, I remain your devoted,

Louise Stapfer[16]

John and Louise were married in San Francisco on January 19, 1914. 'Abdu'l-Bahá was pleased with the union, for He wrote a Tablet to them, signed His name in Persian and in English, and addressed it to the newly married couple:

> To his honor Mr. John D. Bosch and the maid-servant of God, Louise Bosch, Geyserville, California.
> Upon them be Baha'u'llah el Abha!
> He is God!
> O ye two souls of pure spirit!
> Praise be to God that you have spread the feast of union and prepared the banquet of rejoicing. It is blessed. I beg of God that this union be eternal and the means of everlasting happiness, thus, in all the divine worlds ye may live together!
> Upon ye be Baha El Abha!
> [Signed in English alphabet]: abdul "Baha" abbas
> Mount Carmel, Haifa
> March 31, 1914[17]

When John and Louise went on pilgrimage in 1921, Louise was fifty-one years old and John was sixty-six. A reunion with 'Abdu'l-Bahá must have reminded John of the time when he traveled by train from California to New York in 1912 to meet 'Abdu'l-Bahá. The following account of that meeting is comprised from John's detailed handwritten notes; the words are his, but the present writer has combined these accounts to render the narrative chronologically. These are pilgrims' notes, and while they may convey deep spiritual significance, they are not authoritative. John begins by telling of his longing to meet 'Abdu'l-Bahá:

When I heard that Abdul Baha intended to visit America, and was on the ocean [from Alexandria, Egypt], I felt a strong desire to meet him, not to meet him for curiosity or a novelty, but for a longing to see him.

Informed that he would reach New York on April 11th, I started to make arrangements for over two weeks and tried to make up a round trip ticket for a reasonable rate to the Chicago Convention but could not arrive at conclusions, until April 11th, the arrival of Abdul Baha in New York. Then the thought suddenly came to me, why not try to meet him in Washington or New York and without any further consultation with my own mind I just walked into the Union Pacific office and purchased a ticket on the shortest and fastest route, the Overland Limited and Pennsylvania Rail, and departed on April 12th Friday at 10:00 am. On account of the snow storms in the Rocky Mountains the train was three hours late and I had to take a later train out of Chicago on the 15th at 5:30 pm. Arriving at Washington on the 16th at 5:00 pm I made arrangements at the hotel and believing that Abdul Baha might be in Washington I telephoned to Mr. Remey for information. In an hour he called at the hotel and said all was quiet in Washington and no news about the movements of Abdul Baha.

So, I thought best to continue my trip to New York on the next train at 9:00 pm arriving there at 3:50 am, Wednesday, April 17th. The passengers had to remain on the train until 5:00 am, at which time I made myself ready to walk to the Hotel Ansonia, which was about 30 blocks from the Pennsylvania Depot. I arrived at the Hotel Ansonia by 6:00 am and after engaging my room there I requested the Clerk to find out for me if Dr. Fareed is up at this early hour and the Bell Boy reported that he is up and the door open. Without further formalities I started for the 5th Floor and found Dr. Getsinger and the door was open to Abdul Baha's apartments. Dr. Fareed introduced me to [Dr.] Getsinger, Sayed Assad 'Ullah and Mirza Mahmud and said that Abdul Baha would be in the room shortly. In a few minutes I was called into his Parlor. I had in mind to enter cool and resigned as into a business office.

Dr. Fareed introduced me as John D. Bosch of California. With a warm wholesome handshake Abdul Baha greeted me and said, "I have been longing to see you." He offered me a chair and to be seated close where he was seated. I said that I am greatly pleased and fortunate to have the opportunity and privilege to meet him so early in New York and that I travelled 3,000 miles to see him. To which he smilingly replied that he has come 8,000 miles to see me.

Abdul Baha ordered the tea served (of the most delicious brew.) I had a pocketful of questions from the West, but never gave them to Abdul Baha, for he told me all that I wanted to know.

I said to Abdul Baha: I regret very much that I have not the capacity as a teacher and am by nature rather reserved in talking and that the work I have been doing in the cause was mostly in the line of Universal Peace and by circulating books and pamphlets.

Abdul Baha looked directly at me, put his hand on my shoulder and said: "You are doing well, you are doing better than talking. It is not always the elaborate talking, the movement of the lips, that would accomplish results. It is the heart that is powerful. With you it is not words. Your heart talks. Wherever you go your heart radiates, which is even more than the movements of the lips. With you often silence talks and radiates. You are doing very well, to live, to act is the real true response. Your station, your name is Nurani, illumined, enlightened, light, radiant."[18]

While in New York, 'Abdu'l-Bahá told John that he was as a member of 'Abdu'l-Bahá's family, and this sentiment turned out to be a true characterization of the way in which John and Louise were received when they arrived in Haifa in November 1921. For instance, a custom of 'Abdu'l-Bahá was to host a weekly evening gathering called "The Persian Meeting," where He would discuss various aspects of Bahá'u'lláh's teachings and laws to as many as sixty friends at one time. 'Abdu'l-Bahá invited John to attend the meeting that was held on November 19, 1921, and John was the only Western believer present that evening. Dr. Luṭfu'lláh Ḥakím took notes during the meeting, while Mírzá Muḥammad-'Alí Afnán translated. Here is a portion of what 'Abdu'l-Bahá said at that gathering, which was His last public meeting at His home before His passing. 'Abdu'l-Bahá opened the meeting by speaking directly to John:

Although you are here with these assembled friends and cannot speak with them nor they with you, yet you can speak with one another through the heart. The language of the heart is even more expressive than the language of the tongue and is more truthful and has a wider reach and a more potent effect. When lovers meet it may be that they cannot exchange a single word, yet with their hearts they speak to one another. Thus do the clouds speak to the earth and the rain comes down; the breeze whispers to the trees; this is the way in which the hearts of the friends talk together. It is the harmony between two persons and this harmony is of the hearts. For instance, you were in America and I was in the Holy Land. Although our lips were still, yet with our hearts we were conversing together. The friends here love you very much. They have a real attachment for you, although with the tongue they cannot express it.[19]

John was, indeed, a man of few words. In fact, on one occasion when 'Abdu'l-Bahá was in New York in 1912, John found himself at a complete loss for words when 'Abdu'l-Bahá pulled John into a taxi for a ride through the city. John recounts the scene as it took place just outside the Hotel Ansonia:

I was amazed to see the people, numbering about 200, in the lobby, arise in respect to Abdul Baha as he was just passing [through the lobby]. There were three taxis awaiting him and his party. Abdul Baha stepped into the first, with Mirza Mahmood, and Sayed Assad 'Ullah, and there being a seat vacant, Sayed Assad 'Ullah motioned me to come, and as I neared the taxi Abdul Baha put out his hand and pulled me right in. He seemed very tired, and he immediately put his arm around my waist, put his head on my left shoulder, and with a big sigh, fell asleep. We were bound for the home of Mr. and Mrs. Edward Kinney for dinner, and the believers expected that the drive would afford Abdul Baha an opportunity to see the streets and public buildings of New York, but instead of looking at all the big buildings, to our surprise he had a restful nap.[20]

'Abdu'l-Bahá had rested on John's left shoulder as they drove through the city streets of New York in 1912, and it would not be the last time that He would rest on John's shoulder. Nine years later, in 1921, the day after the passing of 'Abdu'l-Bahá, a special honor—one that he could never have imagined—awaited John; it was the sacred privilege of helping to place the precious body of the Master into His coffin and to assist in bearing the coffin upon his right shoulder as it was carried from the room where the Master had ascended. John's account of the preparation of the Master's body and the funeral procession which followed is held at the United States Bahá'í Archives and printed here in part:

The hour for the funeral had been set for nine-o'clock the next morning, Tuesday, November 29th [. . .] By eight o'clock the house, yards and garden were filled with mourners. They came in great numbers to attend the funeral. At half past eight a picture was taken of the room and the bed wherein Abdul-Baha had passed away. In this picture the ladies of the family appeared. Then another photograph was taken, with the sons-in-law and some others of the household surrounding the bed.

At a quarter to nine a sudden command was given to the hundred or more people who were standing in the large center hall. Instantly they all moved toward the front door, but Louise, Johanna [Hauff] and myself, not understanding what had been said, remained standing by the wall. In a moment Mirza Jalal, known to the believers as the son of the King of the Martyrs, appeared, and walking toward me, motioned for me to accompany him. I did not know what he wanted, but I followed as he led the way to one of the north rooms. As we entered the room I saw, to my surprise, a casket. It was very

plain, of white wood, unpainted. We carried it across the hall
to the room in which lay the body of Abdul Baha. We placed it
upon two chairs, and when it was uncovered I observed that it
was zinc lined. Two of the persons present placed in it a most
exquisite silken comforter, leaving the sides hanging over.
Turning to the bed, I noticed that the body of Abdul Baha was
wrapped in three white silken sheets which were folded over
him from both sides. Rouhi Effendi and others then prepared
to place the body in the casket. They were at the head, Mirza
Jalal at the center, I at the feet. We gently laid it [the body
of 'Abdu'l-Bahá] in the casket and someone put a silken pillow under the head. The best attar of rose was sprinkled over
Abdul Baha, then both sides of the comforter were drawn up
and laid over him. The cover was then placed upon the casket
and at once, as from an invisible command, six of us raised it
to our shoulder, I, being at the head. We carried it to the large
room outside and lowered it to the floor. A beautiful ivory silk
cover was laid over it, also one of the many wreaths that had
been sent. A call was given, the doors were opened, and many
people entered the room [. . .]. Sharply at nine o'clock the
casket was lifted from the floor by the appointed pallbearers,
who carried it out the front door, down the steps and through
the gate, along the short street about the length of two of our
city blocks, to the road which led up Mount Carmel.

About 40 carriages were waiting at the gate to join in
the funeral cortege, but only about five were occupied, as all
who possibly could, wished to honor the Master they had
loved by humbly walking after his remains. Even the British
High Commissioner, who had come specially from Jerusalem,
walked with the others. Beside him, in full uniform, was the

Chief of Police of Haifa, who had left his horse standing in the street near the house of Abdul Baha. The Governor of Phoenicia also walked. There were men of all nations, of all creeds, of all walks in life, high and low, rich and poor. It seemed that never had there been such a funeral procession before. So great was the desire to help carry the casket up the mountain that some of the men were wrangling for the privilege of only touching it with their fingertips. For an hour and a half that great mass of people slowly moved along the winding road up the steep incline of Mount Carmel.

It was a perfect day, one of the most beautiful one could imagine. As I turned and looked back now and then many were the thoughts that came to me as I watched all those people wending their way up the mountain. Ahead was the Tomb of the Bab. Behind were the blue Mediterranean and the bay of Haifa, and nine miles away was the old city of Akka, and in the far distance the Lebanon Mountains. Never can I forget that scene.[21]

Of the thoughts that came to John in that scene, one must have been the memory of the Master asleep on his shoulder while riding in an automobile through the city of New York in 1912, and the gratitude for such a privilege. Louise wrote to Ella Cooper of this glorious privilege bestowed upon John: "Tomorrow it will be one week since we carried our blessed Lord's earthly temple to Mount Carmel. John had the great privilege that day to assist in carrying the coffin into the room which our Lord lay, and John also assisted in placing the holy body into the coffin. This is John's everlasting bounty for his services rendered to the Cause, and because of the privilege he had of lifting the holy body of his Lord, John can never be the same being any more. And he is and looks different, too."[22]

The news of the ascension of 'Abdu'l-Bahá spread rapidly through the city, the region, and indeed throughout the whole world. Thousands of people of various faiths, races, and ranks gathered for His funeral; any differences of religion, race, and rank receded behind the unifying forces released by the Master's ministry. Shoghi Effendi wrote that the passing of 'Abdu'l-Bahá "brought to a close the ministry of One Who was the incarnation, by virtue of the rank bestowed upon Him by His Father, of an institution that has no parallel in the entire field of religious history, a ministry that marks the final stage in the Apostolic, the Heroic and most glorious Age of the Dispensation of Bahá'u'lláh."[23]

No one had anticipated the passing of 'Abdu'l-Bahá, even though 'Abdu'l-Bahá Himself made various allusions to His approaching death. In *The Priceless Pearl*, the wife of Shoghi Effendi, Rúhíyyih Khánum, confirms that "a few weeks before 'Abdu'l-Bahá died, suddenly He came into the room where Shoghi Effendi's father was and said, 'Cable Shoghi Effendi to return (from Oxford) at once.' His mother told us that on hearing this she consulted with her mother and it was decided that to cable risked shocking Shoghi Effendi unnecessarily and so they would write to him the Master's instruction; the letter arrived after He had ascended."[24]

Although we cannot know for certain what was in the mind of 'Abdu'l-Bahá in the days preceding His passing, one cannot help wondering if the presence of the six Western believers in the holy land at that time was providential. Marzieh Gail, who knew John and Louise Bosch, wrote that "John was one of those whom 'Abdu'l-Bahá chose as a companion for the time when He should leave the world. Afterward, the friends saw that the Master knew the moment of His passing and had prepared for it. Some who had asked permission to visit Him at that time, He had gently turned away, but to John and Louise He had written 'I am longing to see you.'"[25] In the following account of the last time in which John was in the presence of 'Abdu'l-Bahá before His passing, John expressed how unworthy he felt of such a bounty:

The last time Abdul Baha spoke to me was in the morning of [Friday] November 25, 1921, when I longed to have a glimpse of him. I entered the garden near his house where he gave instructions to the gardener and then he walked up and down the lane on the north side of the house taking exercise like most any morning, then picking a few oranges and mandarins from the trees with his own hands, giving them to the visitors there—several Persians, Hindus and Arabs were standing there—and then when he approached me he gave me one mandarin and said in English with his usual smile, "Eat! Good!" I always remember his words in the magnetic tone he spoke them to me. He seemed to be very happy at that time and smiled at me. I wondered then if I was worthy of that smile of our Master, not knowing then that I would be called to help laying his earthly body in the casket in the morning of the fourth day after this occurrence. He then walked into his house and at the same day at noon he came to lunch at the Pilgrim House where he spoke to several of us, and when serving rice when we only took a small portion he always said in English, "Again, again" meaning that we should again take rice and eat plenty. How wonderful it was to be a guest of the host of the world during his last days on earth. Never shall

I forget the farewell of the Master. When he rose from the chair and after his usual ablution as is the custom there after meals, he proceeded towards the door, then turned to us and standing in a majestic position outstretching his hands toward us and then raising them to his forehead, his face illumined, said in a smiling way to all of us, three times, "Good afternoon. Good afternoon. Good afternoon." And with each time stretching his hands forward, palms upward, and raised them to his forehead. How happy we were to see him happy and how little we knew then that those were his last words to us.[26]

In the same account, John describes the night he and Louise were called to the house of the Master just moments after His soul ascended:

After midnight, we were awakened in the Pilgrim House by a few loud knocks given in rapid succession and we wondered what had happened. My watch pointed to 1:20 o'clock. My wife said, "Something must have happened to Abdul Baha. Let us hurry and find out what this unusual call is." In a few minutes we were running to the house of Abdul Baha where we found that it was only too true that our Master had just passed away. Doctors were leaving the house and we entered the room finding all of the family of Abdul Baha there, Abdul Baha resting in bed as though he were still alive. Approaching the bed I could not resist to take his hand, not trusting he was dead. It was warm and life-like. Then I touched his forehead and hoped that he still might utter a word, but it was only too true that our Master had passed away, his spirit had departed. The Greatest Holy Leaf then kindly reached her hand to me and motioned me to sit beside her, which I did. The room became filled with friends and people from the town and the antechamber and the hall too became filled. It is indescribable to describe the sorrow and weeping uttered by the people in that hour. To me it seemed that thousands of thoughts went through my mind in those moments. Sometimes there comes to all of us feelings that sigh for expression when only our silence really registers the depth of our emotion, and our moist eyes suggest what words could never reveal, so I cannot express the deep stirrings within me when all in deep silence I arose again and touched the hand and forehead of Abdul Baha still warm. I said, "Oh Abdul Baha!" And Rizwanieh said later how they loved it that in the deep silence someone called the name of the Master. Again I was seated alongside the Greatest Holy Leaf who through her calmness was an example to us all. Through her poise and calmness a change came over me, a relief, the thought that our Master was at last released and relieved from all the persecutions and the answering to questions of all the friends and inquirers and curiosity seekers. I felt that his precious body now was at rest, his spirit alive, that we were all equal now regardless of position, that each and every one of us could find him and serve him only in spirit and in his teachings, the greatest of privileges and also the greatest of obligations![27]

Louise reflected on the unworthiness she felt at the privilege of being in the room of 'Abdu'l-Bahá moments after His ascension. She wrote, "I had then the feeling that we believers—excepting the holy family—that we believers, myself included, were standing in a room and in a presence to which no known privilege had given us entrance; I felt that this one time surely we had literally rushed in where angels feared to tread, and that the shock of Abdul Baha's sudden passing was the cause that had removed certain barriers and restrictions."[28]

Louise adds further spiritual insight to the sanctity and significance of the ascension of 'Abdu'l-Bahá. As has been mentioned previously, the Guardian characterized the Master as the "moon" of the Bahá'í Dispensation.[29] The moon has no inherent light of its own; rather, it achieves all of its brilliance by reflecting the light of the sun. Louise observed the night of the ascension of 'Abdu'l-Bahá was a moonless night, and she wrote in a letter to Ella Cooper dated December 5, 1921: "We [. . .] were in the room together with the holy family, and the Holy Mother [Monireh Khánum, the wife of 'Abdu'l-Bahá] held my husband's hand and the Greatest Holy Leaf held mine. After a time we went back to the Pilgrim House, leaving the holy family alone. It was still night—no moon at all. Not long afterward the dawn broke, and at last the sun rose with great effulgence over the scene of this memorable night."[30]

The Universal House of Justice has elaborated on the imagery associated with 'Abdu'l-Bahá as the "Orb" of Bahá'u'lláh's Covenant and has referred to the passing of Bahá'u'lláh as "the setting of the Sun of Bahá" and noted the relationship between the sun and moon as analogous to the relationship between Bahá'u'lláh and 'Abdu'l-Bahá: "With the setting of the Sun of Bahá, the Moon of His Covenant rose in reflected glory, lifting the darkness of a night of despair, and lighting the path to the unity of all humankind."[31]

In *The Priceless Pearl*, Rúhíyyih Khánum explains that after the passing of 'Abdu'l-Bahá, the members of the holy family looked for burial instructions for Him and "discovered His Will—which consists of three Wills written at different times and forming one document—addressed to Shoghi Effendi. It now became the painful duty of Shoghi Effendi to hear what was in it; a few days after his arrival they read it to him."[32] Shoghi Effendi was at Oxford when he received news of his Grandfather's passing, and due to passport difficulties, he could not arrive in the holy land until December 29, 1921, one month and a day after the passing of his beloved Grandfather.[33] Adib Taherzadeh, in his book *The Child of the Covenant*, explains the details of the reading of the Master's Will:

> Although the Will and Testament of 'Abdu'l-Bahá was read out to Shoghi Effendi soon after his arrival in Haifa, it had to be formally presented to the members of the family and others in the Holy Land. On 3 January 1922, in the presence of nine persons, mainly senior members of 'Abdu'l-Bahá's family, and in Shoghi Effendi's absence, the Will and Testament was read aloud and its seal, signature and handwriting were shown to those present. Later, the Greatest Holy Leaf sent cables to Persia and America—the two major communities at that time— informing them that according to the Will and Testament of 'Abdu'l-Bahá, Shoghi Effendi had been appointed "Guardian of the Cause of God."[34]

A few days after the formal reading of the Will, a public reading was held at which John was present. He described the occasion in detail:

> On January 7th, just 40 days after the passing of Abdul Baha, at nine in the morning, we were invited to assemble in the large hall of the residence of Abdul Baha to listen to the reading of the will and testament of Abdul Baha. It was in Arabic.*

---

* According to Dr. Omid Ghaemmaghami, Associate Professor of Arabic and Near Eastern Studies at Binghamton University, each of the three parts of the

Jusuf Khan of Tihran, Persia, began to chant the first part of the testament. He began at 9:55 and finished at 10:50. That part of the testament (which had been affected by many years of dampness) had been written by Abdul Baha when Shoghi Effendi was [a boy], and therein Abdul Baha referred to him as "the young and tender branch." The second part was chanted by Muhammad Taki of Cairo. That part was finished at 11:20. Then followed the chanting of the third part by Jusuf Khan, which he finished at a quarter to twelve o'clock.

At this reading of the testament there were 120 persons present. Many had come specially from Cairo, Alexandria, Port Said, Jerusalem, Damascus, Beirut, Persia, India and England. Six Americans were present: Dr. and Mrs. Krug, Mrs. Hoagg,* Curtis Kelsey of New York, John D. and Louise Bosch of California.[35]

Bahíyyih Khánum was very much aware of the Master's affection for John and Louise, and she invited the Bosches to stay with the holy family during a 40-day period of mourning. The privilege of such intimate association with the family of 'Abdu'l-Bahá at such a calamitous time calls to mind 'Abdu'l-Bahá's words to John in New York when He said that John was like a member of the family.

---

Will and Testament of 'Abdu'l-Bahá contains sections revealed in Arabic and sections revealed in Persian. (Via email, July 20, 2019.)

   * Imogene Hoagg was in Egypt on the night of the ascension. She had returned to Haifa in time for the public reading of the Master's Will. For further information on Imogene Hoagg, please see http://bahaiblog.net/2016/12/emogene-hoagg-spiritual-giant/.

Nearly two months had passed since John and Louise's arrival in Haifa. Their unique pilgrimage and extended stay with the Master's family had come to its end, and the time had come for John and Louise to prepare for their reluctant departure from the holy land. John kept an hourly record of the events that followed: At 5:30 am on January 17, 1922, he visited the tomb of the Báb and 'Abdu'l-Bahá. At 8:30 am, John and Louise bid their farewell to the holy family and then to Shoghi Effendi, who took them to view the picture of Bahá'u'lláh. Then the Guardian made an extraordinary request of the Bosches: he entrusted a copy of portions of the Will and Testament of 'Abdu'l-Bahá to the worthy care of John and Louise Bosch, and he asked that they deliver this document to the Bahá'í National Convention in Chicago to be held in April of that year.[36]

It is important to note that it was the Greatest Holy Leaf, and not John and Louise, who would first communicate to the American Bahá'ís the contents of the Master's Will. The Greatest Holy Leaf cabled the United States on January 16, 1922: "'In Will Shoghi Effendi is appointed Guardian of the Cause and Head of the House of Justice. Inform American friends.'"[37] Furthermore, John and Louise were not the only individuals to whom the Guardian gave early copies of the Will and Testament. Rúḥíyyih Khánum wrote that immediately after the events following the Master's ascension,

Shoghi Effendi selected eight passages from the Will and circulated them among the Bahá'ís; only one of these referred to himself, was very brief and was quoted as follows: "O ye the faithful ones of 'Abdu'l-Bahá! It is incumbent upon you to take the greatest care of Shoghi Effendi [. . .] For he is, after 'Abdu'l-Bahá, the guardian of the Cause of God, the Afnán, the Hands (pillars) of the Cause and the beloved of the Lord must obey him and turn unto him." Of all the thundering and tremendous passages in the Will referring to himself, Shoghi Effendi chose the least astounding and provocative to first circulate among the Bahá'ís. Guided and guiding he was from the very beginning.[38]

One can only imagine how John and Louise felt when the Guardian entrusted portions of the Will and Testament to them. So astonishing is this honor, so sacred the privilege, so astounding the significance of bearing the Master's Will and Testament to the United States, that it is important to pause this narrative of John and Louise's experiences in the holy land and consider the singular importance of the Will and Testament of 'Abdu'l-Bahá—a document the Guardian describes as the Master's "greatest legacy to posterity, the brightest emanation of His mind and the mightiest instrument forged to insure the continuity" of Bahá'u'lláh's Dispensation.[39]

Shoghi Effendi explained that the Will and Testament of 'Abdu'l-Bahá is unique in the history of religion, describing it as "the Document establishing that Order, the Charter of a future world civilization, which may be regarded in some of its features as supplementary to no less weighty a Book than the Kitáb-i-Aqdas; signed and sealed by 'Abdu'l-Bahá; entirely written with His own hand."[40] Furthermore, the Guardian explained that the Will and Testament of 'Abdu'l-Bahá is the distinguishing feature of the Bahá'í Dispensation and the believers are urged "to grasp the fundamental difference existing between this world-embracing, divinely-appointed Order and the chief ecclesiastical organizations of the world."[41] The Guardian clarifies further the unique distinction of the Will and Testament of 'Abdu'l-Bahá:

Unlike the Dispensation of Christ, unlike the Dispensation of Muḥammad, unlike all the Dispensations of the past, the apostles of Bahá'u'lláh in every land, wherever they labor and toil, have before them in clear, in unequivocal and emphatic language, all the laws, the regulations, the principles, the institutions, the guidance, they require for the prosecution and consummation of their task. Both in the administrative provisions of the Bahá'í Dispensation, and in the matter of succession, as embodied in the twin institutions of the House of Justice and of the Guardianship, the followers of Bahá'u'lláh can summon to their aid such irrefutable evidences of Divine Guidance that none can resist, that none can belittle or ignore. Therein lies the distinguishing feature of the Bahá'í Revelation. Therein lies the strength of the unity of the Faith, of the validity of a Revelation that claims not to destroy or belittle previous Revelations, but to connect, unify, and fulfill them. This is the reason why Bahá'u'lláh and 'Abdu'l-Bahá have both revealed and even insisted upon certain details in connection with the Divine Economy which they have bequeathed to us, their followers. This is why such an emphasis has been placed in their Will and Testament upon the powers and prerogatives of the ministers of their Faith.[42]

Of the Will and Testament of 'Abdu'l-Bahá, Shoghi Effendi said, "We stand indeed too close to so monumental a document to claim for ourselves a complete understanding of all its implications, or to presume to have grasped the manifold mysteries it undoubtedly contains."[43] The Will and Testament of 'Abdu'l-Bahá is so unrivaled in the history of religion that it takes one's breath away to imagine the unique bounty and singular blessing bestowed upon

John and Louise Bosch by the Guardian when he asked them to be the bearers of this document, which was the blueprint for the future world civilization and an invaluable guide for the American Bahá'í community—a community that the Guardian would later describe as the "cradle of the Administrative Order."[44]

The Guardian's commendation of this weighty and precious document into the hands of John and Louise is a demonstration of the deep trust he had in them—a trust that had its beginnings during the Master's visit to the United States when the Master told John that he was "one of the family now." It was a trust that also had its beginnings when May Maxwell gave birth to her daughter Mary Maxwell (Rúhíyyih Khánum), as it was Louise (Stapfer) Bosch who was like an aunt to little Mary. When Shoghi Effendi and Mary Maxwell were married on March 24, 1937, uniting forever the believers of the East with those of the West, John and Louise Bosch sent a cable to Haifa that read, "Illustrious nuptial thrilled the universe," to which the Guardian cabled a reply on March 31, 1937 that read, "Inexpressibly appreciative thrilling message. Deepest Love, Shoghi."[45] Two months after her marriage to Shoghi Effendi, Rúhíyyih Khánum wrote a most precious, handwritten letter to John and Louise:[46]

Haifa, Palestine
May 26, 1937
My Dear Ones:

Your lovely letter made me very happy. Indeed I love you both so much and have always felt so close to you and during these weeks when the infinite Bounty of Baha'u'llah has been so unexpectedly and abundantly showered upon me, I who have never deserved it in any conceivable way! My thoughts have often gone out to you both.

This union of East and West is so far above personality. I feel myself only an instrument caught up in the power and majesty of the Plan of God; I can only pray, and ask others to pray with me, that I may become worthy and render our beloved Cause great services. It seems to me I stand at the bottom of a mountain—my privilege and responsibility to climb ever higher, and I hope you will pray for me.

My love I send you both, always.

Rúhíyyih[47]

With a copy of portions of the Will and Testament of 'Abdu'l-Bahá in their protective care, John and Louise, along with their young traveling companion, Johanna Hauff, departed Haifa at 10:00am on Tuesday, January 17, 1922. The party of three journeyed first to Jerusalem, where they stayed the night. The next day, they traveled by carriage to Bethlehem, where they visited the Church of the Nativity. The day after that, they traveled in an overland automobile to the Dead Sea, Jericho, and the Lamentation Mountains where Christ fasted and prayed for forty days. They concluded the day with a trip to the Mount of Olives. On Friday, January 20, Johanna Hauff returned to Haifa (where she stayed until February) and John and Louise returned to Jerusalem. On Saturday, January 21 they departed for Cairo and arrived at 11:00pm.[48]

They stayed in Cairo for one week as the guests of Muḥammad Taqí Isfáhání, whom they had met in Haifa. (Muḥammad Taqí Isfáhání was the one who chanted in Arabic the second part of the initial reading of the Will and Testament of 'Abdu'l-Bahá in the Master's residence in Haifa.)[49] They had several meetings with the friends there, and they visited the gravesites of Lua Getsinger and

Mírzá Abu'l-Faḍl. The reader may recall that Lua Getsinger considered Louise Bosch one of her special five souls she nurtured in the Cause; while travel-teaching for the Cause, Lua died unexpectedly in Cairo on May 1, 1916 and is buried there.

Mírzá Abu'l-Faḍl was the beloved servant of 'Abdu'l-Bahá who, at the Master's request, traveled to Paris and to the United States with Laura Clifford Barney (who compiled a collection of 'Abdu'l-Bahá's responses to questions on religious topics in the book *Some Answered Questions*) in order to ensure that the new believers had a clear understanding of the teachings and laws of Bahá'u'lláh's Revelation. Mírzá Abu'l-Faḍl died in Cairo while visiting at the home of Muḥammad Taqí Isfáhání. Of Mírzá Abu'l-Faḍl's book *The Brilliant Proof*, the Master said that the Bahá'ís should "memorize and reflect upon" this book so that "when accusations and criticisms are advanced by those unfavorable to the Cause, you will be well armed."[50] It should be noted that in December 1942, the Guardian announced the successful transfer of Lua Getsinger's remains from a Christian cemetery in Cairo to the Bahá'í cemetery in Cairo.[51] Her grave now adjoins the grave of the "far-famed Abu'l-Faḍl within a lofty tomb where, as suggested by Hand of the Cause Ḥasan Balyuzi, "the East and the West meet."[52]

From Cairo, John and Louise traveled to Alexandria and Ramleh, where they spent two days meeting with the Bahá'í friends there. On Saturday, January 28, the friends came to the Windsor Hotel to bid them farewell, and John and Louise departed on the *SS Adriatic* to sail through the Mediterranean Sea toward Europe.[53] Their travel teaching efforts continued to be inspired by the direction given to them in 'Abdu'l-Bahá's *Tablets of the Divine Plan*, where He called upon the believers to travel to Europe after the Great War and spread the teachings to those longing souls:

This world-consuming war has set such a conflagration to the hearts that no word can describe it. In all the countries of the world the longing for universal peace is taking possession of the consciousness of men. There is not a soul who does not yearn for concord and peace. A most wonderful state of receptivity is being realized [. . .] Therefore, O ye believers of God! Show ye an effort and after this war spread ye the synopsis of the divine teachings in the British Isles, France, Germany, Austria-Hungary, Russia, Italy, Spain, Belgium, Switzerland, Norway, Sweden, Denmark, Holland, Portugal, Rumania, Serbia, Montenegro, Bulgaria, Greece, Andorra, Liechtenstein, Luxembourg, Monaco, San Marino, Balearic Isles, Corsica, Sardinia, Sicily, Crete, Malta, Iceland, Faroe Islands, Shetland Islands, Hebrides and Orkney Islands.[54]

In Italy, John and Louise organized public meetings on the Bahá'í Faith in Naples, Rome, Florence, and Como. From there they passed into Locarno, Switzerland and made their way toward Zurich, Louise's birthplace, and then to St. Gallen, the place of John's birth, where they stopped for one week.

From Switzerland they traveled to Germany, where they stayed for nearly a month and focused their teaching efforts on the cities of Stuttgart, Esslingen, and Bad-Mergentheim because these were cities that had been visited by 'Abdu'l-Bahá in 1913. Germany was beloved of the Master, as His assurances to the German people testify. For instance, in the *Tablets of the Divine Plan*, the Master associated Germany with His wish that He Himself could travel to these countries:

Miss Knobloch traveled alone to Germany. To what a great extent she became confirmed! Therefore, know ye of a certainty that whosoever arises in this day to diffuse the divine fragrances, the cohorts of the Kingdom of God shall confirm him and the bestowals and the favors of the Blessed Perfection shall encircle him.

O that I could travel, even though on foot and in the utmost poverty, to these regions, and, raising the call of "Yá Bahá'u'l-Abhá" in cities, villages, mountains, deserts and oceans, promote the divine teachings! This, alas, I cannot do. How intensely I deplore it! Please God, ye may achieve it.[55]

When John and Louise visited Germany, they spent a great deal of time with Wilhelm Herrigel (with whom John had corresponded regarding the translation of Thornton Chase's book *The Bahá'í Revelation*). Herrigel was beginning to question the Administrative Order outlined in the Will and Testament of 'Abdu'l-Bahá, but his dissent had little effect on dividing the Bahá'í community in Germany—a community that remained firm in its acceptance of Shoghi Effendi as Guardian of the Cause. In a letter written two years after the ascension of 'Abdu'l-Bahá, the Guardian reassured the friends in Germany to remain steadfast and to set their sights on the greatness promised them by 'Abdu'l-Bahá. Here is the letter, in part:

December 4, 1923
To the dearly-beloved friends throughout Germany
Care of the National Spiritual Assembly
My well-beloved friends:
    What a joy to correspond with you again, and express, after a long and unbroken silence, my warm sentiments of love and affection for those tried, and yet steadfast, lovers of 'Abdu'l-

Bahá! Your trials and sufferings have been a constant source of anxiety and painful sorrow, not to me alone, but to the Ladies of the Household as well as to the friends at large.

True, humanity is to-day widely afflicted with unprecedented ills and calamities, but you, the chosen and favoured children of 'Abdu'l-Bahá, have, by some wisdom inscrutable to us all, received the fullest measure of this distress, and are carrying the burden of your cares with heroic fortitude, unflinching faith, and undaunted courage worthy of the admiration of even the most severely tried of your fellow-sufferers in far-away Persia.

Your only consolation lies in the ever-living words of our departed Master, who confidently declared that the days are not far distant when Germany will shake off her present humiliation, and will emerge, mighty, united and glorious, not only to take her destined place in the councils of nations, but to raise high the triumphant banner of the Cause in the very heart of Europe.

Your ceaseless activities since His departure from our midst have been steadily extended as your tribulations and anxieties have multiplied, and I feel hopeful that ere long the true Faith of God will blaze forth in that land, and will herald publicly the Message of Salvation to that distracted continent.

. . .

The members of the holy family and myself have joined lately the resident friends in the Holy Land in contributing towards the relief of the present distress in Germany, and we trust our modest efforts will mitigate to some extent the rigours of this coming winter in that afflicted country.

Hoping to hear from you, individually and collectively, and remembering you always in my prayers.

I am your brother and co-worker[56]

Perhaps the most touching example of the steadfastness of the German Bahá'í community can be seen at the onset of World War II when the Bahá'í Faith was officially banned in June, 1937. Two years before the ban, Miss Mary Maxwell pioneered to Germany in 1935; she was twenty-five years old. Of her early experiences there, she wrote to the American Bahá'í community the following:

The first contact that I made with the Bahá'ís of Germany was on the occasion of the Esslingen Summer School in August of 1935. Of all the many and varied impressions that flowed into my mind the deepest and most sacred was that of hearing the meeting opened by a reading of a Bahá'í prayer in German. Though I could scarcely understand it, the power and beauty of the creative Word was distinct and a consciousness of the innate and glorious oneness of the followers of Bahá'u'lláh the world over streamed into me with a sense of joy and gratitude.[57]

Having had a successful month-long teaching campaign in Germany, John and Louise departed for the United States on April 11, 1922, sailing on the *SS Resolute*. In his papers, John makes a special note about their ship being "the first large Steamer departing Germany since the War, under the American Flag." They were at sea for twelve days, arrived in New York on April 23, and were met by Miss Nelly Lloyd at the pier. Together they made their way to the train depot where Mrs. Safa Kinney and Mrs. Valeria Kelsey were waiting to join them on the train to Chicago. There, John and Louise Bosch would, as requested by the Guardian, deliver a portion of the Will and Testament of 'Abdu'l-Bahá to the Convention in Chicago. In his journal, John wrote, "On April 24 we arrived Chicago at 2pm Monday and at Convention about 3pm, just in time when my name as a delegate of Geyserville was called. How happy we were to meet all the friends from so many states of the United States of America."[58]

After the Convention, they traveled to Portland and visited their good friends, the Latimers. From there, they took the train to San Francisco and arrived at their home in Geyserville in May, 1922. In July they received a letter from Soheil Afnán, a member of the family of 'Abdu'l-Bahá. (The Guardian would not have been in the holy land at this time, as he had already left on his sojourn to Switzerland on April 5, 1922).[59] Here is the letter, in part:

Haifa, Palestine
June 30, 1922
My Dear Mr. and Mrs. Bosch,
I was very glad to see some time ago the photo of Mr. Bosch among a group of whole-hearted German friends and I could not but realize what faithful servants Divine Love has wrought. One can hardly believe that a group of conflicting Westerners could unite under no common bond of friendship save devotion to our Eastern Lord and conviction in His sublime Cause.[60]

Such a letter must have reassured them of the success of their journey—especially to the country of Germany and its people for whom the Master had promised so many glorious spiritual victories. Furthermore, the letter must have also brought back to their minds the fragrance of the holy land and the bounty of being in the presence of the Master one last time on this earth. Home in Geyserville, John and Louise must have reflected on the year-long journey that began with an intention to make a pilgrimage and ended with a most unique experience of being present at the passing of 'Abdu'l-Bahá and present at the public reading of His Will and Testament. For each of them, their thoughts must have returned to the first time each of them met 'Abdu'l-Bahá—Louise during her pilgrimage in 1909, and John upon visiting 'Abdu'l-Bahá' at the Hotel Ansonia in New York in 1912 with a pocketful of questions to ask.

'Abdu'l-Bahá had a special affection for John and bestowed upon him blessings beyond measure. In the following Tablet addressed to Mrs. Helen Goodall on August 17, 1909, the Master wrote, "Exercise on My behalf the utmost kindness and love to John D. Bosch. With the utmost humility I pray to the Kingdom of Abhá that that soul may become holy, find capacity to receive the outpouring of Eternity and become a luminous star in the West."[61]

In another instance, when 'Abdu'l-Bahá was visiting the east coast of the United States, John thought to invite 'Abdu'l-Bahá to visit him in his home in Geyserville, which was on the west coast of the United States. John explained to 'Abdu'l-Bahá that his home in Geyserville was not a palace but that he would be highly honored if 'Abdu'l-Bahá could visit. John wrote that 'Abdu'l-Bahá responded, "With you," and repeated, "With you I would sleep in the basement."[62]

On another occasion, John reported to his close friend Mr. Thornton Chase: "Have received a letter from Mrs. Goodall in which she writes that Abdul Baha sends me this message: '*Give the glad tidings of the Bounties of the Supreme to Mr. John D. Bosch.'* Isn't that short and impressive: it is more to me than a long letter."[63]

John died on July 22, 1946, just two weeks shy of his ninety-first birthday, and Louise died on September 6, 1952 at the age of eighty-two. They were forever changed by their experience in Haifa in 1921 and dedicated the remainder of their lives entirely to the promotion of the Cause of Bahá'u'lláh.

In 1935, the National Spiritual Assembly of the Bahá'ís of the United States and Canada began formalizing its membership records by asking the Bahá'ís to fill out a card that was called the "Bahá'í Historical Record Card." The decision to issue the cards was recommended by the delegates at the 1934 United Stated Bahá'í National Convention in an attempt to get a "thorough and complete Bahá'í census" of the Bahá'í community—particularly its survey of racial, cultural and religious backgrounds. The result was that about 1,813 believers—representing about 60% of the body of believers in America at that time—filled out the card.[64] The information is important archival information for future Bahá'í historians to study the remarkable circumstances under which these early Bahá'ís accepted Bahá'u'lláh as the Manifestation of God for this Day. In *Century of Light,* a document prepared under the supervision of the Universal House of Justice, the spiritual resolve of the Bahá'ís of both East and West in the first decades of the twentieth century is surveyed:

Their response arose from a level of consciousness that recognized, even if sometimes only dimly, the desperate need of the human race for spiritual enlightenment. To remain steadfast in the commitment to this insight required of these early believers [. . .] that they resist not only family and social pressures, but also the easy rationalizations of the world-view in which they had been raised and to which everything around them insistently exposed them. There was a heroism about the steadfastness of these early Western Bahá'ís that is, in its own way, as affecting as that of their Persian co-religionists, who in these same years, were facing persecution and death for the Faith they had embraced.[65]

On the front side of the Historical Record Card are questions about name, date of birth, and date of acceptance of the Bahá'í Faith. On the back side of the card is this question: *General information you would like to have preserved in this historical record (about Bahá'í services, connection with the Cause in early days, special talents, etc.).* John answered this question as follows:

Was privileged to be sent to that early Chicago Temple Convention of 1909 as delegate of the Californian and Hawaiian believers. Was first Californian believer who went to New York to meet 'Abdu'l-Baha in 1912. Was travelling in 'Abdu'l-Baha's party from New York to Washington D.C. and was in the same party again 6 days afterward from Washington to Chicago. Was in Wilmette at the Laying of the Cornerstone of the Mashriqu'l-Adhkar. Was present in Haifa at the Passing Away of 'Abdu'l-Baha. On Day of His Funeral was called to assist with the Laying of the Body of 'Abdu'l-Baha into the Coffin.[66]

Had the card been large enough, John could have added many more distinctions, had he wished. For instance, not only was he the traveling companion of 'Abdu'l-Bahá during His visit to America in 1912, but he was told by 'Abdu'l-Bahá that he was to be considered as a member of the family of 'Abdu'l-Bahá and that 'Abdu'l-Bahá Himself gave John the name "Núrání," which means "luminous," and wrote it on a piece of paper for John in His own handwriting.[67] Moreover, John and Louise were invited to stay with the holy family for two months after the ascension of 'Abdu'l-Bahá, and upon their departure from the holy land in January, 1922 the Guardian entrusted portions of the Will and Testament of 'Abdu'l-Bahá into their care so that John would deliver it to the United States Bahá'í National Convention in 1922. John participated in some of the most pivotal and sacred events of the first centenary of Bahá'í history, yet his genuine humility is an example of his selfless devotion to the Cause of Bahá'u'lláh.

In the introductory pages of *God Passes By*, Shoghi Effendi described the first century of Bahá'í history, 1844–1944, by dividing it into four periods: "These four periods are to be regarded not only as the component, the inseparable parts of one stupendous whole, but as progressive stages in a single evolutionary process, vast, steady and irresistible."[68] The fourth period in that evolutionary process spans from 1921 to 1944; its commencement is marked by the conclusion of the Apostolic Age with the passing of 'Abdu'l-Bahá in 1921, and punctuated by the implementation of the provisions of His Will in the years that followed—and it would be America that would become the cradle of that Administrative Order described in the Will and Testament of 'Abdu'l-Bahá.

Yet the services of John and Louise Bosch were not at an end. During the "fourth period" of the first century of the Bahá'í Dispensation, from 1921–1944, John and Louise would offer their most lasting service to the community of the Greatest Name by opening their property in Geyserville, California as a Bahá'í summer school that would provide what the Guardian later described as one "of those initial schools which, as time goes by, will, on the one hand, evolve into powerful centers of Bahá'í learning, and, on the other, provide a fertile recruiting ground for the enrichment and consolidation of its teaching force."[69]

Bahá'u'lláh directed His followers to look to 'Abdu'l-Bahá as the perfect exemplar of a pattern of Bahá'í life. There was no other person in John and Louise's life who had a greater influence on the pattern of their lives. 'Abdu'l-Bahá showed great kindness and love toward both of them, particularly toward John. For instance, after John's visit with 'Abdu'l-Bahá in New York, Washington D.C. and Chicago, he prepared to say good-bye to 'Abdu'l-Bahá, and in doing so received the unaffected kindness of the Master. John described it in this way:

> I thanked Abdul Baha for the privilege of traveling with him from New York to Washington, and thence from Washington to Chicago. Abdul Baha replied, "I wanted you to come," and then he rose and took from the table a big cake 12 or 14 inches in diameter, which he handed to me. Also, some bananas, apples, and oranges until my arms were packed full to overflowing. That was goodbye.[70]

In the space of five words—"I wanted you to come"—'Abdu'l-Bahá had filled the cup of John's heart.

When John and Louise requested to visit 'Abdu'l-Bahá in 1921, just after their return from a short-term pioneering trip to the Island of Tahiti, the Master had sent two communications to John and Louise: a telegram and a Tablet. The telegram said "Bosches permitted, Abbas," and was received by John and Louise in April, 1921. It was upon receiving this telegram that John and Louise prepared for a pilgrimage that began in November 1921. They were unaware that 'Abdu'l-Bahá had sent a Tablet on May 1, 1921, and the Tablet was not translated until a year after the passing of 'Abdu'l-Bahá. What a touching confirmation it must have been for John and Louise to receive this Tablet more than one year after the ascension of 'Abdu'l-Bahá—and a heartwarming assurance to them that their presence during the Master's ascension was His wish:

> To his honor Mr. Bosch and Mrs. Bosch
> Upon them be Bahá'u'lláh El Abha!
> He is the El Abha!
> O ye two blessed souls,
> . . . You have permission to come into the presence in the coming winter or spring. 'Abdu'l-Baha is in the utmost longing to see you.
> Upon ye be Baha El Abha,
> (Signed) 'Abdu'l-Baha Abbas.
> May 1, 1921
> Acca, Bahji
> Translated by M. A. Sohrab
> December 14, 1922
> Los Angeles, California[71]

# 2 / Dr. Florian and Grace Krug

In the spring of 1921, Dr. Florian and Grace Krug decided to move to Haifa, Palestine. Their decision was a remarkable one because it was entirely life-changing, and it attracted ridicule in the newspapers. In one instance, a full-page syndicated article, which was published in newspapers from New York to San Francisco, was sharply sardonic in its crude exaggeration of Dr. and Mrs. Krug's character: "When Dr. Florian Krug, the eminent New York surgeon, announced recently his determination to sell his rich holdings in the Metropolis of America, and, with his wife, to go to the Far East . . . all eyes in the large circle of his professional and social acquaintances focused for a time on Bahaism, to ascertain just what stuff the new lodestone is made of. It was astounding news. Neither the surgeon nor his wife was ever accused of gullibility. Not even a voice was ever heard imputing to man or wife the faintest intimation of fanaticism."[1]

There was a time when such scrutiny by the press would have wounded Florian Krug's pride. Gullible he was not, nor was he inclined to be persuaded by mysticism, and he certainly was not a fanatic. He and Grace could have stayed in New York City, where Florian was a successful surgeon with five medical offices in the city, where Grace often entertained guests in their well-appointed Park Avenue flat, where they had a maid and a cook to serve them, and where they often played golf—with both of them competing in country club golf tournaments with success. However, their desire to serve 'Abdu'l-Bahá was greater than all these material considerations. In the newspaper interview, Grace explained:

> I became interested in the Baha'i movement nearly twenty years ago. The more I studied its tenets, the more convinced I became of the importance of its demands for a universal peace. Had I needed further proof of the necessity for such new power in the troubled world today, I could easily have found it in the world war. While I needed no proof of the necessity and potential power of this great movement, nevertheless the world war has everywhere emphasized the great, urgent need of cooperation along every line, such as the Baha'i movement insists upon, for the successful bringing about of universal peace."[2]

Not to be gainsaid by the newspaper reporter's effort to impugn their decision to forsake their homeland in order to serve a Cause universally respected and dedicated to promoting the oneness of mankind, Grace explained further:

> Today the number who follow Baha'i teachings because they are convinced of the practicality of the program that all races and creeds should unite in a movement for world peace, is estimated at thirty thousand, and the movement is growing

54

rapidly in every country on earth. One of the cardinal points in the teachings of Baha'u'llah demands the abandonment of prejudice—religious, patriotic and racial—as the influence most destructive of human society. White doves and gray doves associate with each other in perfect friendship. Man draws imaginary lines on the planet and says: 'This is a Frenchman, a Mussulman, an Italian.' Upon these differences wars are waged. Men are fighting for the possession of the earth. They fight for that which becomes their graves, their cemeteries, their tombs.[3]

Grace Crossman was born in Brooklyn, New York on April 29, 1870 and was the daughter of New York City coffee importer William Henry Crossman. In appearance she was the example of simple elegance, and her dark brown eyes shone with a brightness that did not go unnoticed by those who knew her. Grace was a naturally unselfish person; sincere love was the foundation of her being. Many years later, Mrs. Coralie Franklin Cooke—writer, intellectual, and one of the most prominent contemporary Bahá'ís of African descent—observed that "Mrs. Grace Krug lays particular emphasis upon the necessity and beauty of love, and everyone who knows her is ready to aver that she is a living example of her own teaching."[4] In many ways, she was the embodiment of her name, "Grace": she had an innate sense of courteous goodwill, dignity, and conviviality.

Florian Krug was born in Mayence, Germany, on December 12, 1858. He was raised in Germany, where he attended Freiburg University. He was a member of the Hasso-Borussia Corps, which was a fraternity of students who, in the tradition of the Mensur, practiced a type of swordsmanship in which two opponents, confined within a fixed "mensur" or measure from one another, would deliberately strike the other's face with his sword. The objective for each swordsman was to demonstrate unflinching determination by stoically enduring a wound to the cheek or forehead. The scar to the face would remain as a permanent token of the bearer's firmness of opinion and purpose. In short, the Mensur was as much a mental exercise as it was a physical one: its aim was to train the student to stand his ground against any idea that was in opposition to his own, whether the idea be ideological, philosophical, or religious. Florian fought forty-seven duels and had a deep scar running almost the length of his left jawbone.[5]

Florian emigrated from Germany in 1885 and began a successful practice as a physician and a medical researcher in obstetrics and gynecology in New York. When Florian and Grace married in 1904, it was a second marriage for both of them. Florian had three children from a former marriage; the two younger children, Louise and Charles, were raised by Grace. That same year, Grace began studying the Bahá'í teachings with a Bahá'í friend named Miss Annie Boylan. Florian made it clear to Grace that he was not interested in her newfound Faith, which he dismissed as a dubious social movement that amounted to nothing more than a metaphysical pastime. But Grace stood her ground and was not deterred by her husband's prejudgments of the Bahá'í Cause.

Grace and Florian honeymooned in Italy in the northeastern village of Madonna di Campiglio in the summer of 1904, and it became a tradition for the Krug family to return to Campiglio every summer. In fact, it was there, while hiking in the Alps, that Grace realized the truth of the Revelation of Bahá'u'lláh, and she began teaching the Bahá'í Faith in Campiglio. The first person she taught was Tommaso Gallarti-Scotti, the Prince of Molfetta.* He had recently graduated college and had begun to write articles about the need for the Catholic Church to reconcile science and religion. Although he did not declare his belief in Bahá'u'lláh, he was sympathetic to His teachings.

Florian was a shrewd and discerning man, and although he did not object to Grace's teaching work, he was skeptical at first. He had lived long enough in the world to know how people can be easily taken in by an idealistic philosophy that merely begins and ends in words. He wanted to see the Bahá'í teachings in action.

Grace attended Bahá'í meetings throughout the year in New York City, and she formed close bonds with the believers there, especially Juliet Thompson, who had only recently returned from Paris where she learned of the Bahá'í Faith through May Bolles Maxwell. Miss Thompson became an enthusiastic teacher of the Cause and attracted many seekers to her home art studio at 48 West 10th Street in Greenwich Village. A friend of Juliet Thompson wrote, "Never will these meetings be forgotten. Those who were fortunate enough to assemble there in those pioneer days were tasting the spiritual happiness they had always read about, which sings on in the heart regardless of the turbulent waters of the outer world. Every evidence of a worldly atmosphere was absent."[6]

In the summer of 1908, the Krug family vacationed again in Madonna di Campiglio. Upon their return to New York City in September 1908, Grace learned from her Bahá'í friends that an

---

* For more information on Prince Molfetta, please see *https://www. geni.com/people/Fulco-Tommaso-Gallarati-Scotti-IV-Principe-di-Molfetta/321308492330004854*; Prince Molfetta: *https://it.m.wikipedia.org/wiki/Tommaso_Gallarati_Scotti*; Prince Molfetta: *https://it.wikipedia.org/wiki/Tommaso_Gallarati_Scotti*.

important event had recently occurred in the Bahá'í world. In the aftermath of the Young Turk Revolution, all political prisoners held either in confinement or house arrest under Sultan 'Abdu'l Ḥámid of the Ottoman Empire were freed. This meant that 'Abdu'l-Bahá, who had been a prisoner for forty years, was now free to leave the prison-city of 'Akká.

The news of 'Abdu'l-Bahá's release became a focal point of unity and excitement among the believers in New York City as it introduced the possibility that 'Abdu'l-Bahá would at last be free to travel to all parts of the world and spread the teachings of Bahá'u'lláh, and this was cause for rejoicing. Howard MacNutt hosted a gathering at his home to inform the believers of the news.[7] Bahá'ís and their friends filled the living room of the MacNutt residence in Brooklyn, New York. Although Grace missed attending the gathering because it took place while she was en route to the United States from Italy, she would have heard about the spiritual excitement generated at the meeting, as it was reported in the New York "Bahá'í Bulletin":

A splendid evidence of the vitality of the Bahai Cause was expressed in the gathering of Believers at 935 Eastern Parkway, Brooklyn, on Saturday, August 30th, to celebrate the "freedom of Abdul Baha." Although this was a practically midsummer meeting, and notification of it informal and hasty, the house was filled and the occasion a memorable one in Bahai history. . . . [The guests who were not Bahá'ís] were visibly moved and affected by the evidence of love and spiritual fragrance, manifested by the people of Baha, toward everybody.[8]

Many of the believers present at that meeting shared their thoughts on what 'Abdu'l-Bahá's freedom meant to them. One was Mr. William Hoar, who first heard of the Bahá'í Faith at the World Parliament of Religions in Chicago in 1893.* He spoke of his pilgrimage in 1902 and gave the history of 'Abdu'l-Bahá's imprisonment and exile. Mrs. Isabella Brittingham, who had visited 'Abdu'l-Bahá in 1901, shared a Tablet she received from the Master. Mrs. Julia Grundy expressed how she felt that 'Abdu'l-Bahá's liberation was analogous to humanity's liberation from the bonds of superstition and religious uncertainty. Mrs. Mary MacNutt said that on her pilgrimage to 'Akká in 1904, 'Abdu'l-Bahá had said, "Though my body is imprisoned, my spirit is ever free."[9] Mrs. Sarah Harris, whose husband Hooper Harris had recently spent a year teaching the Bahá'í Faith in India at the request of 'Abdu'l-Bahá, reviewed the spiritual victories that had been achieved by Bahá'ís all over the world and said that 'Abdu'l-Bahá's release was the result of these spiritual victories. Howard MacNutt concluded that "the influence from the announcement from the East enkindled Bahá'í hearts with new fire and fervor."[10]

---

* The first mention of the name of Bahá'u'lláh was at the World Parliament of Religions, which took place in Chicago in 1893. A Presbyterian minister named Henry Jessup had written a paper that was read by Reverend George A. Ford of Syria at the Parliament. The paper referred to Professor Edward G. Browne's account of his meeting with Bahá'u'lláh. One of the persons present at the reading of the paper was Mr. William Hoar of Chicago. Shortly after the World Parliament of Religions, Mr. Hoar began studying the Bahá'í teachings in Chicago with Ibrahim Khayru'lláh, a Lebanese immigrant who had learned of the Bahá'í Faith in Egypt. Later, William Hoar moved to New York, where he continued his study of the Bahá'í teachings with Anton Haddad, a friend of Khayru'lláh. Both Ibrahim Khayru'lláh and Anton Haddad learned of the Bahá'í Faith in Egypt from a Bahá'í teacher from Persia named Hájí 'Abdu'l-Karím-i-Tihrání.

No longer confined to the prison-city of 'Akká, 'Abdu'l-Bahá moved to Haifa and received pilgrims at His home at 7 Haparsim Street. Grace Krug's closest Bahá'í friend, Miss Annie Boylan, journeyed to Haifa in October of 1908, and while in the presence of 'Abdu'l-Bahá, Miss Boylan spoke of Grace's acceptance of the Cause of God. The news prompted 'Abdu'l-Bahá to write this Tablet to her:

Through Miss Boylan to Mrs. Florian Krug
He is God!
O attracted one to the Kingdom of God!

The maid-servant of God, Miss Boylan, arrived and stayed here for a few days in the enjoyment of perfect happiness. She spoke eloquently in praising thee. Her expressions of thy excellence exceeds the power of words. She said—That attracted one of God (Mrs. Krug) has a pure heart, a shining face, and a soul and conscience full of joy and happiness through Divine Glad Tidings. Consequently, my Love for thee was set in motion. I prayed with humility and submissiveness to the Divine Threshold that the rain of Favor should descend and the rain drops from the Clouds of Bounty should impart freshness and tenderness to thee beyond measure. So that thou mayest rest under the Shadow of the Tree of Life, make thy tongue eloquent in commemorating the Holiness and Sanctity of the Truth (GOD), and helped and assisted, with all the members of thy family, in doing good deeds and praiseworthy actions. Then they will all find their ways to the Kingdom of GOD, partake of Eternal Life and become manifestations of limitless bounties.
Upon thee be the Glory of ABHA!

(signed) Abdul Baha Abbas
Received October 1908
Translated by M. Enayat'ullah[11]

No doubt, the most prominent thought in the minds of most American believers was that 'Abdu'l-Bahá's release from the prison-city of 'Akká meant that He could make a journey to North America. When asked if He would make such a journey, 'Abdu'l-Bahá made clear that the friends would have to demonstrate unity in order for Him to come. In the meantime, when news came that 'Abdu'l-Bahá had arrived in France in 1911, Annie Boylan sailed for Europe upon the invitation of her friends Hippolyte and Laura Dreyfus-Barney, who had helped arrange 'Abdu'l-Bahá's visit to France. Annie arrived in Thonon-les-Bains, on the shores of Lake Geneva bordering Switzerland, on August 23, 1911, two days after 'Abdu'l-Bahá's arrival to that city.

Miss Boylan's visit was short but profound. 'Abdu'l-Bahá was staying at the Hotel du Parc where He had a chance encounter with the Persian prince, Sultán-Masúd Mírzá Zillu's-Sultán (1850–1918), the eldest son of Násiri'd-Dín Sháh, who was in voluntary exile in Europe, accompanied by his four sons. At various times, the prince had been the governor or governor-general of various provinces in Iran from 1862 to 1907 and had persecuted the Bahá'ís zealously. Hippolyte Dreyfus recounted to Juliet Thompson that upon meeting 'Abdu'l-Bahá, the prince presented his excuses for the executions he authorized. According to Hippolyte Dreyfus, 'Abdu'l-Bahá forgave him by saying, ""'All those things are in the past. Never think of them again.'""[12] Annie Boylan was a witness to this encounter, and in a letter to Mrs. Corinne True, she wrote of how the prince "abased himself before Abdul Baha, kissed the hem of His garment, and begged for permission to call on Him. Then his son, Prince Ismail, told Abdul Baha he was ashamed of the actions of his family in reference to the Bahais."[13]

In her letter to Corinne True, Annie also reported that 'Abdu'l-Bahá would come to North America under one condition: that the believers become united in their devotion to the Covenant. Unity among the believers, she wrote, would attract 'Abdu'l-Bahá like a magnet. Annie's letter concluded with a suggestion that Corinne do her part to unite the believers in Chicago while Annie would do her part in New York City to "unite with anyone and all to try to attract 'Abdu'l-Bahá."[14]

In the early days of the Bahá'í Faith in North America, the Bahá'ís had only a small number of translated texts from the writings of Bahá'u'lláh. Therefore, the believers had to rely on what they learned from talks given by 'Abdu'l-Bahá or stories from pilgrims who had met Him. When Annie Boylan returned to New York, she shared her experiences with Grace Krug. Annie's stories of 'Abdu'l-Bahá demonstrated His love and forgiveness, nobility and virtue, dignity and humility, and gave Grace further confirmations of His station as the Perfect Exemplar of the teachings of Bahá'u'lláh.

When Annie shared her experiences from her visit to 'Abdu'l-Bahá in France, Grace was most interested in the lessons from 'Abdu'l-Bahá about the principle of the oneness of mankind—the pivotal principle of the Bahá'í Faith, and the principle closest to Grace's heart. Annie Boylan wrote about it in a general letter to the friends in the United States:

At Thonon, France last August, Abdul Baha was asked what answer shall we give the people who are asking who is this Venerable Sheik. Abdul Baha said, "Tell them I am a Baha'i,

then they will ask you what is a Baha'i, you answer, 'A Baha'i
is one who has eliminated all prejudices, all religious prejudice,
all national prejudices, all racial prejudices, all political prejudices, all social prejudices, who is for the unity and harmony
of mankind, for universal peace and against war.'"[15]

During the ministry of 'Abdu'l-Bahá, most of the American
believers accepted the teachings of Bahá'u'lláh by writing directly
to 'Abdu'l-Bahá to declare their Faith. These American believers
never imagined they would meet 'Abdu'l-Bahá in person, in North
America. Therefore, when 'Abdu'l-Bahá made His historic visit to
North America in 1912, it was not only unprecedented, it was an
unimaginable fulfillment of an ardent hope of the American believers. Arriving in New York City on April 11, 1912, 'Abdu'l-Bahá
traveled throughout the United States and parts of Canada, and
He spoke about the teachings of Bahá'u'lláh until His departure
on December 5, 1912. The significance of His journey is given an
extensive overview in *God Passes By*, where Shoghi Effendi wrote
about how 'Abdu'l-Bahá's release from prison opened the way for
Him to journey to the West:

So momentous a change in the fortunes of the Faith was the
signal for such an outburst of activity on His part as to dumb-
found His followers in East and West with admiration and
wonder, and exercise an imperishable influence on the course
of its future history. He Who, in His own words, had entered
prison as a youth and left it an old man, Who never in His life
had faced a public audience, had attended no school, had never
moved in Western circles, and was unfamiliar with Western
customs and language, had arisen not only to proclaim from

pulpit and platform, in some of the chief capitals of Europe and in the leading cities of the North American continent, the distinctive verities enshrined in His Father's Faith, but to demonstrate as well the Divine origin of the Prophets gone before Him, and to disclose the nature of the tie binding them to that Faith.[16]

Twice 'Abdu'l-Bahá spoke at Florian and Grace Krug's home at 830 Park Avenue in New York. As yet, Florian was not convinced of the spiritual station of 'Abdu'l-Bahá. His son Charles Krug recollected how his father vowed, "If that old man comes into this house I'll have the doorman throw him out!" When it was clear that Grace was determined to have 'Abdu'l-Bahá come to their home, despite Florian's opposition, he retorted, "Now I can get my hands on the ringleader of this bunch!" Florian's daughter Louise said, "We were terrified. Charlie and I were standing there by the door as 'Abdu'l-Bahá came in. He put His arms out with that wonderful gesture—you could feel the love pouring out. He walked right up to my father and looked him straight in the face and asked, 'Dr. Krug, are you happy?'" Louise said, "My father simply wilted and looked like a bird that had let its wings down to enjoy the sun. I don't know anyone who opposed the Faith more violently than my father, but 'Abdu'l-Bahá gave him that love that he could not resist." From that time on, Dr. Krug never said a word against the Master.[17]

It is important to note that Florian Krug was not a vindictive man, and although the prominent scar on the left side of his face may be seen as the sign of reckless vanity, he was a man of integrity. In the Mensur tradition, such a scar was a badge of honor and was valued as an outward sign of the inward character of the man. The scar on Florian Krug's face was as imposing as his character: he was a man not to be trifled with, and yet, he was a man for whom no sacrifice was too great if it was in the service of Truth.

When 'Abdu'l-Bahá spoke at the Krug's home on July 15, 1912, He spoke of the spiritual susceptibilities bestowed upon man by God, and that man shows thankfulness to God by exercising these spiritual susceptibilities through good deeds:

God has conferred upon man the gift of guidance, and in thankfulness for this great gift certain deeds must emanate from him. To express his gratitude for the favors of God man must show forth praiseworthy actions. In response to these bestowals he must render good deeds, be self-sacrificing, loving the servants of God, forfeiting even life for them, showing kindness to all the creatures. He must be severed from the world, attracted to the Kingdom of Abhá, the face radiant, the tongue eloquent, the ear attentive, striving day and night to attain the good pleasure of God. Whatsoever he wishes to do must be in harmony with the good pleasure of God. He must observe and see what is the will of God and act accordingly. There can be no doubt that such commendable deeds are thankfulness for the favors of God.[18]

'Abdu'l-Bahá's words must have struck a deep chord of truth with Florian, and although we cannot know what Florian was thinking, it is likely he was measuring the value of his own materialistic philosophy toward life against the spiritual discipline of aligning one's will with the will of God. It could be that Dr. Krug began to realize that the spiritual path was the worthier path, for it required far greater fortitude, courage, and discipline than the material one.

Shortly after 'Abdu'l-Bahá's talk at the Krugs', He visited Dublin, New Hampshire where He stayed as a guest of Mrs. Agnes Parsons.* While there, the Master revealed a Tablet to Grace. It is unclear what prompted such a remarkable prayer written for her in the following Tablet, but clearly 'Abdu'l-Bahá was preparing her for service to the Cause:

To the maid servant of God Mrs. Florian Krug. Upon her be Baha Ollah El Abha.
He is God!
O Almighty! I am the maid servant at Thy Threshold. I am weak and impotent and Thou art the Protector and the Assister of the indigent ones!
O Thou Kind Beloved! Enkindle a fire in the heart and the soul and burn away the veils of superstition. Illumine the eyes by beholding Thy Countenance and make my heart and consciousness the envy of the rose-garden. Release me from every attachment. Confer upon me Inexhaustible Favors, so that I may not see any one save Thee; I may not seek any path except the Path of Thy Love and may not utter aught else save

---

* Agnes Parsons was a Bahá'í from Washington D.C. and is remembered for the task given to her by 'Abdu'l-Bahá during her second pilgrimage in 1920 to "arrange a Convention for unity of the colored and white races." The Convention took place at the First Congregational Church in Washington, D.C. from May 19 to May 21, 1921. Immediately after the close of the Convention, Mrs. Parsons sent the following cable to 'Abdu'l-Bahá: "Convention successful. Meetings crowded. Hearts comforted." For more information, please see "In Memoriam," *The Bahá'í World*, vol. 5, pages pp. 410–14.

the Mysteries of Thy Beauty. Verily Thou art the Seer, the Bestower and the Almighty.

(Signed) Abdul Baha Abbas

Translated by Mirza Ahmad Sohrab, August 7, 1912, Dublin, N.H.[19]

One of the Persian believers who traveled with 'Abdu'l-Bahá was Mirzá Maḥmúd-i-Zarqání who kept a diary of daily events throughout 'Abdu'l-Bahá's journey. On July 26, 1912, 'Abdu'l-Bahá asked Maḥmúd to record a most astonishing prediction about Grace's spiritual destiny, which Maḥmúd wrote in his diary:

In the afternoon 'Abdu'l-Bahá spoke of Hájí Muhammad-Taqí Vakíl'ud Dawlih, the Afnán. He also showed great kindness to some of the American Bahá'ís. About one of them, He said: "Write this in the margin of the book: The time will come when her whole family will be proud of Mrs. Krug and her faith. Her husband is still distant and heedless; the time will come when he will feel himself exalted on account of Mrs. Krug's faith. I see what they do not see. Ere long the whole of her family will consider the faith of that lady as the crown of honor on their heads."[20]

That was not the only time that 'Abdu'l-Bahá praised Grace and intimated great things about her spiritual destiny. On another occasion, right after 'Abdu'l-Bahá was leaving a talk He gave in New York City, he asked Florian's son Carl (Charles) to accompany Him in the taxi ride back to His hotel: "'Abdu'l-Bahá summoned Carl Krug to ride home with Him. Seated in the taxicab, He instructed Carl to write what He was about to say. Then 'Abdu'l-Bahá said:

'You must be very grateful to your mother—you must appreciate her greatly—you do not realize her station now or what a great honor she has bestowed on your household. She will be one of the famous women of America. You must appreciate and love her very much. All will know of her servitude.'"²¹

By saying that "all will know of her servitude," 'Abdu'l-Bahá had painted Grace's character by describing her devotion, humility and meekness toward God. In His writings, 'Abdu'l-Bahá described the requisite selflessness that underlies true servitude: "Servitude to God lieth in servitude to the friends. One must be the essence of humility and the embodiment of meekness. One must become evanescence itself and be healed of every disease of the self, in order to become worthy of thraldom to the Threshold of the Almighty."²²

'Abdu'l-Bahá's visit to America lasted nearly eight months. Two days before His departure, He spoke again at the Krug home. After the meeting, Maḥmúd wrote that Mrs. Krug's home "was filled with many people who had come just to be in 'Abdu'l-Bahá's presence," and that "group after group of older and newer believers sadly and tearfully came to see the Master, encircling Him and weeping at His imminent departure . . . Today the believers were so overcome by emotion that even a stone would be affected."²³ The theme of 'Abdu'l-Bahá's talk was the importance of spiritualizing one's own life before attempting to spiritualize the lives of others. For Florian, this theme must have resonated with his commitment to self-discipline. For Grace, it must have confirmed her resolve to serve the Cause. To all present that afternoon in the Krug home, 'Abdu'l-Bahá was giving a prescription for living a spiritual life. Among the things He said was this: "Until man acquires perfections himself, he will not be able to teach perfections to others. Unless man attains life himself, he cannot convey life to others. Unless he finds light, he cannot reflect light. We must, therefore, endeavor ourselves to attain to the perfections of the world of humanity, lay hold of ever-lasting life and seek the divine spirit in order that we may thereby be enabled to confer life upon others, be enabled to breathe life into others."[24]

As mentioned previously, Florian was a renowned physician who had dedicated his life to healing others through his skill as a surgeon. Therefore, it is likely that he agreed with the spiritual analogy suggested by 'Abdu'l-Bahá's words: one cannot heal others if he himself is sick; therefore, one who is spiritually dead cannot bring spiritual life to others.

After He left the United States, 'Abdu'l-Bahá sailed to Europe where He stayed for six months. He visited Britain, France, Austria-Hungary, Germany, arriving finally in Egypt in June of 1913.[25] On at least four occasions, Grace wrote to 'Abdu'l-Bahá while He was in Europe and Egypt, and despite His busy itinerary, He answered all her letters. Grace received one Tablet addressed to her while 'Abdu'l-Bahá was in London, a second Tablet while He was in Paris, and a third and fourth Tablet while He was in Ramleh, Egypt.[26] 'Abdu'l-Bahá received thousands of letters from believers over the course of His ministry, and no matter how consequential or inconsequential the questions asked in these letters, He answered each as though it were the most important letter to be answered that day.*

---

* Dr. Firuz Khazemzadeh has reported that, "Although 'Abdu'l-Bahá carried out many of His activities through personal contact with visitors and pilgrims and through His travels, He conducted most of His work through a vast and varied correspondence. The Bahá'í World Center currently holds nearly sixteen thousand of His letters to individuals and institutions" ((Khazemzadeh, "'Abdu'l-Bahá 'Abbás," https://www.bahai-encyclopedia-project.org).

In one letter to Him, Grace asked about the best way to advance the Cause in New York, and she suggested that the formation of committees might be an effective approach to the teaching work. 'Abdu'l-Bahá replied:

To the maidservant of God, Mrs. Krug
Upon her be Baha Ollah El Abha!
His God!
O thou my daughter in the Kingdom:
Thy letter was received. Today all the believers of God must think of conveying the Message, and not of the formation of committees; for there will be no result from the organization of the committees. It will be a name without significance. A few days they gather together and then they will be dispersed, but if they engage in teaching they will quicken the souls and in the estimation of the Merciful . . . they will become dear and beloved. This has been experienced in the West that whosoever has become the means of the guidance, the education and the refinement of the morality of the people, he becomes favored in the Divine Threshold and like unto a brilliant lamp he shines amongst all the inhabitants of the world. It is my hope that the friends of God and the maidservants of the Merciful may become conducive to the education of the souls and with a detached heart and a spirit rejoiced with the Glad-Tidings of God may they associate with all the people.

Convey on my behalf my love to thy dear son and thy kind daughter. Likewise, convey my respectful greeting to the revered Doctor. I always think of him.
Upon thee be Baha El-Abha
(signed) Abdul Baha Abbas
Translated by M. Ahmad Sohrab

January 17, 1913
London, England[27]

Even though 'Abdu'l-Bahá had departed from the shores of
North America, He kept His hand on the pulse of the believers,
especially those in New York City, which He named the "City of
the Covenant."[28] From the lessons learned from 'Abdu'l-Bahá's
visit, Grace had come to understand that to be firm in the Covenant
of Bahá'u'lláh required more than merely accepting Bahá'u'lláh's
teachings. It required the believer to accept Bahá'u'lláh as the Manifestation of God and the provisions of Bahá'u'lláh's Covenant,
which named His son, 'Abdu'l-Bahá, as His divinely appointed
successor and sole interpreter of the holy text of Bahá'u'lláh.* Such
firmness in the Covenant protects the unity among the believers
and safeguards the Cause so that the Bahá'ís may, in turn, be the
cause of spiritual unity among all the nations of the world. In fact,
at the conclusion of the Bahá'í Temple Unity Convention on April
30, 1912, 'Abdu'l-Bahá prayed for "this American nation" and
asked God to "Confirm this revered nation to upraise the standard
of the oneness of humanity, to promulgate the Most Great Peace,
to become thereby most glorious and praiseworthy among all the
nations of the world."[29] Agnes Parsons,** a Bahá'í from Washing-

---

* In His Will and Testament, 'Abdu'l-Bahá named His grandson, Shoghi
Effendi, as Guardian of the Cause of God. Several years after the death of the
Guardian, the Universal House of Justice was elected according to the provisions
outlined in the Will and Testament of 'Abdu'l-Bahá.

** Although Grace lived in New York City and Agnes lived in Washington
D.C., it was 'Abdu'l-Bahá's wish that the two women work closely together in
the promotion of the Cause. In their correspondence to one another, they frequently noted that their friendship was an eternal one because they were united

ton D.C. who hosted 'Abdu'l-Bahá several times during His stay in North America, wrote to Grace about how 'Abdu'l-Bahá's prayer for America inspired her to work alongside women in the Cause in order to establish greater unity among the believers. Grace replied to her letter enthusiastically:

February 1st, 1913
My dear Mrs. Parsons,
I agree most heartily with your suggestion to exchange monthly letters with our Sisters in the other assemblies. Any inter-change of ideas will help to unite us, and that is very important. Our Beloved Abdul-Baha will be pleased to hear of your plan. I wrote Him a long letter yesterday and told Him about it.

I am happy to tell you, my dear Sister, that the Cause in New York is growing in the most wonderful way.

Ever since the departure of Abdul-Baha I have worked with heart and soul to bring about real unity. So many of the people are easily led into all kinds of pit-falls. The Word of God is the life-giver. The responsibility of accepting the Teachings of today is very great indeed. You, my dear, impress upon the friends to grow out of all their old superstitions. A Baha'i must be able to beautify his or her character. Some of our New York women shine like brilliant stars.

---

by 'Abdu'l-Bahá. In 1919, Grace lamented that she had "neglected the duty that our Beloved Abdul-Baha laid upon me of corresponding with you," and in another letter she rejoiced that "our blessed Master brought us together for eternity" (Letter from Grace Krug to Agnes Parsons, April 4, 1919; letter from Grace Krug to Agnes Parsons, undated).

I am thinking of you . . . and what glorious days those spent in the Sun-Shine of our Master's Heavenly love. Such blessings as He showered upon us, how privileged we are to know Him. What Bounty from God to have had our eyes opened.

Oh! My dear, work and teach, never be disheartened. Let your pure heart sing the Glad-tidings. In the End, what a glorious Victory awaits us.

'Abdu'l-Bahá's Divine Spirit overwatches us, always counseling us to be brave, to be courageous and to be patient.

I suppose you have received all the Press articles from London—how beautifully He has been treated.

With Bahai love and greetings,

Yours in His Service,

Grace Krug[30]

Indeed, 'Abdu'l-Bahá was well-received in London, where He continued to promote Bahá'u'lláh's teachings. On one occasion, He spoke about the high station of women, saying that "The woman is indeed of the greater importance to the race. She has the greater burden and the greater work. Look at the vegetable and the animal worlds. The palm which carries the fruit is the tree most prized by the date grower. The Arab knows that for a long journey the mare has the longest wind. For her greater strength and fierceness, the lioness is more feared by the hunter than the lion. . . . The woman has greater moral courage than the man; she has also special gifts which enable her to govern in moments of danger and crisis."[31]

The Master's genuine love and concern for every believer is strongly felt in these precious Tablets. For instance, it appears, from 'Abdu'l-Bahá's reply to her in the following Tablet, that Grace had asked about whether her travel plans to Carlsbad, Czechoslovakia to recuperate from an illness could include some kind of service to the Cause. What a confirmation this Tablet must have been for Grace to read of 'Abdu'l-Bahá honoring Florian, who still had not surrendered his heart to the Cause of God. Here is the letter, in part:

Rue St. Didier 30
Paris, France
March 12, 1913
To the maidservant of God, Mrs. Florian Krug, New York City
Upon her be Baha-o-llah El Aba!
He is God!
O thou who art firm in the Covenant. Your letter was received. I was affected by the news of thy indisposition. Praise be to God it has disappeared by this time.

As regards your voyage to Carlsbad, it is very agreeable. You will thereby have a good recreation. But pass through London and while there meet and associate with the maid servants of the Merciful. There are several honorable ladies whose meeting will confer much joy.

I will pray to God that divine Blessings may descend upon you and your honorable husband . . . Convey my greeting and kindness especially to Miss Boylan and thy beloved daughter.

Upon thee be Baha El Abha!
(Signed) Abdul Baha Abbas
Translated by M. Ahmad Sohrab
March 12, 1913
Paris, France[32]

The mention of Grace's Bahá'í teacher, Annie Boylan, and Grace's stepdaughter, Louise Krug, is a remarkable detail. When one considers the myriad of people 'Abdu'l-Bahá met throughout His travels to the West, it is astounding how He made sure that no detail was overlooked in His remembrance of each and every soul associated with the Cause.

On April 26, 1913, Grace hosted the Fifth Annual Temple Unity Convention at her home in New York City, where a recent Tablet from 'Abdu'l-Bahá concerning firmness in the Covenant was read. The occasion was reported by Alice Ives Breed* in *Star of the West* magazine. Mrs. Breed's description of Grace's hospitality gives one a picture of how Grace's home must have appeared when 'Abdu'l-Bahá visited nearly five months prior:

> The fifth annual Convention of the Bahai Temple Unity was opened with a breakfast given at the home of Mrs. Florian Krug, 830 Park Avenue, New York, Saturday, April 26th, at 12:00 o'clock noon to the Executive Board of the Bahai Temple Unity of nine members, and the sixteen members of the New York Committee of Arrangements. Twenty-five of those invited sat around a long, beautifully appointed table, decorated with three low mounds of gorgeous pink roses, interspersed with vases of sweet peas, while asparagus vines trailed gracefully over the white cloth.

---

* Alice Ives Breed was a prominent member of the American Women's Club Movement, which was a social movement in the nineteenth century aimed at giving women an opportunity to shape public policy at the community level. She was the mother of Florence Breed Khan.

The breakfast consisted of the dishes Abdul-Baha used to have in this home: Vegetable soup, chicken, rice, salad, ices— all perfectly prepared and served.

The hostess declared it to be the happiest day of her life, and certainly her radiant face expressive of the illumined soul, confirmed the statement. To look up and down that table, at those glowing faces, was an inspiration and joy. The opportunity for conversing and exchanging ideas concerning the approaching convention; the great idea for which the building of the Mashrak-el-Azkar stands; Abdul-Baha [. . .] bidding all to arise and serve, was a scene, the memory of which will remain in the minds and hearts of those present.

The hostess called upon various ones to speak and all responded appropriately, concluding with the reading of the Tablet recently sent by Abdul-Baha concerning firmness in the Center of the Covenant.

The Executive Board went into session at two o'clock in another part of this beautiful home, while a reception to all the visiting and resident Bahais was held from three to five o'clock. Beautiful music, refreshments, fragrant flowers and illumined faces made everyone happy.[33]

By June 1913, 'Abdu'l-Bahá was in Egypt where He had a wide range of appointments, including a meeting with the Khedive (ruler of Egypt, 1867–1914, governing as a viceroy of the sultan of Turkey), the Muftí (the Muslim authority in Egypt), Persian nobles, members of the Turkish Parliament, and editors of newspapers in Cairo and Alexandria.[34] It is heartwarming to see how much attention 'Abdu'l-Bahá gave in the following Tablet to Grace, despite His busy schedule in Egypt, in which He made a reference to having "received exceedingly good news" about her. While it is unknown what that news was, it is likely that He received a report of the joyous convention she hosted in her home.

'Abdu'l-Bahá used a metaphor of the "harp and lyre" in this Tablet. As a traditional literary symbol, the harp is the instrument of the angels and often used to symbolize joy and worship while the lyre is often used as a symbol of peace, wisdom, and moderation.[35] It is possible that the Master used the symbol as a metaphor for quickening the spirit, and in doing so, offered Grace a glimpse of her spiritual destiny and the service He inspired her to achieve:

To the maid-servant of God who is enkindled with the Fire of the Love of God and attracted to the Fragrances of God, Mrs. Florian Krug, New York City.

Upon her be Baha Ollah El Abha!

He is God!

O thou my beloved daughter!

His Holiness Baha Ollah bears testimony that not for one moment have I been disengaged from thy remembrance. Whenever some news is received about thee, the utmost happiness is produced. For example, today I received exceedingly good news about thee, therefore, with infinite joyousness I write thee this epistle; so that thou mayest realize how beloved thou art in this Court: because it is my hope that in the world of woman thou mayst render a great service according to my wish. That service is: Mrs. Krug may become a magnetic power whereby to attract all the hearts; that she may carry in her hand the lamp of the Kingdom of God, conferring illumination upon the eyes; that she may adorn the meetings; that she may take hold of the Harp and lyre of the Love of God and sing such a melody as to quicken the spirit and cause the bodies to be exhilarated and be moved with joy and happiness.

Convey to thy dear son and daughter my infinite kindness. Likewise announce to the honorable Doctor my utmost respect, my sincerity of intention and my heartfelt attachment to all the members of his household for ever and ever.

Upon thee be Baha El Abha
(Signed) Abdul Baha Abbas
September 1st, 1913
Ramleh, Egypt
Translated by Mirza Ahmad Sohrab[36]

The mention of Florian was never omitted in the Tablets to Grace. As Grace's attachment to the Cause grew, she hoped that her husband would become attracted to the Cause as well. In the following Tablet, 'Abdu'l-Bahá assured Grace of Florian's potential to be attracted to the Kingdom of God. The Tablet ended with a prayer for the success of the women's meetings Grace was hosting at her home:

To the Maidservant of God Mrs. Florian Krug, New York City.
Upon her be Baha Ollah El Abha.
He is God!
O thou affectionate daughter!

Thy letter was received. Thy services to the Kingdom of Abha are more than thou hast written; indeed thou hast no thought or mention except Baha Ollah. Thou art strengthened and confirmed. I give thee promise in the clearest text and I hope that thou wilt be made successful in rendering abundant services.

The efforts of all the people whom thou seest from the king to peasant are like unto inscriptions made upon water; they write on one hand while from the other it is effaced. In this infinite creation consider how many thousand million kings and queens and illustrious men came and exerted themselves night and day in order to gain a result from life. But in the end they and their traces were effaced and vanished and are forgotten. Their results proved transitory and of no permanency. But praise be to God thou art building an edifice which is everlasting and shall never be laid waste nor forgotten. Its foundation has been laid in the Kingdom of Abha out of heavenly gems. Thank thou God.

As to thy honorable daughter: indeed she is worthy of glorification and thy loving son is qualified to enter into the Kingdom of Abha. As to the doctor, thy dear husband, if thou canst make him thy companion in soaring upwards be thou assured that he will soar to the great zenith. When one of the pair of doves takes to flight, the other will likewise fly. Now that thou hast taken wing I hope that the doctor will also fly swiftly.

With the permission and sanction of the doctor, invite the beloved of God some day and convey unto them all the message of my love and longing and say: I expect that New York be blessed, that the voice of firmness in the Covenant and Testament may reach all regions from that city, and that it may become distinguished in all ways.

O Thou King of kings! Make Thou New York blessed. Make the friends affectionate to one another; sanctify the souls; make the hearts free; illumine the world of thoughts; gladden the spirits; confer a heavenly power and bestow a Divine Confirmation; spread a merciful carpet, in order that

that city of Baha may flourish; and New York may find the blessing of the Kingdom of Abha; that land may become a delectable Paradise; a Divine garden; a heavenly plantation and a merciful flower field.

O Thou King of kings! Make Thou Mrs. Krug a maidservant of Baha, a fortunate daughter and a shining light. Illumine that household and make that family the manifestors of Infinite Bounties, in order that the maidservants of the Merciful One may celebrate there a meeting with the utmost joy and fragrance, and hold a festivity with infinite happiness and cheerfulness. Thou art the Giver, the Bestower, the Compassionate.

Upon her and upon them be Baha El Abha.

(Signed) Abdul Baha Abbas.

Received December 1913

Translated by Mirza Ali Kuli Khan[37]

'Abdu'l-Bahá's prayer that God "Illumine that household and make that family the manifestors of Infinite Bounties" was eventually realized. Grace's stepson, Charles Krug, grew up to be an active teacher of the Cause. He served on the Northeastern States Teaching Committee and traveled throughout the northeastern United States giving public lectures on the Bahá'í Faith. In a newspaper article announcing one of his lectures, Charles was described as "exceptionally well informed on world matters and is expected to touch on a solution of the problem confronting the world today."[38] His lectures were aimed at demonstrating how the Revelation of Bahá'u'lláh gives a prescription for the world's ills, with topics ranging from "Man's True Approach to God" and "God's Newly Revealed Law" to "The Promised Day is Come" and "The Truths of World Unity," where he told his audience, "By world unity I mean the establishment of a definite divine international world order possessing all the authority and power necessary to conduct the affairs of the world."[39] Charles and his wife Ernestine also taught a course at Green Acre Bahá'í School called "The Essentials of the Bahá'í Faith."[40] Charles died in 1980 and is buried at Beaverdale Memorial Park in New Haven, Connecticut. He was eighty-eight years old.

In 1916, the Krugs' daughter, Louise, married Russell Lee Steinert, director of Steinert and Sons piano manufacturer and president of the Jewett Piano Company. They had a daughter named Barbara, who was born in 1917. Tragically, in 1919, Russell was fatally injured while attempting a dive in shallow water off Sandy Point in Ipswich, Massachusetts. He was only twenty-eight years old. Ten years later, Louise married a man named Elliot Tucker Sayward, who died unexpectedly in 1940. Her daughter Barbara Steinert died in 1971, and in a recorded interview in 1974, she explained that all her life she relied on the memory of being in the presence of 'Abdu'l-Bahá in order to get through tests and difficulties. She said, "It has been such a wonderful help in my life because I have had quite a few tragedies that I have lived through and that memory [of 'Abdu'l-Bahá] has helped me to carry on."[41] She lived to be ninety-seven years old and was buried on November 8, 1988 at Forest Hills Cemetery in Jamaica Plain, Massachusetts. She remained faithful to the Cause of Bahá'u'lláh all her life.

Since His visit to the Krug home in 1912, 'Abdu'l-Bahá kept in close contact with the Krugs and continually checked how their lives were progressing. For instance, when word came to Him that Louise was engaged to Russell, 'Abdu'l-Bahá sent a Tablet to Annie Boylan in which He sent blessings to Louise. The Tablet was written in 1916, but it was not mailed to Grace until October of 1918.

'Abdu'l-Bahá's secretary, Mírzá Aḥmad Sohrab, explained that the Tablet was returned "owing to the declaration of war between Germany and the United States." The portion of the Tablet addressed to Grace and translated by Aḥmad Sohrab read as follows: "Convey my utmost kindness to the attracted maid servant of God, Mrs. Krug. It is a long time that we have heard no news from her. Of late we received the news that her daughter has the intention of marriage. We hope that this marriage will be a blessed one! In brief, that dear daughter is always remembered."[42]

This was not the only time that 'Abdu'l-Bahá wrote of His good memories of being in the Krugs' home. In a Tablet to Annie in 1916, 'Abdu'l-Bahá wrote about His hope that Grace was continuing with her teaching efforts by hosting meetings for women interested in the Bahá'í Faith:

Convey to the dear daughter Mrs. Krug my respectful greeting . . . It is hoped that her illumined meeting is still continued and the maid servants of the Merciful gather in that assembly and are occupied in the commemoration of His Highness, the Almighty, and are engaged in the promotion of the Divine Teachings and exerting themselves in the establishment of unity and concord. Those days that meetings were held in her [Mrs. Krug's] home and I used to present myself therein, and talk with the friends of God, shall never be forgotten. Upon thee and upon her be greetings and praise.[43]

'Abdu'l-Bahá took a great interest in the teaching efforts of individual believers. Both Annie and Grace had been teaching the Faith to seekers on Monday evenings at the Bahá'í Library at 416 Madison Avenue in New York City. Not only did they receive direct encouragement from 'Abdu'l-Bahá, but they also received direction from Him on the attitude they should have while teaching the Cause:

To the maid-servants of God: Mrs. Krug and Miss Boylan, New York City, USA
Upon them be Bahá ullah 'il Abhá
c/o The attracted maidservant of God, Juliet, upon her be Bahá ullah 'il Abhá.
He is God!
O ye my two beloved daughters!

Throughout these long years where communication was severed, I ever recalled you and have not forgotten you and have supplicated from the Divine Kingdom bounty and assistance. Although material communication was interrupted, yet spiritual sentiments were continuously being exchanged.

I ask from the Bounties of the Abhá Kingdom that your gathering may remain in the utmost joy and spirituality, that you may be kind to all, strive for the welfare of every human individual, exercise kindness toward the afflicted, be like unto a physician of body and soul for the sick, that ye may bestow sight to the blind, hearing to the deaf, attention to the heedless and life to those who are dead. Therein lies my hope and I am awaiting good news to emanate from your meeting.

Convey on my behalf the utmost longing to Dr. Krug. I always await the time when he undertakes a voyage to the East and makes a tour in these regions so that interview with him may be realized.

Convey the most wonderful Abhá greetings to all the friends and the maid-servants of the Merciful.

Upon ye be Bahá Ullah 'El Abhá.

Home of Abdul Bahá Abbás
Haifa, Palestine
April 4, 1919[44]

As it happened, Florian did undertake a voyage to the East. He and Grace formed a party of ten friends who traveled to Haifa in April, 1920, where they stayed as the guests of 'Abdu'l-Bahá for twenty-four days.[45] The Krugs' U.S. passport application required that they give a reason for their travel to Palestine. Grace wrote "spiritual education" as her purpose, and Florian wrote "spiritual upliftment."[46] After visiting 'Abdu'l-Bahá for more than three weeks, Florian was spiritually transformed and decided that he not only wanted to be a Bahá'í but that he wanted to dedicate the remainder of his life serving 'Abdu'l-Bahá.[47]

When the Krugs returned to New York City, Grace began hosting Bahá'í activities at her home. On Friday afternoons, she hosted and taught a children's class—which she described as glorious. On Mondays, she hosted a Bahá'í meeting in the afternoon, and she facilitated another meeting at the New York City Bahá'í Library on Monday evenings.[48] Grace must have written to 'Abdu'l-Bahá about Florian's and her efforts to educate themselves spiritually because 'Abdu'l-Bahá answered in the Tablet that follows below. It is of interest to note that this Tablet was also published in Reality Magazine, which was a publication of the New York City Bahá'í community. The cover of the magazine read "REALITY: A Magazine Devoted to the Elimination of Prejudice, Religious, Racial, and Class."[49] Also, the Tablet mentions the name of thirteen-year-old Adeline Nicholai. She was one of the children in Grace's study class, and Grace must have written to 'Abdu'l-Bahá about her. He wrote:

To the dear maidservant of God, Mrs. Florian Krug, unto her
be the Glory of God, the Most Glorious.

He is the Most Glorious,

O thou revered dear daughter:

They letter has been received. Praise be unto God on your
return to America, you went with the utmost enthusiasm and
rapture, I hope that these people whom you have converted
will, every one, become a corner-stone in the great Edifice.
The maidservant of God, Adeline Nicholai, is mentioned in
the Kingdom of Abha and is bestowed with the effulgence of
Favor.

His honor, Dr. Krug, my dear friend, is always in mind.
I do never forget him. It is my hope that he has become
a teacher of divine philosophy; that he speaks of the realm
of the Kingdom; that he is charmed by Truth, forgetting
entirely the world of nature; that he will prove to be a banner
of Guidance, and the propagator of the Light of the Higher
Realm. Unquestionably it becomes so.

Praise be unto God the Cause of God is developing in New
York and the friends are in unity and concord. Mr. and Mrs.
Deuth are exerting their utmost to the publication journal
"REALITY." The friends should help them.

Praise be unto God the fasting was observed with the utmost
pleasure. It is my hope that all the divine Commandments will
be practiced in that continent.

Unto thee be Abha Glory!

(Signed Abdul Baha Abbas)

May 28, 1921

Haifa, Palestine

Translated by Aziz 'Ullah Khan S. Bahadur, Haifa, Palestine[50]

By the time Grace received this Tablet, she and Florian had already decided to move to Haifa. Among Grace's personal papers is a copy of a cable from her to 'Abdu'l-Bahá, dated June 21, 1921, that read, "GRATITUDE FOR BOUNTY."[51] Presumably, the cable indicated that she and Florian had 'Abdu'l-Bahá's permission to come to Haifa.

Florian and Grace departed from New York on the 15th of October, 1921 and arrived in Haifa on the 18th of November, ten days before the passing of 'Abdu'l-Bahá. Their ship anchored in the Bay of Haifa, and they were met by Rúḥí Afnán and Saichiro Fujita.* They were taken to the Western Pilgrim House at 4 Haparsim Street, where 'Abdu'l-Bahá greeted them and said He was happy they had come. Then, He walked out of the Western Pilgrim House and asked Grace and Florian to come with Him. Grace described it this way: "He led the way out of the house, up the street to the gate of His own residence, into His garden, and up a flight of outside stairs to a room over the garage that had been built during our absence of the past year. He turned, and smiled and said, 'Now I am going to give you and Dr. Krug my room.' I burst into tears, I don't know why, such a feeling of apprehension came over me. His grandson, Ruhi Afnan, tried to comfort me by saying, 'The family are all very happy, Mrs. Krug, that the Master has decided to move back into the big house, as we were anxious about His sleeping out here alone.'"[52]

---

* Rúḥí Afnán was a cousin of Shoghi Effendi. His mother was Tuba, one of the daughters of 'Abdu'l-Bahá. Saichirō Fujita grew up in Japan; he immigrated to the United States in the early 1900s, where he learned of the Bahá'í Faith. When 'Abdu'l-Bahá visited the United States, Fujita traveled with Him to various cities. After the Great War, 'Abdu'l-Bahá arranged for Fujita to live in Haifa.

There are several accounts from those present in the household of 'Abdu'l-Bahá suggesting that He knew of His approaching ascension, but, as a kindness, He prepared His household slowly through subtle allusions to His approaching death. 'Abdu'l-Bahá had several dreams that foreshadowed His ascension, and Shoghi Effendi explained one of them in this way:

Through the dreams He dreamed, through the conversations He held, through the Tablets He revealed, it became increasingly evident that His end was fast approaching. . . . Whilst occupying a solitary room in the garden of His house, He recounted another dream to those around Him. *"I dreamed a dream,"* He said, *"and behold, the Blessed Beauty* (Bahá'u'lláh) *came and said to Me: 'Destroy this room.'"* None of those present comprehended the significance of this dream until He Himself had soon after passed away, when it became clear to them all that by the "room" was meant the temple of His body.[53]

It was not through dreams alone that 'Abdu'l-Bahá foretold His ascension. Knowing the shock that His passing would produce, He made subtle efforts to prepare those closest to Him for the inevitable. The following story related by Shoghi Effendi illustrates how carefully and deliberately 'Abdu'l-Bahá intimated His departure from this earthly life:

About two weeks before His passing He had spoken to His faithful gardener in a manner that clearly indicated He knew His end to be nigh. *"I am so fatigued,"* He observed to him, *"the hour is come when I must leave everything and take My flight. I am too weary to walk.*" He added: "*It was during the closing days of the Blessed Beauty, when I was engaged in gathering together His papers which were strewn over the sofa in His writing chamber in Bahjí, that He turned to Me and said: 'It is of no use to gather them, I must leave them and flee away.' I also have finished My work. I can do nothing more. Therefore must I leave it, and take My departure.*"[54]

Grace noted these intimations from 'Abdu'l-Bahá, but only in hindsight. She said, "He so veiled the knowledge of his passing that we did not know it until the very hour."[55] Indeed, it was unexpected. Grace wrote that she had feelings of sadness in the days leading up to the ascension of 'Abdu'l-Bahá—a feeling that she could not explain until afterward:

The last nine days in which we were blessed with His presence on earth, His life from hour to hour was so busy and beautiful to watch, that after my early morning visit each day to the Shrine of the Bab, I stood at my window to catch as many glimpses of the Master as possible. In the morning He would seat Himself in the garden, under the grape arbor, to receive the many visitors seeking His wisdom. There were Generals in gaudy uniforms, Arabs, again a poor man or woman seeking alms. He was so beautiful and serene, with a sweetness of spirit that I had never noticed before. There was an air of finality and completeness around Him. The first private interview that Dr. Krug and I had with the Master in His reception room, I knelt at His feet and held my miniature up to Him to bless. He looked at it intently with an expression on His dear face unutterably sad and said, "It is most beautiful, put it away, do not wear it while you are in Haifa as my enemies will use it against me." Then He chanted a short commune, placed the miniature upon His heart for a moment and returned it to me. Again that same feeling of sadness came over me.[56]

It was Florian who was called to the bedside of 'Abdu'l-Bahá at the moment of His passing. Because he and Grace were lodged in the room that 'Abdu'l-Bahá had built for Himself as an addition to the house, Florian was only a flight of stairs away from the entrance to the main house and to the room where 'Abdu'l-Bahá slept.[57] At the request of the holy family, Florian wrote a formal statement pronouncing the death of 'Abdu'l-Bahá. The medical evaluation was written in Florian's own handwriting and concluded that the Master died of natural causes.[58]

The importance of such a formal statement by Florian cannot be underestimated. In the absence of an official evaluation of death, the enemies of the Cause might have taken opportunities to make seditious claims about the cause of death. In His lifetime, 'Abdu'l-Bahá was surrounded by enemies who, He wrote, "do not doubt the validity of the Covenant but selfish motives have dragged them to this condition. It is not that they do not know what they do— they are perfectly aware and still they exhibit opposition."[59] In the opening lines of His Will and Testament, 'Abdu'l-Bahá made clear the importance of safeguarding the Cause against those whose selfish motives become the cause of dissension:

All-praise to Him Who, by the Shield of His Covenant, hath guarded the Temple of His Cause from the darts of doubtfulness, Who by the Hosts of His Testament hath preserved the Sanctuary of His most Beneficent Law and protected His

Straight and Luminous Path, staying thereby the onslaught of the company of Covenant-breakers, that have threatened to subvert His Divine Edifice . . .[60]

Florian's professional role as a medical doctor led him to be able to perform a valuable service for the holy family. In a letter to his son Charles, Florian described the honor of being able to serve the Master and the privilege of an intimate parting with the Master at the moment of His passing:

> We arrived at Haifa on November 18th and were most heartily welcomed by the Beloved Master, His family and all the friends. He bestowed the great honor upon us of assigning to us his own room, which had only recently been built as an annex to His mansion and which He had occupied but a few weeks, instead of us being installed in the Pilgrim house for American and European guests.
>
> I noticed upon our arrival a great change that had taken place in His physical condition. He was tired and weary although mentally as youthful as ever.
>
> Nine days we spent in His presence, while He showered kindness and love upon us. Shortly after 1 o'clock A.M. on Monday the 28th of November I was hastily summoned to His bedside. He was beyond any medical help. I had the great privilege of perceiving His last earthly breath and of closing His loving eyes. The scene of agony, grief and sorrow after His departure are indescribable and unforgettable.[61]

Of the moment of the Master's passing, Shoghi Effendi wrote:

At 1:15 A.M. He arose, and, walking to a table in His room, drank some water, and returned to bed. Later on, He asked one of His two daughters who had remained awake to care for Him, to lift up the net curtains, complaining that He had difficulty in breathing. Some rose-water was brought to Him, of which He drank, after which He again lay down, and when offered food, distinctly remarked: *"You wish Me to take some food, and I am going?"* A minute later His spirit had winged its flight to its eternal abode, to be gathered, at long last, to the glory of His beloved Father, and taste the joy of everlasting reunion with Him.[62]

Even though 'Abdu'l-Bahá gave many signs of His imminent death, it was not enough to quell the grief that overcame the members of the household. Shoghi Effendi wrote, "The news of His passing, so sudden, so unexpected, spread like wildfire throughout the town, and was flashed instantly over the wires to distant parts of the globe, stunning with grief the community of the followers of Bahá'u'lláh in East and West. Messages from far and near, from high and low alike, through cablegrams and letters, poured in conveying to the members of a sorrow-stricken and disconsolate family expressions of praise, of devotion, of anguish and of sympathy."[63]

Florian and Grace remained in Haifa until February, 1922. Having planned to give their life to serving 'Abdu'l-Bahá in Haifa, they suddenly felt like homeless wanderers and would have to find another path of service than the one they had anticipated. After giving their wholehearted support to Shoghi Effendi as the one whom 'Abdu'l-Bahá appointed as Guardian of the Cause, Florian and Grace decided that Florian would visit Freiburg, Germany, his old university town, and Grace would journey back to the United States to be present at the National Convention in May, 1922 where she could share the experiences of being in the presence of 'Abdu'l-Bahá during the days before His ascension. In his report of the Convention, Louis Gregory wrote that Grace Krug "gave a graphic and powerful description of the funeral of Abdul-Baha, the officials and dignitaries that took part in honoring him, the eloquent eulogies that were delivered by the representatives of various religions and the mass of weeping and moaning humanity, to the number of ten thousand, who followed his body, borne aloft by loving hands to its resting place in the Sacred Shrine on Mount Carmel."[64]

Florian's health weakened after the passing of 'Abdu'l-Bahá, and he contracted pneumonia. His decision to visit Freiburg was in the hope that he would regain his health and come to terms with his grief. His thoughts may have wandered back to how he had been faintly mocked in American newspapers for his decision to move to Palestine to serve the Master. One headline had read "Luxury Sacrificed by Surgeon" and had stated that "one of America's wealthiest and most celebrated surgeons is going to leave his practice and his house in New York to devote the remainder of his life to religion."[65] Indeed, Florian had been completely transformed by religious faith. He had found a Cause worthy of his service and self-sacrifice, and he had given up all material attachments in order to do so. There was no jewel more precious to Dr. Florian Krug than 'Abdu'l-Bahá, as Florian himself related in this story of a time when he took a photograph of the Master without His permission:

In April 1920, a feast of Rizwan was given at the house of Enayatullah Esphahani. When our Beloved Master entered the garden, this snapshot was taken by me. The Master turned and said in English, "You are a thief." Later in the house He referred to this incident jokingly saying, "There is a thief among us. I shall have him delivered to the judges for punishment." To which I replied, "I am ready to receive the severest punishment, because I have stolen the most precious thing on this earth, namely the picture of our Beloved Master."[66]

What a transformation from Florian's days as a Mensur swordfighter! He had surrendered to 'Abdu'l-Bahá and now would have to find a way to live without the presence of his Master.

After the Convention, Grace sailed for Europe on May 27, 1922 and arrived in Freiburg on June 8, 1922, where she joined Florian. Grief weighed heavily on their hearts as they tried to contemplate a future entirely different than the one they had planned in Haifa. They traveled to Madonna di Campiglio, the village in the Tyrolean Alps where Grace had her spiritual awakening, and the place where the Krug family had spent nearly every summer as a family since 1904. The villagers there spoke both German and Italian, and, over the years, Florian and Grace developed friendships with many who were interested in learning about the Bahá'í Faith.

While in Campiglio that summer of 1922, an extraordinary opportunity arose to renew an acquaintance with Tommaso Gallarti-Scotti, the Prince of Molfetta. The reader may recall that it was in Campiglio in 1904 that Grace had begun an investigation into the truth of Bahá'u'lláh's Revelation and had mentioned the name of 'Abdu'l-Bahá to the prince.[67] The prince had written articles about how the practice of the Catholic Church should become reconciled with modern science. After his articles were condemned by the Holy See, he capitulated, but he did not abandon his interest in spiritual progress. Since the prince was the first person to whom Grace gave

93

the message of Bahá'u'lláh, she never forgot him. Writing seventeen
years after first teaching the prince, Grace described the story of
his receptivity to the Faith and how she and Florian renewed their
friendship with him so many years later:

This is my seventeenth summer here. I love it better than any
place on Earth with the exception of Haifa. I am praying most
earnestly to Abdul Baha to make an international Centre of
Campiglio. Charming people from all over Europe as well as
America gather here. Seventeen years ago the first person I
spoke to about Abdul-Baha was an Italian Prince, an ardent
Truth Seeker. He seemed so interested in the teachings that
the following summer, when Miss Boylan was on her way to
visit Acca, I sent her to see Prince Molfetta in Milan. She had
a long interview with him and during her stay with the Master
she told Him of her experiences in Milan. The Master at once
revealed a glorious Tablet for the Prince, telling him he was
the first non-believer He had ever written to.

Years passed by, not a word did we hear of the Prince. I
thought he was dead. Upon my arrival in Campiglio, I at once
asked a mutual friend what has become of Prince Molfetta and
heard to my delight that he was well and expected to arrive here
by the very next day with his charming wife and two beautiful
children. We have met and have had a long talk about the
Revelation. The seed our Divine Father planted when He sent
the Prince that glorious Tablet is taking root. God be pleased!
The first word the Prince said was the letter from that wonderful man in Palestine was his most treasured possession.

. . . Please give my devoted love to all the friends and ask
them to pray that the doors of teaching will be opened more

and more to me and the Madonna di Campiglio will become a great Center of Light.[68]

Grace and Florian found a purpose in their teaching opportunities in Campiglio, but Florian's health continued to decline. His battle with pneumonia persisted, and they moved to Merano where Florian could receive medical attention. Sadly, Florian passed away in Merano, Italy on August 20, 1924. He was sixty-five years old.

To heal her wounded heart, Grace decided to make a pilgrimage to Haifa. She wrote about her plans to Agnes Parsons:

Hotel Finstermunz
Merano, Italy
October 2, 1924
Dear Mrs. Parsons,

Since your dear and welcome letter reached me dated June 16th I have lived through severe trials—I have thought of you often my dear and wanted to write but the incessant care and anxiety of my beloved husband's illness during those months before he left this plane of life prevented me. Now, I can answer all your questions when we meet.

I sail for Haifa on October 16th. I want to first heal my wounded heart in the Holy Shrine of our Divine Father, Abdul-Baha. I shall remain with the Holy family until after Ascension Day, November 28th. Then I hope, through the power of His love and Bounty, to return to New York refreshed in body and spirit ready to work for the Holy Cause as never before!

I am taking a radiant soul to Haifa, Fraulein Focke of Freiburg, Germany who assisted me in the care of Dr. Krug for so many months before his death . . . I am looking forward with such joy to my meeting with our Beloved Shoghi Effendi. Thank God he is back again in Haifa . . . Upon my return, I hope to have the joy of seeing you—I shall be the guest of my sister Mrs. Florence Roe at the Hotel Plaza in New York for several months. I shall sail from Bremen, Germany in the S.S. Columbus the first part of January, 1925.

. . . My Bahai love and greetings to all the Washington friends. I would like to write to you in detail of all that has happened, but I am overwhelmed with letters of condolence to answer.

Until we meet,

Lovingly, Grace Krug[69]

Among the Krug papers held at the United States Bahá'í Archives, no pilgrims' notes exist from Grace's visit to Haifa in 1924. In a letter to Agnes Parsons, she wrote, "I am very hungry for spiritual communion with those who know how the tests of this life have been very severe for all of us since the ascension of Abdul-Baha."[70] Surely her time in Haifa was spent in personal reflection and spiritual renewal in order to continue her teaching efforts under the guidance of Shoghi Effendi.

Grace returned to the United States on January 25, 1925, accompanied—as she mentioned in her letter above—by Hannah Focke. Grace and Hannah stayed with Grace's sister, Mrs. Florence Roe, for some months and then settled in the small town of Chester, about one hundred miles from New York City. Grace continued to travel to Italy once a year and spent most of her time in a modest apartment in Merano, Italy—the town where Florian was buried. She corresponded a great deal with Agnes Parsons, to whom she wrote, "I have had much pain in the region of my heart."[71] Although Grace was speaking literally of the health of her heart, she was also speaking figuratively of living with a broken heart. In that same letter, she wrote of her reliance on 'Abdu'l-Bahá for spiritual and physical strength: "I am under the protection of His loving Wings and I absolutely trust Him!" In a letter to her friends Doris and Horace Holley, she wrote, "I am so far away from my friends and active service in the Cause, struggling to recover my health that I often wonder if the day will ever come when I can return to America strong enough to travel through the United States on a Teaching tour."[72]

Even though Grace felt that her health kept her from being active in the teaching work while she was in Merano, she was effective in attracting receptive souls. She wrote to Agnes, "I have been favored in giving the Message to some German Americans here as well as the Minister and his wife of the little English Church in Merano." In addition to hosting interested seekers in her apartment, she did not neglect the education of her own soul. She read Bahá'u'lláh's Epistle to the Son of the Wolf, which was written in 1891, one year before the passing of Bahá'u'lláh. It is an epistle written to Áqá Najafí, a Muslim cleric in Isfahan who was the son of the cleric responsible for the execution of two brothers who would later be known as the "King of Martyrs" and the "Beloved of Martyrs."[73] The Guardian explained that the Epistle to the Son of the Wolf is "the last outstanding Tablet revealed by the pen of Bahá'u'lláh, in which He calls upon that rapacious priest to repent of his acts, quotes some of the most characteristic and celebrated passages of His own writings, and adduces proofs establishing the validity of His Cause."[74] When Grace finished her first reading of the Epistle to the Son of the Wolf, she picked it up again and read it a second time.[75] Perhaps she read it twice because the book is the culmination of the Revelation of Bahá'u'lláh written at the end of His life, or perhaps she was interested in understanding Bahá'u'lláh's sorrow over the death of the two brother-martyrs. Either way, her close reading of the Epistle to the Son of the Wolf showed the depth of her longing for the vivifying Word of Bahá'u'lláh.

Grace continued to serve the Cause until her death in Chester, New York, on December 30, 1939. In the last years of her life, she was able to fulfill a long-held wish of setting out on a Bahá'í teaching tour to various cities in the United States, including in her home state of New York where one newspaper introduced her as a "world traveler" who would speak on the subject of the Bahá'í Revelation.[76]

In 1944, the National Spiritual Assembly of the Bahá'ís of the United States and Canada published a review of the first hundred years of the Bahá'í Faith called *The Bahá'í Centenary: A Record of America's Response to Bahá'u'lláh's Call to the Realization of the Oneness of Mankind.* It was a lengthy review and covered the history of the central figures of the Cause, the history of the Bahá'í Faith in the United States and Canada, the development of administrative institutions, and the history of the teaching work. In the section called "Teaching Activity from 1912–1921," the National Spiritual Assembly wrote, "With the ascension of 'Abdu'l-Bahá in 1921, the Bahá'í Faith passed into another and distinctly different period of development. The Tree of the Covenant continued to grow, and from His Supreme Heights of Glory 'Abdu'l-Bahá must have witnessed how His wishes were being fulfilled. He had said, 'When I leave the world I want My heart to be assured that the Blessed Beauty (Bahá'u'lláh) has self-sacrificing servants who, in the utmost reverence, arose to serve the Cause of God.' Many self-sacrificing servants and maid-servants did arise and serve, and historians of the future will record the stirring details of their loyal services."[77] Following this statement was a list of those Bahá'ís who "made a beginning of the future record of teaching activity" in North America. Among the sixty-four names listed were Thornton Chase, Lua Getsinger, Howard MacNutt, Helen Goodall, Agnes Parsons, May Maxwell, and Grace Krug.[78]

When one contemplates the lives of Grace and Florian Krug, one cannot help but be struck by their courage to change their lives. Although Florian was at the height of his professional career and Grace was at the height of her social career, they made a conscious decision to sever themselves completely from their material aspirations. A few months before Grace and Florian left New York City in 1921 to live in Haifa, the New York Herald published an article that began with the headline "Doctor to Give Up all for Bahaism" followed by an article that read, "Dr. Florian who has offices at 615 Madison avenue and is one of the best known surgeons in America, is to abandon his large practice and his home here next autumn and devote himself to the Bahai movement, to which he has become a convert. Mrs. Krug said that she and her husband would make their future home in Haifa, Palestine, the home of Abdul-Baha, who they believe fulfills the prophecy of the New Testament and has come upon earth to lead mankind to truth."[79]

In a letter to Grace, Carl Scheffler, Treasurer of the National Spiritual Assembly of the Bahá'ís of the United States and Canada, thanked her for her contribution to the Temple Fund and added a personal note to her at the close of his letter: "I think of you and Dr. Krug very often and of the Doctor's service to our beloved Abdul-

Baha at the time of His passing. This was a wonderful bounty to you both, for I am quite sure that future generations will know all of the details of this that happened to you in the Blessed Presence."[80]

Florian and Grace Krug's plan to live in Haifa was a dream that lasted only nine days. Their journey may not have ended up as they planned, but for such souls, Bahá'u'lláh promises a great spiritual destiny: "O My servants! Sorrow not if in these days and on this earthly plane, things contrary to your wishes have been ordained and manifested by God, for days of blissful joy, of heavenly delight, are assuredly in store for you. Worlds, holy and spiritually glorious, will be unveiled to your eyes. You are destined by Him, in this world and hereafter, to partake of their benefits, to share in their joys, and to obtain a portion of their sustaining grace. To each and every one of them you will, no doubt, attain."[81]

# 3 / Johanna Hauff

Atop a hill above the city of Stuttgart, Germany, stands a country villa in the shape of a fairy-tale castle. Its steep gable roof, its robust towers topped with weather vanes, its spiral staircases, its loggias, and its alcoves give one the sense that the villa is alive, with a consciousness of its own existence. At one time, a blanket of vineyards and a fruit orchard wrapped around the shoulders of the hill and partially encircled the castle in green. The villa is reached by a curving path that turns and climbs gently until it stops at a wooden medieval front door that is braced with imposing iron hinges. To the eye, it is a pleasing combination of medieval and modern, gothic and romantic, castle and cottage; and it was the place that Johanna Hauff called home.

Villa Hauff is now owned by the city of Stuttgart and is located on Ulandshohe hill at Gerokstrasse 7 in Stuttgart.[1] Originally called "Villa Regina," it was built in 1904 for Johanna's mother, Maria Regina, and designed by architect Karl Hengerer, who was inspired by Romanesque, Gothic, and Renaissance styles and solid craftsmanship.[2] The mixture of architectural styles so fancifully rendered were intended as a reflection of the people who lived there. In its day, it was an unusual design for Stuttgart, the capital city of the Kingdom of Württemberg, a German state within the area that is now Baden-Württemberg. This was a city rapidly becoming a place characterized by the deep aristocratic traditions of the past and the rising industrial innovations of the future.

Johanna Hauff's father was renowned industrialist Dr. Friedrich (Fritz) Wilhelm Albert Hauff (1863–1935), a chemist who made his fortune patenting chemicals for use in plate photography, which preceded photographic film on rolls.[3] By the early 1900s, Fritz Hauff joined the Württemberg society of new millionaires, with a fortune estimated at eight million gold marks and an annual income of one million gold marks ($250,000).[4] It was not uncommon at that time for the new industrialist millionaires to seek out connections with the aristocratic hereditary elites. Both sides benefited from an alliance; one side gained social status and the other gained access to the capital that was often needed for supporting the vast parcels of land they owned. When Fritz Hauff married Württemberg aristocrat Maria Regina Elisabeth Freyin von König, it was indeed a marriage of industrial wealth with ancestral legacy, but it was also a marriage of love. Life in Villa Hauff was idyllic. The inside of the castle was filled with Fritz's whimsical household inventions, an art studio for Maria Regina, and a workshop in which their four children could play.

To understand the events that led to Johanna Hauff being present in the house of 'Abdu'l-Bahá on the night He ascended, it is important to understand how she became a Bahá'í and the Bahá'í community in which she became rooted in the Cause. The Bahá'í Faith had its beginnings in Germany as early as 1905, when Johanna would have been eleven years old. The date she and her family learned of the Faith is not certain, but it is certain that her family would have learned about the Faith upon 'Abdu'l-Bahá's visit to Stuttgart in 1913 when Johanna would have been nineteen years old.

It so happened that across the street from Villa Hauff was Villa Wagenburg, the home of Bavarian industrialist Johann Heinrich Solivo and his wife Amalie, known as Emma.[5] Their daughter, Frau Alice Solivo Schwarz, had become a Bahá'í sometime around 1911. Eventually, her husband, Albert Schwarz, who was Honorary Consul for Norway in the Kingdom of Württemberg, became a Bahá'í, and together they did much to advance the Faith in Stuttgart and were instrumental in petitioning 'Abdu'l-Bahá to visit Stuttgart in 1913.[6] A very special occasion with 'Abdu'l-Bahá would take place on April 6, 1913 in the garden of Villa Wagenburg, across the street from Villa Hauff. It would be an occasion that the Bahá'ís of Stuttgart would remember for the rest of their lives and whose recollection would be passed down from generation to generation. 'Abdu'l-Bahá's influence on the Bahá'í community of Stuttgart would inspire Johanna Hauff to make a pilgrimage to Haifa, which would culminate in the honor of being present in the house of 'Abdu'l-Bahá on the night of His ascension in 1921.

The first teacher of the Bahá'í Faith in Stuttgart was German-born Karl Edwin Fischer (1861–1936) who became a Bahá'í in New York in 1903.[7] Early in 1905, he traveled on pilgrimage to meet 'Abdu'l-Bahá and was encouraged by Him to return to Germany and teach the Cause there.[8] Edwin Fischer arrived in Ludwigsburg in April, 1905 and opened a dental practice in Stuttgart about 1906. He was successful in attracting some people to the Cause, but soon realized he needed help with the teaching work. It is likely that he wrote to 'Abdu'l-Bahá for assistance because in 1907, 'Abdu'l-Bahá wrote to

Aḥmad Sohrab in Washington D.C. to look for a Bahá'í suitable to go to Germany.[9] When German-American Alma Knobloch of Washington D.C. responded to the call to Germany, 'Abdu'l-Bahá wrote a Tablet to her family wherein He said, "Truly, I say, Miss Alma Knobloch will show forth and demonstrate on this trip that she is a beloved maid-servant in the Threshold of Oneness, is wise and intelligent and spiritual in the Kingdom of the True One."[10]

Miss Alma Knobloch arrived in Stuttgart on August 9, 1907 and immediately formed a teaching team with Miss Margarete Döring, a local Bahá'í. The women shared a home together and Alma regarded her friendship with Margarete as one of the most important friendships of the fourteen years she lived in Germany.[11] Miss Döring was a member of the Frauenclub (Women's Club), and it was there that Miss Knobloch and Miss Döring hosted the first Bahá'í public meeting in Stuttgart on October 29, 1907.[12] By March of 1908, the Stuttgart community had grown to over thirty believers, and they formed a "Bahá'í-Vereinigung," which was a Bahá'í Association that could organize the growing Bahá'í community there.[13] Although not formally a Local Spiritual Assembly at that time, it was one of the first Bahá'í consultative bodies to be formed in Europe. When the community celebrated Naw Rúz that year at the Women's Club, it was, perhaps, the first Bahá'í holy day commemorated in Germany.[14]

Alma Knobloch hosted Bahá'í meetings nearly every night of the week. Sometimes she was invited to host the gatherings at other people's homes, sometimes she would host them in her own home, and sometimes she would host Friday evening talks at the city museum.[15] As there were limited translations of the Bahá'í writings in German, Alma asked for help from her sister Fanny in Washington, D.C., and together they translated some of 'Abdu'l-Bahá's Tablets from English into German. By 1908, four Tablets of 'Abdu'l-Bahá were published in German in a pamphlet called the "Tabelle Allgemeiner Belehrung" (Table of Instructions), which outlined the basic teachings of the Bahá'í Faith. In 1909 the Bahá'ís of Stuttgart published a translation of the Hidden Words and a book on the history of the Bahá'í religion.[16] At the meetings, Bahá'í prayers and writings were read, and talks were given by resident Bahá'ís of Stuttgart or by one of the various traveling teachers who came through Stuttgart, such as Sidney Sprague in 1907 and Marion Jack in 1908, both of whom had come from North America. Later, in 1911, Lady Blomfield of England and Hippolyte Dreyfus from France gave talks at these gatherings, which deepened the believers' understanding of the Cause.[17] Perhaps the most anticipated of these traveling teachers was Mr. Louis G. Gregory, who was sent to Stuttgart by the Master Himself.

Louis Gregory became a Bahá'í in Washington, D.C., through the teaching efforts of Alma Knobloch's sister, Pauline Knobloch Hannen, and her husband Joseph Hannen. Louis Gregory's biographer, Gayle Morrison, notes "the tributes that 'Abdu'l-Bahá and Shoghi Effendi paid him [Louis Gregory] meant the most. But after theirs, no one's high regard could have meant more than that of Joseph Hannen, his teacher and his close friend."[18] The Knobloch sisters were like family to Louis Gregory, so when Mr. Gregory arrived in Stuttgart, the welcome he received from Alma Knobloch must have felt like a homecoming.

Louis Gregory had arrived from Egypt, where he had been a guest of 'Abdu'l-Bahá in Ramleh, near Alexandria. From Ramleh, 'Abdu'l-Bahá had sent Louis Gregory to Palestine to visit the holy shrines of Bahá'u'lláh and the Báb. After his pilgrimage to the holy shrines, Louis Gregory returned to Egypt, where he stayed with 'Abdu'l-Bahá for two weeks. Louis Gregory wrote of his time with 'Abdu'l-Bahá in his diary, which he called *The Heavenly Vista*. The following was recorded in his diary on his last day in 'Abdu'l-Bahá's presence:

> April 29. At the close of a visit among the friends in Cairo that was both pleasant and interesting, I proceeded again to Ramleh. 'Abdu'l-Bahá received me with gracious kindness and asked, "What day were you at 'Akka?" Greetings from the friends at the various points visited were delivered and He was also told of the beginning of the Feast of Ridvan. Mention was also made of the great kindness and love found in the hearts of the friends. He repeated, "You must visit Persia." He also directed me to visit Stuttgart, Paris, London, and various points in America. 'Abdu'l-Bahá appeared hard-worked and weary. At our parting He lavished His great affection upon me, although the unworthiest of His servants.[19]

Louis Gregory traveled from Egypt to Stuttgart and arrived in early May, 1911, where he was the honored guest at meetings held on at least four occasions.[20] The Bahá'ís of Stuttgart had embraced the Cause of Bahá'u'lláh and had devoted themselves to the Center of His Covenant. They had come to love 'Abdu'l-Bahá without ever meeting Him, so naturally, they were eager for any details of 'Abdu'l-Bahá that Mr. Gregory could share with them. Louis Gregory had penned a description of 'Abdu'l-Bahá after his pilgrimage, and if he shared anything close to this pen-portrait with the believers in Stuttgart, they were sure to have clung to every word:

When . . . I saw him for the first time he was about sixty-seven years of age, about the medium height, with a strong frame and symmetrical features. His face was deeply furrowed and his complexion about the shade of parchment. His carriage was erect and his form strikingly majestic and beautiful. His hands and nails were shapely and pure. His silver hair touched his shoulders. His beard was snow white, with eyes light blue and penetrating, his nose somewhat aquiline. His voice was powerful, but capable of infinite pathos, tenderness and sympathy. His dress was that of the Oriental gentleman of rank, simple and neat, yet very graceful. The color of his apparel was light, the outer robe being made of alpaca. On his head rested a light fez surrounded by a white turban. The meekness of the servant, the majesty of a king, were in that brow and form.[21]

Herr Friedrich Schweizer, one of the Stuttgart Bahá'ís who hosted Louis Gregory in his home, wrote that Louis Gregory "came to us from the presence of Abdul-Baha, throbbing with new life and light."[22] In His writings, Bahá'u'lláh quotes Muḥammad who said, "Blessed the man that hath visited 'Akká, and blessed he that hath visited the visitor of 'Akká."[23] How glorious it must have been to also hear of Mr. Gregory's pilgrimage to the shrines, and how much more glorious to be blessed by his visit, for he had come to Stuttgart after his pilgrimage to 'Akká.

Alma Knobloch's roommate, Margarete Döring, must have written to 'Abdu'l-Bahá of Louis Gregory's spiritual potency, because 'Abdu'l-Bahá responded to her with a Tablet in which He explained the source of that spiritual power—and He seems to suggest to Miss Döring that she too could learn from Louis Gregory's example of spiritual enlightenment:

August 15, 1911

. . . To the maidservant of God, Margarethe Döring, Stuttgart.

HE IS GOD!

O daughter of the Kingdom!

Your letter arrived, and its contents showed that Mr. Gregory, by visiting the blessed Tomb [the Shrine of Bahá'u'lláh], hath received a new power, and obtained a new life. When he arrived at Stuttgart, although black of color, yet he shone as a bright light in the meeting of the friends. Verily, he hath greatly advanced in this journey, he received another life and obtained another power. When he returned, Gregory was quite another Gregory. He hath become a new creation. Reflect on the Grace of the Kingdom of ABHA and see how it enlightened such a person. It has made him spiritual, heavenly, divine and a manifestor of the graces of the world of humanity . . ."²⁴

In his diary *The Heavenly Vista,* Louis Gregory wrote that the Master had spoken directly to him about race. Referring to a prior Tablet He had sent to Louis Gregory, 'Abdu'l-Bahá said, "'Do you remember My Tablet to you?'" And Louis Gregory replied, "'Yes, I have committed it to memory.'" Whereupon 'Abdu'l-Bahá said, "'I liken you to the pupil of the eye. You are black and it is black, yet it becomes the focus of light.'"²⁵ 'Abdu'l-Bahá hoped that Louis Gregory would be a leader in guiding the friends toward the kind of complete racial harmony envisioned by Bahá'u'lláh. Although the community of Stuttgart had little experience with racial diversity, it is unlikely that Louis Gregory avoided the subject of race during his visit. Louis Gregory's confidence as a teacher of the Cause came from this assurance given by 'Abdu'l-Bahá, who said to him, "'I hope that your insight will become so clear that you will not need a teacher; but the Holy Spirit will guide you in all things.'"[26]

As directed by 'Abdu'l-Bahá, Louis Gregory visited Paris and London after his visit to Stuttgart. London Bahá'í Arthur Cuthbert noted that the London Bahá'ís were spiritually edified by his visit, adding, "To meet such a great soul, so filled with the Bahai spirit in any man is an inspiration; but when this man is a negro . . . and proud of his colour, then it is a revelation impressive with great significance as one contemplates the difficult problems existing between the white and black populations. How these problems can be changed by a few such men aflame with God's Word!"[27]

Although it may seem that racial harmony was not prominent in the minds of Europeans in 1911, there were a great many people interested in advancing discussions on race unity. In fact, two months after Louis Gregory's visit, the First Universal Races Congress was held in London, July 26 to July 29 in 1911. More than two thousand people attended the congress, and, according to Mr. W. Tudor-Pole, "a great interest was aroused on Thursday during the discussion on Abdu'l-Bahá's letter to the congress."[28]

When the Bahá'ís in Stuttgart hosted Louis Gregory in May of 1911, they could not have known that within three months 'Abdu'l-Bahá would make a journey to the West that would begin with a visit to parts of Europe, then to the United States and Canada, followed by a return to Europe again. The believers in Stuttgart never imagined that 'Abdu'l-Bahá would visit Germany upon His return to Europe, but when they learned that 'Abdu'l-Bahá was in Paris in 1913, they wrote to Him and asked if He would come to Germany and ". . . give His blessing to the work that had been accomplished there."[29] 'Abdu'l-Bahá replied that He was not certain He could

109

make the trip to Stuttgart, as He had been suffering from a severe cold and had been forced to receive visitors as He lay in bed.[30] In the meantime, 'Abdu'l-Bahá gave permission for the Stuttgart Bahá'ís to visit Him in Paris. Several of the Bahá'ís traveled to Paris in early March and returned to Stuttgart with the hope that 'Abdu'l-Bahá would visit Stuttgart sometime soon.[31]

They did not have to wait long. On March 30, 1913, 'Abdu'l-Bahá and four of His attendants traveled to Stuttgart. They arrived early in the evening of April 1st at the old Stuttgart train station.* The city of Stuttgart was, and still remains, a city of contrasts, where one finds centuries-old architectural styles alongside modern buildings. The old Stuttgart train station was a good example of this contrast. Although it no longer functions as a train station today, when 'Abdu'l-Bahá walked through the station lobby, He would have stood in a spacious foyer, with a central nave supported by numerous double-pillars topped with corbel arches bracing the ceiling, and a large central dome painted with mosaic designs.[32] It looked very much like the interior of the Great Mosque of Córdoba, which was reminiscent of the architectural influences of Islam. From the train station, 'Abdu'l-Bahá and the four Persians who traveled with Him took rooms at the Hotel Marquardt, an enormous 150-room hotel that was adjacent to the train station.

The Bahá'ís of Stuttgart had not been informed of 'Abdu'l-Bahá's departure from Paris, as He had wished to arrive unannounced. According to Ḥasan Balyuzi's account, 'Abdu'l-Bahá wanted His arrival in Stuttgart to be a complete surprise. Although 'Abdu'l-

---

* 'Abdu'l-Bahá's four attendants were Siyyid Aḥmad-i-Báiroff, Mírzá Maḥmúd-i-Zarqání, Siyyid Asadu'lláh, and Mírzá Aḥmad Sohráb. (Cited in Ḥasan Balyuzi, *'Abdu'l-Bahá: The Centre of the Covenant of Bahá'u'lláh*, p. 379.)

Bahá wore His robe and turban, He told His four Persian attendants "to change completely from Eastern garb to European dress, and to discard their oriental headgear."[33] Furthermore, He instructed that there should be no attempts to obtain newspaper publicity during His stay.[34]

From the Hotel Marquardt, 'Abdu'l-Bahá's attendants made telephone calls to some of the believers in Stuttgart, and soon—despite 'Abdu'l-Bahá's attempts to obscure His arrival—the hotel was flooded with visitors. In his book *'Abdu'l-Bahá: The Centre of the Covenant of Bahá'u'lláh*, Hand of the Cause Ḥasan Balyuzi describes the scene at the hotel where so many friends streamed into the lobby to meet their visitor from the East, and how 'Abdu'l-Bahá joked that the crowds of Bahá'ís would frighten away the hotelier:

> 'Abdu'l-Bahá remarked that the hotelier might leave his hotel and seek refuge elsewhere, because of such numbers pouring in. Indeed the staff of the hotel were shaken and astonished to see so many of their countrymen pay such attention and respect to an Easterner who, as it seemed, had come from nowhere. One of the Bahá'ís asked 'Abdu'l-Bahá what to say when people enquired who He was. Tell them, He said, that He was a person calling men to the Kingdom of God, a promoter of the Faith of Bahá'u'lláh, a herald of peace and reconciliation, and an advocate of the oneness of humanity.[35]

No one could have been more astonished by His arrival than Miss Alma Knobloch. It had been nearly a decade since Edwin Fischer had brought the teachings of Bahá'u'lláh to Germany. His efforts had been amplified so successfully by Alma Knobloch and the growing number of local believers in Stuttgart that by the time

'Abdu'l-Bahá visited Stuttgart, well over two hundred people were there to meet Him.[36] Alma wrote to her family in the United States about 'Abdu'l-Bahá's surprise visit and said, "Our joy was beyond measure! We had been working and serving at the break of the New Day and now the Light of the Sun of Truth flooded the land and we were grateful. 'Abdu'l-Bahá's words gave new impetus to the Cause in this country."[37]

On the first day of His arrival, 'Abdu'l-Bahá wasted no time in addressing the immediate concerns of the believers in Stuttgart. The looming clouds of war and the darkness of ignorance was being felt on all sides, but He reminded them that they were living under the protection of the Sun of Reality, which was none other than the teachings of Bahá'u'lláh. Although it is not certain whether Johanna was present at His talk, to a young person such as herself, 'Abdu'l-Bahá's words would have furnished hope for the future, despite the approaching clouds of war, and would have given her strength for the dark years ahead. His talk is given here, in part:

Praise be to God! Because your faces are radiant with the light of the Glory of God; your hearts are attracted to the Kingdom of ABHA. Thank God that you have heard the call of God. You are living in the days of the radiances of the Sun of Reality. The rays of the Sun have poured into your hearts and souls. Your hearts are illuminated, your inner vision clear. Your spirit rejoiced in the glad tidings of the Kingdom of God. Thank God that you are the elect of God. He has elected you because of His own love. The mercies of God have surrounded you. You must live in accordance with the teachings of BAHA'O'LLAH. Be loving to all Mankind. Consort with all religions in amity and fragrance. You must be the cause of the education of the world of humanity. At present the world is still very dark. From one side there threatens the darkness of ignorance; from the other side we hear of war and rumors of war. We must, like a candle, shine with the light of BAHA'O'LLAH, in order that through your efforts this darkness may be dispelled. The light of the love of God can illumine the East and the West. It can change hatred and enmity into love and friendship. The clouds which veil the rays of the Sun of Reality must be dispelled and made to disappear. The world must be rejuvenated. Eternal life must be made possible. The rays of the Kingdom must shine forth. The breath of the Holy Spirit can quicken the dead. I shall always pray for you and I shall supplicate for divine confirmations for each one of you, in order that ye may become more enkindled day by day, more attracted, so that each one of you will become a herald of the Kingdom. This is the eternal glory. This is the eternal life. This is the entrance into the Kingdom of God, the dominion which will last forever.[38]

'Abdu'l-Bahá's visit to Germany in 1913 included Stuttgart, Esslingen, and Bad Mergentheim.[39] Alma Knobloch and Alice Schwarz arranged very special gatherings for Him, including a memorable visit to nearby Esslingen, where a large children's party was held in a hall in the city museum on April 4, 1913. Alice Schwarz also arranged for 'Abdu'l-Bahá to visit her grieving mother, Frau Emma Solivo, whose husband, Heinrich Solivo had passed away the month before. The reader may recall that Frau Solivo lived at Villa Wagenburg, which was across the street from Villa Hauff. The Villa Wagenburg was built in 1863 and was one of the first of the great hilltop villas built in Stuttgart. Although Villa Hauff survived both world wars, Villa Wagenburg did not; it was destroyed by bombing in World War II. In its day, Villa Wagenburg was a traditional garden style country house and stood in picturesque contrast to the tall and narrow castle profile of Villa Hauff.[40] The Villa Wagenburg featured wide garden porches, wide dormers and window shutters, wood detailing, and decorative steeples rising above the enormous roof. Its rural style gave one the feeling of living in an open space, even though it was situated in the center of the city.

Frau Emma Solivo's spirits were surely lifted when more than one hundred believers and friends arrived on April 6th at Villa Wagenburg to be in the presence of 'Abdu'l-Bahá. They gathered in the garden where 'Abdu'l-Baha consented to be photographed, but because there were so many people who attended, the photographs had to be taken in groups—which 'Abdu'l-Bahá arranged Himself.[41]

The garden at Villa Wagenburg delighted 'Abdu'l-Bahá, and He said that He wished that offshoots of various fruit trees and an almond tree could be sent to Haifa if the opportunity arose, so that He could cultivate them in His own garden.[42] Before leaving the garden at Villa Wagenburg, 'Abdu'l-Bahá spoke to every adult, youth, and child there. Johanna Hauff would have been nineteen years old at the time, and although it is not certain she was there, it is hard to imagine that she would not have been at the gathering, since it was a short walk across the road from her home. It was a most memorable day for 'Abdu'l-Bahá, as noted by Alma Knobloch:

It was remarked by 'Abdu'l-Bahá on several occasions that it was well that He came to Germany in the spring. When looking over Stuttgart, the hills were covered with blossoming fruit trees. In the evening the lights threw a beautiful illumination over the mountainsides. 'Abdu'l-Bahá said, "Truly it is worthy to become a paradise." 'Abdu'l-Bahá was kind and thoughtful to all and His Great Love penetrated all the hearts. His spirituality and nobility never failed to express themselves in authoritative Words and countenance. We all felt that a new life had begun and that now the Cause in Germany was established. Before leaving 'Abdu'l-Bahá said, "The Cause has thrown so universal a reverberation through the pillars of the earth that the Divine Power of Bahá'u'lláh shall encircle the globe. Be assured."[43]

It was in this vibrant community environment that Johanna Hauff and her sister Julia became confirmed believers. Yet, despite the ominous signs of continental conflict looming on the horizon, they could not have known that the year ahead would bring about the greatest change in the story of their lives. 'Abdu'l-Bahá alluded to such a change when He spoke on April 3rd to a large audience in the upper hall at the city museum. He explained that change is the natural condition of all things and that the process of disintegration and decay is the natural precursor to new growth and integration. In His wisdom, 'Abdu'l-Bahá was preparing the Bahá'ís for the world crisis to come and the unforeseen spiritual victories that would follow. His talk is given here, in part:

Everything in the world is subject to change. But this transmutation and change are requirements of life. See, for instance, these flowers before us. They come forth from a seed. They grow to perfection, but when they have reached the state of perfection they go back again. This is the invariable law of creation. Likewise man develops until he has grown to maturity. When he reaches beyond the state of maturity he begins to decline. All religions of God are subject to this same law. They are founded in order to blossom out and develop and fulfill their mission. They reach their zenith and then decline and come to an end . . .

This should show you that religion is subject to change. So, also, religion is full of superstition. There is today nothing more than tradition to feed upon. Therefore our souls must strive day and night in order that the foundations of divine religion may again be newly revivified. These traditions and these dogmas are like the husks surrounding the kernel. We must release the kernel from the husk. The world of humanity is in the dark. Our aim is to illumine mankind. It is natural that after the darkness of every night the brilliant day will come. It is our hope that this darkness may be dispelled and that the rays of the Sun of Reality will shine again. We are confident that the darkness will again be followed by the brightness of the day. It is our hope that after the cold winter a new spring will come, giving new life to nature, so that the trees of humanity will again sprout and become verdant in the gardens, so that they may bring forth leaves and blossoms and fruit . . .

Therefore, I desire that all may be united in harmony. Strive and work so that the standard of the world of human Oneness may be raised among men, so that the lights of universal peace may shine and the East and the West embrace, and the material world become a mirror of the Kingdom of God, that eternal light may shine forth and that the day break which will not be followed by the night."[44]

When Archduke Franz Ferdinand of Austria was assassinated in the city of Sarajevo in June of 1914, the fuse to the "Great War" was ignited between the Central Powers of Germany and Austria-Hungary and the Allied Powers of France, Russia, Great Britain, and eventually, the United States.

Confined to Haifa during the war, and cut off from communication with the Bahá'í world, 'Abdu'l-Bahá wrote the *Tablets of the Divine Plan*. Comprised of fourteen Tablets and written in 1916 and 1917 during the darkest days of the war, each Tablet was addressed directly to the believers in the United States and Canada. In these Tablets, 'Abdu'l-Bahá called upon the followers of Bahá'u'lláh to arise and spread the teachings of God throughout North America and the globe. The scope of the Divine Plan was at once broad and specific as the Master mentioned cities, regions, and countries by name and outlined the spiritual victories to be achieved by the believers. Furthermore, in these Tablets, 'Abdu'l-Bahá identified American believers who had already answered such a call, so that the believers residing in the United States and Canada might be inspired by their example. One such pioneering teacher named by 'Abdu'l-Bahá in the *Tablets of the Divine Plan* was Miss Alma Knobloch, who gave up her American citizenship in order to stay in Germany during the war.[45] The Master wrote, "Miss Knobloch traveled alone to Germany. To what a great extent she became confirmed! Therefore, know ye of a certainty that whosoever arises in this day to diffuse the divine fragrances, the cohorts of the Kingdom of God shall confirm him and the bestowals and the favors of the Blessed Perfection shall encircle him."[46]

After the war, severe reparations were imposed on Germany by the Treaty of Versailles, which went into effect in January, 1920.

The cost to Germany was felt in every aspect of daily life. All citizens, high and low alike, lived in need of food and goods—and wealthy families such as the Hauffs and the Schwarzs were no exception. Furthermore, Fritz Hauff's lucrative business producing chemicals for plate photography was surpassed by new technology in roll film, which made plate photography obsolete. In addition, Germany was in a postwar economic crisis due to the devaluation of its currency.

Like most of the residents of cities throughout Germany, the Hauffs were visibly impoverished. Despite the privations, the Bahá'ís in Germany continued to carry out the activities of Bahá'í community life. For instance, in the summer of 1920, a special devotional feast was announced to be "Given to the believers in Germany and to those attracted to the Bahai Cause, in the ballroom of the Krone Hotel in Esslingen, Württemberg, on Sunday afternoon, August 15th 1920, at half past four o'clock."[47] Over three hundred people attended, including Johanna Hauff and her sister Julia, who played piano and violin for the occasion.[48] So many guests were expected that they had to move the meeting from the ballroom to the gardens outside. The Bahá'ís decided to build a miniature model of the 'Ishqábád Bahá'í House of Worship and place it as a decoration in the center of the garden where the devotional meeting would take place.* The unified effort of the Bahá'ís was reported to the *Star of the West* magazine in the United States:

---

* The Guardian wrote that the building of the House of Worship in 'Ishqábád was one of the chief objectives of 'Abdu'l-Bahá's ministry. In *Directives from the Guardian*, p. 1, a letter on behalf of Shoghi Effendi read, "As to the three aims which Shoghi Effendi has stated in his America and the Most Great Peace to have been the chief objectives of 'Abdu'l-Bahá's ministry, it should be pointed out that the first was: The establishment of the Cause in America; the erection of the Bahá'í Temple in 'Ishqábád, and the building on Mt. Carmel of a mausoleum marking the resting-place of the Báb, were the two remaining ones."

Under the present existing conditions here in Germany, the matter of getting together sufficient food at one time for such a gathering was difficult. Nevertheless the friends solved the problem by going to a number of shops, getting as much as possible from each, until the necessary amount was secured. At an early hour, the morning of the feast, practically the entire Esslingen group of Bahais assembled for work. There are but few horses now left in Germany, so the friends came drawing wagons themselves, transporting provisions, flowers, chairs and the many things required; all worked diligently and by early afternoon the model of the Mashrekol-Azkar had been placed in the center of the garden, the tables and chairs arranged, decorations in place, and all other things were in readiness for the arrival of the people.[49]

Several times, the Bahá'ís of the United States sent relief funds to the Bahá'ís in Germany. In August 1921, Alice Schwarz wrote the following letter, on behalf of the Stuttgart Bahá'í community, to the Bahá'ís in Urbana, Illinois who sent financial assistance to Stuttgart:

Dear Friends,

On behalf of my husband, who is out of town for a few days, I want to thank you most heartily for your transmission of a third food-draft for the Bahais. How kind and good it is of the Bahais over there to remember the German friends! We have many needy people in our group who are made happy by your kind help. All groups—as Esslingen, Zuffenhausen, Reutlingen, Göppingen, Gera, Leipzig, etc.—are being provided with the American "love offerings" (Liebesgaben), so that love is building a bridge from country to country. In Germany we now have to do without a great many things that seemed to belong to the necessities of life, for instance, milk, which is only available for infants and people over 70 years of age. The butter rations are infinitesimal, while bread is not to be had and so forth. Finally, one gets used to everything and is content even so.

We are very, very busy here. The ground has been ploughed to receive the seed of the new teaching so that our circle is widening more and more.

With kind greetings to the whole Urbana group, and best regards also from my husband.

Yours in El-Abha,

Alice T. Schwarz[50]

There was frequent communication between the Bahá'ís of Germany and the Bahá'ís of the United States. Susanne Pfaff-Grossmann explained that the German people, "already impoverished as a result of the war, were now confronted with utter destitution and misery owing to the approaching onset of hyperinflation."[51] Her father, Hermann Grossmann (future Hand of the Cause of God) wrote to the Bahá'ís of the United States in August 1923 and explained the grave conditions faced by the Bahá'ís in Hamburg, where he lived. The purpose of his letter was to invite the Bahá'í friends to come visit because there were many opportunities to teach the Cause in postwar Germany:

The hearts of men are open, because they must endure much privation and many trials . . . Although our circle is small, yet the friends are very active in spreading His Teachings. It is a great joy to us when letters or, better still, friends, from other cities come to us. We heartily beg therefore that when any of you come to Europe and to Germany you will not forget our little group. It gives us much strength and will make it easier for us to overcome the difficulties which every new day brings.[52]

After the war, traveling Bahá'í teachers began to arrive in Stuttgart again. In 1921, John and Louise Bosch of Geyserville, California were permitted to make a pilgrimage to see 'Abdu'l-Bahá. As part of their journey to Haifa, they made a teaching trip through parts of Europe, which included a stop in Stuttgart, where they visited the Hauff family. The Great War had deprived everyone of material comforts, but not of spiritual strength. According to Dr. Faramarz Abrar, who knew Johanna Hauff, sometime after the war Johanna wrote a letter to 'Abdu'l-Bahá asking permission to go on pilgrimage, which was granted. Her heart was aflame with the love of the Cause, and in her letter she expressed her joy in having the grace to recognize the message of Bahá'u'lláh.[53] In August, 1919, Johanna received the following Tablet from 'Abdu'l-Bahá in which He addressed her desire to be a servant of the Cause:

To Johanna Hauff
Stuttgart, Germany
He is God!
O Thou who art the leaf of the Tree of Life!
By the Tree of Life recorded in the Holy Book is meant His Holiness Baha'u'llah, while the daughters of the Kingdom

constitute the leaves of that Blessed Tree. Praise thou God therefore that thou hast been related to that Tree, and hast become verdant, fresh, tender, and green.

The doors of the Kingdom are wide open and every soul that seeketh entrance secures a seat at this Table and hast partaken of this heavenly bestowal. Thou art engaged in serving the Kingdom and art quickened by the Breezes of the Abha Paradise. Strive as much as possible to guide the souls and eat of the Bread that has descended from Heaven. That is why Christ says: I am the Bread that has descended from Heaven; he who eats of that Bread shall never die.

Convey on behalf of Abdul Baha to thy mother and sister the utmost kindness. I pray in their behalf and beg from the Kingdom of the merciful everlasting Bounty,

Upon thee be Baha u'llah!

(signed) Abdul Baha Abbas

August 24, 1919[54]

Although Johanna was twenty-seven years old when she made her pilgrimage to Haifa in 1921, she had grown up with the benefits of wealth but also a degree of isolation from the world. She and her parents had the means to vacation away from Stuttgart, but their vacations were at exclusive hotel resorts. So when the Bosches arrived Stuttgart en route to Haifa, Johanna's parents approved of her trip to Haifa because she could be chaperoned by John and Louise Bosch.

After traveling from Stuttgart to Venice, Johanna and the Bosches boarded a steamer to Haifa. On November 14, 1921 a representative of the household of 'Abdu'l-Bahá met them at the dock, and they were taken to the Western Pilgrim House on Haparsim Street, just a short walk away from the house of 'Abdu'l-Bahá. It was the rainy season in Haifa—a welcome respite from the heat of the Palestine summer. Johanna Hauff was one of the first German Bahá'ís to visit 'Abdu'l-Bahá in Haifa, and one of the youngest, too. Her youthful enthusiasm was as welcome as the rain.

Many years after her unique pilgrimage, Johanna recounted her memories of being in the presence of the Master. She recalled that the two weeks before the passing of 'Abdu'l-Bahá were days of complete spiritual fulfillment for Johanna. The Master treated her with deep appreciation and respect and made her feel like she was a daughter to Him.[55] Her days were spent in nearness to the holy shrines, and the evenings were spent in the presence of 'Abdu'l-Bahá around the dinner table in the Western Pilgrim House. Johanna recalled one evening, when she sat quietly at the table, her heart was filled with questions she wanted to ask 'Abdu'l-Bahá. She reported that the Master looked knowingly at her with His penetrating blue eyes and asked her to speak her thoughts. She said, "'My thoughts are in Germany and the question of how, as a poor creature, can I do justice to this holy cause.'" She said that, to her surprise, 'Abdu'l-Bahá replied that He too had been thinking about this and that He said, "'I wish that you learn Arabic and Persian well so that you can translate the holy scriptures of Bahá'u'lláh into your mother tongue. That is my personal wish for you. And since the time is very precious, a teacher will be selected for you here in Haifa so that you can get your first Persian course right away.'"[56] 'Abdu'l-Bahá wrote a Tablet to Johanna's sister, Julia, praising her attraction to the Kingdom of God and expressing that He hoped that she and Johanna would become exemplary servants in the heavenly Kingdom.[57] He also wrote to Johanna's mother and reassured her that Johanna had arrived safely in Haifa. He added that He would guide

Johanna in serving the Cause and that he would teach her so that she could become enlightenment to others.[58]

Johanna Hauff had a keen interest in languages. In addition to her native German, she spoke English, French, Spanish and later she learned Persian and Arabic.[59] She had an interest in the Hidden Words, and as indicated in the following Tablet addressed to her, she undoubtedly wrote to 'Abdu'l-Bahá asking about the meaning of a passage in the Hidden Words. The original Tablet was sent to her, along with an English translation, and sent via Frau Alice Schwarz. A copy of the Tablet has been in the possession of Dr. Faramarz Abrar in Germany, to whom Johanna Hauff entrusted her papers before her passing:

Through the consort of His Honour, Consul Schwarz, upon her be the Glory of God, the most Glorious, to beloved daughter, Miss Johanna Hauff, upon her be the Glory of God, the most Glorious:

*He is God.*

O my dear daughter!

If thou art able to study Persian, it will be appropriate provided that you would study in Stuttgart itself when one of the Persian friends would be sent there.

As to the section of the Hidden Words, it is meant that as long as a person in not thirsty, water cannot be appreciated by him, no matter how sweet and wholesome it may be. Therefore, one must first produce thirst (in him) and then give him the sweet water of the Euphrates.

Today the majority of the people are not thirsty. Souls should be made thirsty through Baha'i deeds, words, and conduct. Then one should offer a chalice from the Fountain of Life.

Convey, on my behalf, the utmost kindness, love and longing to thy honoured father, mother and other members of the family, especially to Julia!

Upon thee be Baha-el Abha

(signed) abdul Baha abbas

Translated by Azizullah S. Bahadur, Haifa (Karmel)

May 5, 1920[60]

Johanna stayed in Haifa for three months, and she learned Persian well enough to translate the Persian portions of the Hidden Words into German. Many years later, Johanna said that translating the writings of Bahá'u'lláh was not merely an exercise in knowing Persian and Arabic; rather, it was an exercise in developing the spiritual capacity to translate the Creative Word. She felt that one could never perfect the art of translation because it was a skill that could always be refined as one grew spiritually.[61]

It just so happened that on the night that 'Abdu'l-Bahá passed away, Johanna was given permission to stay in the house of 'Abdu'l-Bahá, rather than return to the Western Pilgrim House. Due to this blessing, she was able to witness events as they unfolded. In her letters home to her parents, she described these events. While her voice in these letters shows her youthful lack of reserve, one cannot help but perceive from her words an emerging wisdom and maturity as she tells of what she has witnessed. The following letter, translated from German, is an especially poignant example of her state of mind, as it was written on the very day of the ascension of 'Abdu'l-Bahá:[62]

Monday, November 28

What terrible hours were these tonight at the deathbed of the beloved Master! At one o'clock at night (Monday morning) we were called and told the Master was very low. Quickly we went down into the sorrowing house, to His bedside; for a long time I did not know whether He was still with His body or had ascended into His Kingdom. He is no longer among us! Oh, no, we must not say this; His spirit is perhaps a thousand times nearer to us; but it is incredible, unbelievable, because this great loss came so swift—so unexpected. We are all as stunned. I cannot say anything; I do not know what will happen!

Rouha Khanum told me—weeping at His bed where He lay still, unspeakably beautiful and as if sleeping—that she had asked him only in the evening whether I might stay here for some time and that He had replied: "She may stay; she will be a beautiful teacher." But I don't know what will happen now; the heart, the mind, the spirit of this town, this country, our whole world is no longer in a human body!

When this letter reaches you, the sad news will have reached the whole world. We stand in the spirit of Him whose life was a loving martyrdom, from the first to the last minute, for us and for the world, but who is now released from His sufferings and has entered into the eternal Glory.

Friday and Saturday the Master had some fever, Saturday it was worse, Sunday He was all right again. The cause of death is not known; it was general weakness probably. Half an hour before death, there was difficulty in breathing, Shortly before passing away He told his daughter that He was going across.[63]

126

Indeed, within hours of His passing, the entryway of His house was crowded with mourners from Haifa, and expressions of grief were sent from all around the world. These condolences were not solely from Bahá'ís. Messages poured in from prominent officials such as the British Secretary of State for the Colonies, from the High Commissioner of Palestine, the High Commissioner for Egypt, the Council of Ministers in Baghdad.

Newspapers around the world published articles about His passing, which in turn introduced countless readers to the teachings of Bahá'u'lláh. The London newspaper *The Times* published the headline that 'Abdu'l-Bahá "'. . . was prisoner for many years for preaching the brotherhood of man,'" and that the Bahá'í Faith teaches "'. . . all religions are basically one, that differences in them have arisen through the corruptions of theology and dogma.'"[64] Shoghi Effendi explained in *God Passes By* that tributes to 'Abdu'l-Bahá transcended national boundaries and confirmed a universal recognition of 'Abdu'l-Bahá's appeal to the longing of humanity to see its peoples as one human family: "Many and divers newspapers, such as the London 'Times,' the 'Morning Post,' the 'Daily Mail,' the 'New York World,' 'Le Temps,' the 'Times of India' and others, in different languages and countries, paid their tribute to One Who had rendered the Cause of human brotherhood and peace such signal and imperishable services."[65]

As many as ten thousand people attended the funeral procession of 'Abdu'l-Bahá, and Johanna Hauff was among them. One can imagine her, a young German woman, twenty-seven years old, wearing the clothes of the Occident, walking with crowds of mourners adorned in the clothes of the Orient. She understood what she was witnessing: an unprecedented event that would be remembered and commemorated far into the future. The magnitude of the scene made her feel small and worthless—the kind of worthlessness that inspired her to reshape her life in a way that was worthy of humanity. Four days after the funeral, she wrote of her feelings to her parents:

Haifa, Palestine
December 3, 1921
As in a dream these last days have passed. Since I wrote to you on Monday [November 28], after the incredible had happened—incredible because it happened so unexpectedly— much has come to pass. Before I tell you something about it, I wish to thank you from the bottom of my heart, that you let me come here, that I was allowed to be here during these wonderful, hard and indescribably beautiful times. . . . Only after I have been here for days, an understanding gradually arose within me of what it meant, and it was so indescribably spiritualized in the human form—always kind, always loving; already partly absent, yet among us and talking to us.

I am not worth it, that those radiant, luminous, penetrating blue eyes should have rested on me, that that kind mouth should have spoken loving, beautiful words to me—and useless my life would appear to me if the power of the experience does not give me strength to really remold my life and to lead it to a high purpose.

Mr. and Mrs. Bosch, Dr. and Mrs. Krug and I, were almost constantly in the most intimate family circle. On Monday night, we were permitted to see the face of the Master once more—the only ones besides the family. How beautiful it was! Such peace! Such rest! I do not believe that I shall ever in my life see again such an unspeakably beautiful face as that of Abdul-Baha in life and in death. All day long and the night afterwards I was still stunned, hardly able to think, hardly able to bear the grief and look on—until the next morning; then everything changed. We had gone over at eight o'clock and stood once more—for the last time, in the room in which He talked to us when He was not well and in which He passed away—before the bed on which rested the beautiful, white-clad figure . . .

Mr. and Mrs. Bosch and I were alone in the big hall as the sons-in-law passed by to get the casket; they called Mr. Bosch, who helped to carry the casket into the death-chamber and to put the body into it. For a short time the casket was left in the hall and Mohammedan priests, who had asked permission, to come, as did Jews and Christians, said a short prayer.

Then the casket was carried up the mountain on the shoulders of eight men who frequently changed. Never in my life will I forget that walk. More than an hour we followed the bier which covered the human form of the beloved Master—after stormy, rainy days, radiant weather; dark blue the sea, dark blue the sky—slowly, slowly followed the crowd, reverently and shyly they followed the ruler who had gone to deep silence and rest. Whoever could, went along, people and soldiers on both sides of the road. The government and the nobility to accompany "Sir Abbas Effendi"; the poor, their benefactor; the inhabitants of Haifa, their counsellor; others, their greatest scholar, philosopher and sage—men of all languages, nations and creeds, who were but passingly or not at all interested in his Cause, crowded around his casket. A triumphant procession it was, the first fruit, at least the first visible fruit, of his life of sufferings in this region afflicted with spiritual blindness.

But before I noticed all that, the new uplifting feeling had come over me; while we slowly ascended the steep mountain and were looking at the deep, blue sea, the white city of BAHA 'ULLAH (Acca) and the radiant, blue sky, all mourning left me and a feeling of strength and comfort came over me; it seemed as if Abdul-Baha had not gone, as if the spirit of power and beauty that speaks from out his words, had suddenly, inexplicably come over me and was comforting and guiding me past the sorrowing crowd into the nearness of His love and life. (I cannot possibly give an impression of what I felt; nor can I find the words.) Mrs. Bosch had similar feelings and Mrs. Krug said: "It was the most wonderful experience."

On the summit the casket was put down in front of the Tomb of the Bab and about five or six Arabic eulogies and one French address were given—all by non-Bahais who knew little of his teachings. The Frenchman said that all stood deeply moved at the bier of the man who had proclaimed the religion of the soul, whose words and deeds were in perfect harmony, who gave the world the most beautiful teachings of all philosophies and all religions in such a way that it could accept them, and he ended with about these words: "Not only the inhabitants of Acca, Haifa and the Persians in his country, but all civilized people are weeping today at the bier of this great one." The Arabic addresses are said to have been very beautiful, too.

To all in Haifa, to the government which lowered its flag to half-mast, even to the people who were indifferent or opposed him because they could not get away from their fanatical prejudices, to all came the presentiment that one of the greatest had gone from them. Just as at Christ's departure "the curtain of the temple was rent in twain," the curtain which does not let the real light penetrate into the temple of religion. God grant that it may remain rent and that the light can get in! (Two years ago, Abdul-Baha was asked when the carnage and dreadful riots in the world would stop, He answered: "When the world will have become wise enough to accept the teachings of BAHA ' ULLAH.") After the speeches were over, the casket was put down in the Tomb where it will remain until the orders which Abdul-Baha has left in his last Will and Testament will have been read, which will be done by his oldest grandson [Shoghi Effendi] who is shortly expected back from London.

The heart-breaking grief of the family . . . It is an irreplaceable loss for them. It had come so suddenly for all of them, although the Master had spoken for months continually of his going—they had not understood, probably because they simply could not believe it. Now only do they begin to realize it.

And he was so weary, so tired! He said it to us, he said to everybody. Mrs. Bosch told me even on the first day: "His work is done, completely done, everything has been said; every further day is a gift of grace." We did not dare to ask questions, nor dare to deliver letters, because we heard 400 letters were still lying there unanswered, but in his great love and kindness for Germany he wanted to have them nevertheless and his very last Tablet is going to Germany. The Krugs said too, a veil seemed to be about him, that he was quite different than before. I felt the strangeness at first as something too high, too incomprehensible at the first meeting and later, when his kindness bridged it over, I felt that he was hardly a human being any longer. On Sunday when he was much better again that we were all quite happy, he told his family that he was leaving them now, that they should faithfully serve the Cause of God and should not let any enemies enter therein. He said, "This is my last day." But nobody realized what he meant, they thought he wanted to undertake a sudden journey, as he often did. When he said it, he smiled as if joking, and since he liked to joke they did not take it seriously. Then he told his daughter Rouha that he needed nothing, that he was well and all should go to bed—only she remained with him. At one o'clock at night he complained about difficulty of breathing and she threw back the mosquito netting, and wanted to give him milk, but he said, "You want to give me milk now that I am dying?"

She had Dr. Krug called at once. By this calling I woke up too, but when he got there, the Master had already passed away. "As a thief in the night" was his coming and going, so that this prophecy too should be fulfilled!

But now the time has come for everyone to work, for the Germans particularly whom he loved so dearly, to whom his last message goes—to work in order to maintain unity . . . and become worthy to enact the Master's will.[66]

The Bahá'í National Archives of Germany is in possession of the Tablet addressed to the Bahá'ís of Stuttgart that was delivered after the passing of 'Abdu'l-Bahá. This Tablet is the one to which Johanna Hauff refers in her description above. The Tablet was dictated in Persian by 'Abdu'l-Bahá, and He passed away before reviewing it; therefore, the Tablet was not signed by Him. Nevertheless, the Tablet was translated into German and sent to the Bahá'ís of Stuttgart. In the first part of the Tablet, 'Abdu'l-Bahá greets "the Friends of God in Stuttgart" and tells them that Mr. and Mrs. Bosch arrived in Haifa and brought with them the love of the believers in Stuttgart, which 'Abdu'l-Bahá acknowledged as the most precious gift He could receive. The second part of the Tablet is introduced and then quoted in part by Shoghi Effendi in *God Passes By*:

> His very last Tablet, graciously revealed for His loved ones in Stuttgart, conveys His reflections upon this transient world, and His counsels to His loved ones that dwell therein:
>
> O ye beloved of the Lord! In this mortal world, nothing whatsoever endureth. The peoples of the earth dwell therein and spend a number of days uselessly, ultimately descending neath the dust, repairing to the home of eternal silence, leaving behind them no achievement, no blessing, no result, no fruit. All the days of their life are thus brought to naught. Whereas the children of the Kingdom sow seeds in the fertile soil of Truth, that will eventually spring up and bring forth many a harvest and shall forever bestow upon mankind its increase and bountiful grace. They shall obtain eternal life, attain unto the imperishable bounty, and shine even as radiant stars in the firmament of the Divine Kingdom. The Glory of Glories rest upon you![67]

When this Tablet was sent to the Bahá'ís of Stuttgart, Alma Knobloch was no longer residing there, but how happy it must have made her to know that Stuttgart was remembered by 'Abdu'l-

Bahá until His last days. After fourteen years of assisting with the expansion of the Bahá'í Faith in Stuttgart and surrounding areas, Alma returned to Washington, D.C., in 1920, where she was able to reinstate her U.S. citizenship. She left behind a Bahá'í community that she had nurtured and strengthened by her example of devotion to 'Abdu'l-Bahá, the Center of the Covenant.[68] Alma's success was greatly due to the receptive people she met, who, in turn, became active participants in the teaching efforts. Alma said that when she first arrived in Stuttgart, she observed, "Stuttgart is a beautiful city surrounded by hills which are dotted with fine houses. Here in Southern Germany is situated the Capital of Württemberg. The people are thinkers, and have an extremely religious turn of mind."[69] On April 27, 1913, 'Abdu'l-Bahá Himself had written of the Stuttgart believers, attesting to their constancy and spiritual perception:

> I beseech for you divine confirmation and imperishable glory, so that ye may be so strengthened by His grace as to become wholly detached and freed from everything that pertaineth to the world of nature, so that your earthly cares and attachments may be turned into ease and tranquility. I shall never forget this city, inasmuch as divine fragrances are inhaled from its citizens. Unlike the people of certain cities, the inhabitants of this place are not immersed in the sea of materialism. They are endowed with constancy and spiritual perception. However, there are some cities whose residents are so deeply absorbed in the world of nature that they are wholly bereft of spiritual perception. They occupy themselves with eating, resting, dancing and amusement. They are entirely unaware of the kingdom of heaven. But Stuttgart is not such a city. Therefore, I earnestly hope that it may become illumined.[70]

When 'Abdu'l-Bahá passed away, the German believers demonstrated the qualities of constancy and spiritual perception that He had described of them. For instance, when the Greatest Holy Leaf sent cables to the major Bahá'í centers throughout the world announcing that in His Will and Testament, 'Abdu'l-Bahá had appointed Shoghi Effendi as the Guardian of the Cause of God, the Bahá'ís of Germany were swift to send a reply to assure the Greatest Holy Leaf of their fidelity to the Guardian. The cable read, "'All believers deeply moved by irrevocable loss of our Master's precious life. We pray for heavenly protection of Holy Cause and promise faithfulness and obedience to Center of Covenant.'"[71]

As has been mentioned in chapter 1, Shoghi Effendi was studying in Oxford at the time of the passing of 'Abdu'l-Bahá. He was unable to arrange passage to Palestine until after 'Abdu'l-Bahá's funeral, and he arrived in Haifa on December 29, 1921 with no foreknowledge that 'Abdu'l-Bahá had appointed him Guardian of the Cause of God. Only after the Will and Testament of 'Abdu'l-Bahá was read to him after his arrival in Haifa did he gain this knowledge. Later, when the Will and Testament of 'Abdu'l-Bahá was read aloud to nine members of 'Abdu'l-Bahá's family on January 3, 1922, Shoghi Effendi was not present. The public reading of the Master's Will and Testament took place on January 7, 1922, in which the station of Shoghi Effendi was clearly proclaimed in these words from the Master's Will:

O my loving friends! After the passing away of this wronged one, it is incumbent upon the Aghṣán (Branches), the Afnán (Twigs) of the Sacred Lote-Tree, the Hands (pillars) of the Cause of God and the loved ones of the Abhá Beauty to turn unto Shoghi Effendi—the youthful branch branched from the two hallowed and sacred Lote-Trees and the fruit grown from the union of the two offshoots of the Tree of Holiness,—as he is the sign of God, the chosen branch, the Guardian of the Cause of God, he unto whom all the Aghṣán, the Afnán, the Hands of the Cause of God and His loved ones must turn. He is the expounder of the words of God and after him will succeed the first-born of his lineal descendants.[72]

In a letter from the Universal House of Justice, the significance of the passing of 'Abdu'l-Bahá is noted as a deeply profound moment in history for Bahá'ís. From the standpoint of a century after 'Abdu'l-Bahá's ascension, it is difficult for us to imagine what it would have been like to look at 'Abdu'l-Bahá with one's own eyes and to hear His voice with one's own ears. His passing "took from the Bahá'ís of that era a Figure Who was the object of their ardent love and loyalty; to the faithful of this age, He remains without parallel: a perfect embodiment in word and deed of all that His Father taught, the One through Whom the Covenant of Bahá'u'lláh was 'proclaimed, championed and vindicated.'"[73]

Johanna Hauff came of age during this unique period in Bahá'í history, a period in which the Bahá'í world transitioned from the Heroic Age of the Cause (1844–1921) to the Formative Age of the Cause (1921–the present.) The Heroic Age witnessed the birth and rise of the Cause of God, and the Formative Age was ". . . the Age in which the institutions, local, national and international, of the Faith of Bahá'u'lláh were to take shape, develop and become fully consolidated."[74]

Under the direction of Shoghi Effendi, the expansion of the Cause of Bahá'u'lláh continued according to the goals set out in 'Abdu'l-Bahá's *Tablets of the Divine Plan*. Furthermore, Shoghi Effendi dedicated himself to carrying out the provisions of 'Abdu'l-

Bahá's Will and Testament, which called for the establishment of the Administrative Order. From the beginning of Shoghi Effendi's ministry in 1921, he focused on encouraging the believers to establish and strengthen Local Spiritual Assemblies throughout the world. These Spiritual Assemblies were the necessary foundation of the Administrative Order and upon which the strong pillars of future National Spiritual Assemblies would rest. These pillars would, in time, support the dome of that administrative structure, the Universal House of Justice.[75]

The most significant development of the Administrative Order in Germany came as the result of a landmark letter from Shoghi Effendi, dated March 12, 1923 and addressed "To the beloved of the Lord and the handmaids of the Merciful throughout America, Great Britain, Germany, France, Switzerland, Italy, Japan and Australasia." In it, Shoghi Effendi outlined the specific functions of Bahá'í community life: the responsibility of the Bahá'ís to continually respond to the ever-changing conditions of the world, the importance of every adult believer to participate in the annual election of Local Spiritual Assemblies, the process by which National Spiritual Assemblies were to be elected, the importance of contributing to the Bahá'í Fund, the supervision and development of Bahá'í translations and literature, the promotion of the enlightenment of children and youth, and, above all, "the most essential obligation," which is none other than "delivering far and wide this Message of Salvation to a sorely-stricken world."[76]

The letter would have been read by virtually every Bahá'í in Stuttgart, because, after all, it had been addressed to them. In response to their grief over the passing of 'Abdu'l-Bahá, the greatest service they could do for Him was to heed every word addressed to them by His appointed successor. In Shoghi Effendi's affectionate wisdom, he began the letter in these words: "Over a year has elapsed since that calamitous Hour, when the glorious Person of 'Abdu'l-Bahá was veiled from mortal eyes and His Spirit ascended to the Kingdom of Glory; and I feel that the time is now ripe to take those fresh and momentous decisions which will enable us to fulfill, speedily and faithfully, the last wishes of our departed Master."[77]

Further in that letter, Shoghi Effendi, cognizant of the suffering endured by the Bahá'ís during and after the first World War, encouraged the believers to seize the opportunities to advance the Cause in these countries where the war had left deep wounds waiting to be healed:

> But great achievements still await us in this world, and we feel confident that, by His grace and never-failing guidance, we shall now and ever prove ourselves worthy to fulfill His great Purpose for mankind. And who can fail to realize the sore need of bleeding humanity, in its present state of uncertainty and peril, for the regenerating Spirit of God, manifested this Day so powerfully in this Divine Dispensation? Four years of unprecedented warfare and world cataclysms, followed by another four years of bitter disappointment and suffering, have stirred deeply the conscience of mankind, and opened the eyes of an unbelieving world to the Power of the Spirit that alone can cure its sicknesses, heal its wounds, and establish the long-promised reign of undisturbed prosperity and peace.[78]

It is awe-inspiring to imagine the members of the Bahá'í community of Stuttgart—Johanna Hauff included—reading these words of the Guardian. He was outlining, in no uncertain terms, the necessary steps to be taken by the believers to ensure the spiritual rebuilding of their post-war community. Calling the adult believers to exercise their sacred duty to raise up Spiritual Assemblies, Shoghi Effendi made it crystal clear that this duty was one that could not be neglected: "And, now that this all-important Work may suffer no neglect, but rather function vigorously and continuously in every part of the Bahá'í world; that the unity of the Cause of Bahá'u'lláh may remain secure and inviolate, it is of the utmost importance that in accordance with the explicit text of the Kitáb-i-Aqdas, the Most Holy Book, in every locality, be it city or hamlet, where the number of adult (21 years and above) declared believers exceeds nine, a local 'Spiritual Assembly' be forthwith established."[79]

It did not take long for the German believers to respond to Shoghi Effendi's call for an expansion of the Administrative Order in Germany. Despite the difficulties during the post-war years, Local Spiritual Assemblies were formed across Germany and its National Spiritual Assembly was recognized by Shoghi Effendi in 1923 with its headquarters in Stuttgart.[80*]

Furthermore, Shoghi Effendi called for Spiritual Assemblies to supervise ". . . Bahá'í publications and translations, and provide . . . for a dignified and accurate presentation of all Bahá'í lit-

---

* In 1934, the National Spiritual Assembly of Germany was renamed as the National Spiritual Assembly of Germany and Austria. (See "National Spiritual Assembly of Germany and Austria" online at *https://bahaipedia.org/NSA:Germany_and_Austria*). In May, 1937 the National Spiritual Assembly was officially prohibited by the Reichsfüher SS and Chief of the German Police in the Ministry of the Interior, Heinrich Himmler (Susanne Pfaff-Grossmann, *Hermann Grossmann, Hand of the Cause of God: A Life for the Faith,* p. 55). It was not until April, 1946 that the National Spiritual Assembly was re-established. In 1959, Germany and Austria established independent National Spiritual Assemblies, fulfilling a goal of the Ten Year Plan (Ibid., p. 158).

erature and its distribution to the general public."[81] This portion of the Guardian's letter must have reaffirmed for Johanna her path of service in the Cause. 'Abdu'l-Bahá had given Johanna Hauff a mission to learn Persian and Arabic in order to translate the Bahá'í writings into German as it was the vital link to the teaching work.

Although translations of the sacred writings were desperately needed, they were of value only if they were accurate translations that represented the Word of God with the power and beauty of the original text. In a Tablet to an individual believer in 1906, 'Abdu'l-Bahá wrote, "Regarding the translation of the Books and Tablets of the Blessed Beauty, erelong will translations be made into every tongue, with power, clarity and grace. At such time as they are translated, conformably to the originals, and with power and grace of style, the splendors of their inner meanings will be shed abroad, and will illumine the eyes of all mankind. Do thy very best to ensure that the translation is in conformity with the original."[82]

Johanna Hauff spent the whole of her life studying Persian and Arabic, and she understood that "the splendors of their inner meanings" could best be translated if she herself were constantly engaged in service to the Cause. 'Abdu'l-Bahá wrote:

When the friends do not endeavor to spread the message, they fail to remember God befittingly, and will not witness the tokens of assistance and confirmation from the Abhá Kingdom nor comprehend the divine mysteries. However, when the tongue of the teacher is engaged in teaching, he will naturally himself be stimulated, will become a magnet attracting the divine aid and bounty of the Kingdom, and will be like unto the bird at the hour of dawn, which itself becometh exhilarated by its own singing, its warbling and its melody.[83]

Not only did 'Abdu'l-Bahá set clear standards for translation, He outlined how the translation work should be carried out as part of the global teaching campaign launched by the *Tablets of the Divine Plan:*

> Likewise, whenever it is possible a committee must be organized for the translation of the Tablets. Wise souls who have mastered and studied perfectly the Persian, Arabic, and other foreign languages, or know one of the foreign languages, must commence translating Tablets and books containing the proofs of this Revelation, and publishing those books, circulate them throughout the five continents of the globe.[84]

Johanna did not translate any of the sacred writings without the permission and guidance of Shoghi Effendi and—later—the Universal House of Justice. Nor did she work alone. She collaborated with the Hand of the Cause of God Dr. Adelbert Mühlschlegel, Mr. Manutschehr Zabih, and Mr. Günter Heyd in translating the Hidden Words, and its publication was approved by the National Spiritual Assembly of Germany and Austria in 1948.[85] That year, the National Spiritual Assembly drew up a Five Year Plan under the direction of the Guardian. One of the goals of the plan was to have a series of works by Bahá'u'lláh, 'Abdu'l-Bahá, and Shoghi Effendi translated and published.[86] Johanna translated *Some Answered Questions,* which was published in German as *Gersräche und Lehren* in 1953. Dr. Hermann Grossmann translated *The Seven Valleys* and *Bahá'í Prayers* in 1950.[87] His sister, Elsa Grossmann, had already translated *Gleanings from the Writings of Bahá'u'lláh* and *The Dispensation of Bahá'u'lláh* in the 1930s.[88]

Johanna had a humble regard for the art of translation and never felt that she had completely mastered the magnitude of the task, especially given Bahá'u'lláh's own description of His Creative Word: "O friend of mine! The Word of God is the king of words and its pervasive influence is incalculable. It hath ever dominated and will continue to dominate the realm of being. The Great Being saith: The Word is the master key for the whole world, inasmuch as through its potency the doors of the hearts of men, which in reality are the doors of heaven, are unlocked."[89]

The Guardian's love and encouragement of the Stuttgart friends had no bounds. The Bahá'ís had emerged from the first world war, and the aftermath of its consequences, like a phoenix that had found new life from its own ashes. The Guardian used this very metaphor in his praise of the German believers:

November 27, 1924
To my dearly-beloved brothers and sisters in 'Abdu'l-Bahá.
My most precious brothers and sisters in the love of God!
Your most welcome letter bearing the signatures of those who have attended your Annual Bahá'í Congress recently held in Stuttgart filled my heart with a joy that I cannot express. As I read it over and over again I could feel from every word, nay every syllable, of that soul-stirring message of yours the promised quickening power of the Word of Bahá'u'lláh and the love of 'Abdu'l-Bahá which will, in time, I am certain, achieve the most far-reaching transformation throughout Germany.

Your great and promising country, dear to you all, blest by 'Abdu'l-Bahá's sacred feet, and the object of the hope and affection of Bahá'ís in every land, is in a most startling manner rising phoenix-like from the ashes of humiliation and despair, determined now to raise aloft victoriously and serene the Standard of Bahá'u'lláh and with His love set all the world aflame . . ."[90]

By 1933, the Bahá'ís of Stuttgart had received approval from Shoghi Effendi to publish portions of *The Dawn-Breakers* in its magazine called *Die Sonne der Wahrheit* from 1934 to June, 1937.[91] The stories published therein would inspire and prepare the believers for the spiritual heroism that the second world war would require of them.

The freedom of the Bahá'ís to organize administratively and to read Bahá'í literature was interrupted by the rise of German nationalism in the 1930s. Despite the efforts of the Bahá'ís of Germany to strengthen the Administrative Order of the Cause and to expand the distribution of Bahá'í literature, their institutions were attacked, their meetings forbidden, and their literature confiscated.* By 1937, the Bahá'í Faith was completely banned in Germany, as described here by Shoghi Effendi in 1944 in his book *God Passes By*:

> In Germany, likewise, the rise and establishment of the Administrative Order of the Faith, to whose expansion and consolidation the German believers were distinctively and increasingly contributing, was soon followed by repressive measures, which, though less grievous than the afflictions suffered by the Bahá'ís of Turkistán and the Caucasus, amounted to the virtual cessation, in the years immediately preceding the present conflict, of all organized Bahá'í activity throughout the length and breadth of that land. The public teaching of the Faith, with its unconcealed emphasis on peace and universal-

---

* For a comprehensive account of this period of the history of the Bahá'í Faith in Germany, read Susanne Pfaff-Grossmann's biography *Hermann Grossmann, Hand of the Cause of God: A Life for the Faith.*

ity, and its repudiation of racialism, was officially forbidden; Bahá'í Assemblies and their committees were dissolved; the holding of Bahá'í conventions was interdicted; the Archives of the National Spiritual Assembly were seized; the summer school was abolished and the publication of all Bahá'í literature was suspended.[92]

The authorities of the German National Socialist Party had destroyed all of the records of the National Spiritual Assembly. When the National Spiritual Assembly was permitted to function again, the Guardian asked that the early believers of Stuttgart be enlisted to reconstruct the records of the past. The following was written to Hermann Grossmann on behalf of the Guardian: "The loss of all the records of the National and Local Assemblies is indeed very great, and he hopes that your family, Dr. Mühlschlegel, Dr. Schmidt, Herr Jörn, Anna Köstlin, Frau Schweizer, Frau (Alice) Schwarz—, in fact, all the old believers, will try and reconstruct from memory, and write down, as much of the history of the Cause in Germany as they can remember, so that some accurate records for the future will remain."[93]

In 1923, Johanna married Baron von Werthern, and by the second world war, she was still raising her two teenaged sons, Hans and Manfred. The ban on every aspect of Bahá'í life made it impossible for her to speak about the Bahá'í Faith at home with her husband and children. Johanna's marriage eventually ended in divorce. Their younger son Manfred became an architect and delighted his mother by submitting a design for the Bahá'í House of Worship in Langenhain. Their older son Hans married, but his wife did not allow any discussion about the Bahá'í Faith between them or with their grandchildren.[94]

In 1953, Shoghi Effendi launched the Ten Year Crusade. It was a teaching plan vast in scope, and its aim was to establish the Cause of Bahá'u'lláh in the unopened countries and territories throughout the world. Johanna was fifty-nine years old and had been serving on the National Spiritual Assembly of Germany and Austria (1950–1956) when Shoghi Effendi asked if she would take up a pioneering position in the provincial capital of Tyrol, Innsbruck, Austria.[95] Johanna joined an American Bahá'í named Bertha Matthisen, who was already pioneering in Innsbruck, and they became a teaching team, working together for the proclamation of the Bahá'í Faith. Soon after Johanna's arrival in Innsbruck, she received another letter written on behalf of the Guardian by Rúhíyyih Rabbani in German and dated September 16, 1955, in which Johanna was praised for her steadfastness, her zeal, and her devotion and was encouraged to rely on the power of Bahá'u'lláh to assist her in establishing a nucleus of firm and devoted believers who could become strong bearers of the faith and its institutions.[96]

In time, more pioneers arrived in Innsbruck, and Johanna reported to Shoghi Effendi on the progress of the Bahá'í community. She received a reply in a letter dated March 3, 1956, written on behalf of the Guardian in German, wherein the Guardian expressed that he was pleased that the work in Innsbruck was making progress and that he was sure that, thanks to Johanna's enthusiasm and that of the other dear friends, it would not be long before a flourishing community would emerge in that city.[97]

On April 25, 1959, the delegates of the Austrian Bahá'í community met in the Bahá'í center at Thimiggasse 12 in Vienna to elect the first National Spiritual Assembly of Austria (independent of Germany), of which Johanna became a member. During her service, she was also appointed to the National Spiritual Assembly's translation and review committee.[98] Johanna had never abandoned her study of Arabic and Persian. When she returned from Haifa in 1922, she began her studies at Berlin University in Persian and Arabic, and she took classes in both languages all her life. She had succeeded in fulfilling the wish of 'Abdu'l-Bahá of translating the sacred writings into German and furnishing the German-speaking people with the Word of God, which Bahá'u'lláh described as the "master key" through which "the doors of the hearts of men, which in reality are the doors of heaven, are unlocked."[99] She also had done her part, through her service as a pioneer, to help raise up the National Spiritual Assembly of Austria so that it would become the strong pillars of the future Universal House of Justice.

In 1974, Johanna was in her eightieth year and visibly weaker. She returned to Germany to stay with her son Hans in the town of Hofheim. After a few months, she died on June 29, 1974 and is buried in the forest cemetery in Hofheim. Johanna Hauff von Werthern had lived through a time in the history of the world when the forces of disintegration and integration had unfolded before her eyes. She had witnessed the onset of the destructive forces that would hasten the decline of an outworn civilization while actively working toward building a new one in its stead.

In 1939, Johanna and her sister Julia had decided to sell Villa Hauff to the city of Stuttgart. The house has had a storied life since then.[100] First it was used as a military hospital during the second world war; in 1942, the Nazi military police occupied the home; in 1945, it was occupied by the Americans and used as an American consulate. After the war, the house was used as a youth center for "German Youth Activities."[101] When the house was returned to the city, the city continued to use it as a youth center under the newly founded Stuttgart Youth House Association. Since 1985, the house has been used by the city as a youth center for art production and art education with workshops offered in painting, ceramics, textiles, sculpture, photography, and film. It also has a gallery and a café.[102]

When He visited Stuttgart, 'Abdu'l-Bahá spoke about how change is a law of nature and a necessary process for growth and transformation. The Master's visit marked the early beginnings of Johanna Hauff's Bahá'í life—a life that spanned eighty years and witnessed some of the most significant developments in the Cause of God. No wonder the Master loved the Bahá'ís of Germany so deeply. Of that never to be forgotten visit to Stuttgart, 'Abdu'l-Bahá wrote:

I shall never forget the days I passed in Stuttgart in thy company, for the whole time was given to the diffusion of the reviving breaths of the Holy Spirit. Those wonderful meetings were charged with the surging spirit of divine confirmation which radiated from the presence of Bahá'u'lláh. The light of the Kingdom was shining forth from the Realm of Glory, His invisible assistance was unceasingly vouchsafed, the hearts were filled with gladness, the spirits rejoiced through the revelation of heavenly glad-tidings, and each of the beloved friends was radiant like a candle. Therefore those days shall never be forgotten. Now I fervently hope that following my departure the fire of the love of God may burst into flame more intensely than ever, and that thou mayest raise a heavenly melody at every meeting. I am well pleased with and deeply grateful to the loved ones of God in Stuttgart. They are blessed souls indeed. I will never forget them. Remembrance of them is always a source of joy to me. Convey on my behalf warmest Abhá greetings to all the friends there.[103]

# 4 / Curtis Kelsey

In the winter following 'Abdu'l-Bahá's return to Haifa from His journey to the West, Mírzá Aḥmad Sohrab wrote that one day, 'Abdu'l-Bahá was seated on the veranda next to the window of the Haifa Pilgrim House. According to Sohrab, 'Abdu'l-Bahá gazed out over the bay of Haifa and across the shores of the Mediterranean Sea. With His eyes resting on 'Akká and the vicinity of the shrine of Bahá'u'lláh, the Qiblih of the nations, 'Abdu'l-Bahá said:

The view from the Pilgrim House is very attractive, especially as it faces the Blessed Tomb of Bahá'u'lláh. In the future the distance between 'Akká and Haifa will be built up, and the two cities will join and clasp hands, becoming the two terminal sections of one mighty metropolis. As I look now over this scene, I see so clearly that it will become one of the first emporiums of the world. This great semi-circular bay will be transformed into the finest harbour, wherein the ships of all nations will seek shelter and refuge. The great vessels of all peoples will come to this port, bringing on their decks thousands and thousands of men and women from every part of the globe. The mountain and the plain will be dotted with the most modern buildings and palaces. Industries will be established and various institutions of philanthropic nature will be founded. The flowers of civilization and culture from all nations will be brought here to blend their fragrances together and blaze the way for the brotherhood of man. Wonderful gardens, orchards, groves and parks will be laid out on all sides. At night the great city will be lighted by electricity. The entire harbour from 'Akká to Haifa will be one path of illumination. Powerful searchlights will be placed on both sides of Mount Carmel to guide the steamers. Mount Carmel itself, from top to bottom, will be submerged in a sea of lights. A person standing on the summit of Mount Carmel, and the passengers of the steamers coming to it, will look upon the most sublime and majestic spectacle of the whole world.[1]

Hand of the Cause of God Ḥasan Balyuzi related another instance in which 'Abdu'l-Bahá described the future transformation of the semicircular bay:

The Shrine of the Báb was now a place of pilgrimage. A Bahá'í of 'Ishqábád . . . was moved to offer to defray the expense of building a pilgrim house in the close vicinity of the Shrine. It was on the balcony of this same Pilgrim House, overlooking the town of Haifa, the bay and the plain of 'Akká beyond, that 'Abdu'l-Bahá stood, soon after its completion, and spoke of the vision He had of the future of Mount Carmel and the bay, of the two towns stretched out there before His gaze. Behind Him stood Mírzá Maḥmúd-i-Zarqání, His secretary during

His tour of the Western world and the diarist of that tour. Did Mírzá Maḥmúd see the splendorous scene, He asked. Poor Mírzá Maḥmúd could see nothing but a puny town below, which was Haifa, an almost deserted port that had no harbour facilities, a bare waste of desert and sand round the arc of the bay, in the distance a walled, circumscribed ʻAkká, dimly discernable. But ʻAbdu'l-Bahá could see the two towns joined round the bay, a fine harbour teeming with the ships of all nations, Carmel bathed in light at nightfall, shining like a jewel, great institutions serving the needs and the aspirations of the human race. He saw the world metropolis of the future, sited in a land holy since the days of Abraham.[2]

When ʻAbdu'l-Bahá described how the harbor from ʻAkká to Haifa will be one path of illumination, it calls to mind the location of the shrines of the Báb and Bahá'u'lláh, the "twin Luminaries of the Baháʼí Revelation."[3] The Qiblih, the Point of Adoration for the Baháʼí world, is the shrine of Bahá'u'lláh in ʻAkká and is described by ʻAbdu'l-Bahá as the "luminous Shrine" and "the place around which circumambulate the Concourse on high."[4] Similarly, the shrine of the Báb in Haifa is "the Spot round which the Concourse on high circle in adoration" and the "a focal center of Divine illumination and power, the very dust of which ʻAbdu'l-Bahá averred had inspired Him, yielding in sacredness to no other shrine throughout the Baháʼí world except the Sepulcher of the Author of the Baháʼí Revelation Himself."[5]

Bahá'u'lláh visited Haifa four times between the years 1868 and 1891. On one of those visits He stood with ʻAbdu'l-Bahá on Mount Carmel and designated the spot where the shrine of the Báb should be built. On another occasion, Bahá'u'lláh revealed the Tablet of

Carmel, in which He announced the fulfillment of the greatest, most longed-for heavenly promise in the story of mankind—the advent of the Kingdom of God on earth.[6] In a sublimely poetic apostrophe, Bahá'u'lláh addressed the mountain and spoke of the uniqueness of this Day of God:

> Call out to Zion, O Carmel, and announce the joyful tidings: He that was hidden from mortal eyes is come! His all-conquering sovereignty is manifest; His all-encompassing splendor is revealed. Beware lest thou hesitate or halt. Hasten forth and circumambulate the City of God that hath descended from heaven, the celestial Kaaba round which have circled in adoration the favored of God, the pure in heart, and the company of the most exalted angels. Oh, how I long to announce unto every spot on the surface of the earth, and to carry to each one of its cities, the glad-tidings of this Revelation—a Revelation to which the heart of Sinai hath been attracted, and in whose name the Burning Bush is calling: "Unto God, the Lord of Lords, belong the kingdoms of earth and heaven." Verily this is the Day in which both land and sea rejoice at this announcement, the Day for which have been laid up those things which God, through a bounty beyond the ken of mortal mind or heart, hath destined for revelation. Ere long will God sail His Ark upon thee, and will manifest the people of Bahá who have been mentioned in the Book of Names.[7]

Shoghi Effendi has written that one of the chief objectives of 'Abdu'l-Bahá's ministry was the "building on Mt. Carmel of a mausoleum marking the resting-place of the Báb."[8] He went on to write, "He ['Abdu'l-Bahá] Himself testified, on more than one occasion, that the safe transfer of these remains, the construction of a befitting mausoleum to receive them, and their final interment with His own hands in their permanent resting-place constituted one of the three principal objectives which, ever since the inception of His mission, He had conceived it His paramount duty to achieve. This act indeed deserves to rank as one of the outstanding events in the first Bahá'í century."[9] After the Báb and His companion were martyred in the city of Tabríz in 1850, their mangled remains were left at the edge of the moat outside the city. On the second night after the Báb's martyrdom, their remains were collected by His faithful followers and kept hidden until they could be interred in a shrine befitting the Báb's station.

On Naw-Rúz, 1909, 'Abdu'l-Bahá fulfilled the wish of His Father and announced that "'the holy, the luminous body of the Báb [. . .] after having for sixty years been transferred from place to place [. . .] has, through the mercy of the Abhá Beauty, been ceremoniously deposited, on the day of Naw-Rúz, within the sacred casket, in the exalted Shrine on Mt. Carmel. . . .'"[10] Shoghi Effendi explained that 'Abdu'l-Bahá had arranged for a marble sarcophagus to be placed in the vault of the shrine, and "by the light of a single lamp, He laid within it, with His own hands . . . the wooden casket containing the sacred remains of the Báb and His companion."[11] Describing this scene, Shoghi Effendi wrote:

When all was finished, and the earthly remains of the Martyr-Prophet of Shíráz were, at long last, safely deposited for their everlasting rest in the bosom of God's holy mountain, 'Abdu'l-Bahá, Who had cast aside His turban, removed His shoes and thrown off His cloak, bent low over the still open sarcophagus, His silver hair waving about His head and His face transfigured and luminous, rested His forehead on the border of the wooden casket, and, sobbing aloud, wept with such a weeping that all those who were present wept with Him.[12]

After the remains of the Báb had been laid to rest, another consideration was the illumination of His tomb in a manner that would be fitting for the Herald of Bahá'u'lláh.[13] During the lifetime of the Báb, the Persian authorities had sought to put out the light of His Cause by exiling Him to a mountain fortress, called Máh-kú, which was located in Azerbaijan, in northwestern Iran. This region is separated from Turkey by the craggy cliffs of the Zagros Mountains, and today, wedged in the face of one of its cliffs, are the crumbling remains of the fortress of Máh-kú. The Báb had been sent there as prisoner by the shah's grand vizir, who imagined that he could put an end to the Báb's spiritual influence over the people of Persia.[14]

Instead, the vizir's own design was thwarted, for in those nine months of His confinement within the stone walls of this fortress, the Báb revealed the Bayán, which Shoghi Effendi explained "should be regarded primarily as a eulogy of the Promised One rather than a code of laws and ordinances designed to be a permanent guide to future generations."[15] It is the book wherein the Báb makes clear to His followers the station of Bahá'u'lláh: "'Well is it with him who fixeth his gaze upon the Order of Bahá'u'lláh, and rendereth thanks unto his Lord. For He will assuredly be made manifest. God hath indeed irrevocably ordained it in the Persian Bayán.'"[16] Dark and cold were the days in which the Báb suffered in Máh-Kú, where He was denied even a candle by which to write. In one of the most breathtaking passages of the Persian Bayán, and speaking in the voice of God, He writes, "How veiled are ye, O My creatures . . . who, without any right, have consigned Him unto a mountain . . . there is not at night even a lighted lamp! . . . All that is on earth hath been created for Him, and all partake with delight of His benefits, and yet they are so veiled from Him as to refuse Him even a lamp!"[17]

In one place in His Tablet to the Hague, written in December of 1919, 'Abdu'l-Bahá demonstrated the relationship between material civilization and divine civilization by using the metaphor of a lamp. He wrote, "Material civilization is like a lamp-glass. Divine civilization is the lamp itself and the glass without the light is dark."[18] Light, therefore, is a symbol of the Divine. It is no wonder, then, that 'Abdu'l-Bahá's vision that "the entire harbor from 'Akká to Haifa will be one path of illumination" and the joined cities of 'Akká and Haifa "will be lighted by electricity" is an intimation of a "mighty metropolis" of the future, the glimmerings of which were not far away. Within a few years of 'Abdu'l-Bahá's return from His journey to the West, He began to make plans to install electrical equipment for the illumination of the shrine of Bahá'u'lláh near 'Akká and the shrine of the Báb in Haifa. The story of how the shrines became illumined began with an ordinary person named Curtis Kelsey who had the bounty of rendering this extraordinary service to 'Abdu'l-Bahá.

Curtis Kelsey lived in New York, and after becoming a Bahá'í in 1917 at the age of twenty-three, he was elected to the Spiritual Assembly of New York City. Around that same time, 'Abdu'l-Bahá was making plans to install the first electrical generators for the shrine of the Báb and the shrine of Bahá'u'lláh.[19] One of Curtis's fellow Spiritual Assembly members, Mr. Roy Wilhelm, had been corresponding with the Master about this endeavor. Roy offered to purchase the equipment and have it sent to Haifa. Roy also mentioned to 'Abdu'l-Bahá that he knew someone—a member of the Spiritual Assembly of New York City named Curtis Kelsey—who could travel to Haifa and install the equipment. 'Abdu'l-Bahá approved of Roy's suggestion and sent a cablegram in August of 1921 that read, "CURTIS KELSEY PERMITTED."[20]

Within a couple of weeks, Curtis was bound for Haifa. Dozens of friends from the New York City Bahá'í community came to see Curtis off at the wharf. The scene was a faint reminder of a day in September three years before when his family and friends had bid him farewell as he boarded the *Aquitania* as a private in the American Expeditionary Forces bound for France in 1918 to fight in the Great War. This time, he was traveling on a completely different kind of mission. Friends and family crowded around him, full of pride that their own native son, Curtis, would assist 'Abdu'l-Bahá in the project of illuminating the holy shrines of the Báb and Bahá'u'lláh with light. As he boarded the *Olympic* carrying two suitcases that were loaded heavily with electrical equipment, Curtis waved good-bye. Across his shoulder hung the Graflex camera his mother had given him, and in his pocket was an envelope with $250 from his father.

The *RMS Olympic* was a luxury ocean liner, the best in her class. Built in 1911, she had served as a troopship during the Great War and had earned the nickname "Old Reliable." What a fortunate turn of events it was for Curtis to stroll her decks as a civilian passenger instead of as a uniformed soldier. Under normal conditions, the voyage across the Atlantic Ocean would have taken just over fifteen days, but there was heavy fog one hundred miles from the ship's port of call in Cherbourg, France. The fog caused the ship to be delayed off the coast for a day, and the delay concerned Curtis because he knew that Roy Wilhelm had informed 'Abdu'l-Bahá that he would arrive in three weeks.[21] When the fog cleared and

Curtis set foot on the port dock, he rushed to the ticket office to book passage on the next ship to Alexandria, Egypt. He was told that the next ship would not sail for several weeks, so Curtis took a train to Naples to try his luck at booking passage on a steamship from there.

When he arrived, he had no luck and was told that there were no ships bound for the Middle East. Refusing to give up hope, he asked the ticket agent to call him at his hotel if anything changed. Two days later, the ticket agent called Curtis to tell him that, unexpectedly, a space had become available. The steamship *Esperia,* "the fastest, largest, and most luxurious vessel plying in the Mediterranean" had made an emergency docking at the Port of Naples.[22] One of its passengers was ill with appendicitis and needed immediate medical attention.[23] The ticket agent said that the *Esperia* was bound for Alexandria, Egypt, and he asked if Mr. Kelsey would like to take the place of the passenger who had disembarked. Delighted by the stroke of good fortune, Curtis boarded the *Esperia* as it raised anchor and began its voyage across the Mediterranean Sea toward Egypt.

From Alexandria, Curtis traveled by train through the bustling city of Cairo and then further north and across the border to Palestine, where the arid landscape stretched its arms around the shores of the Mediterranean. As the train made its turn around the point of Carmel in its approach to Haifa, Curtis looked north and could see the view across the bay toward 'Akká. Turning his gaze southeast, he could see the barren slopes of Mount Carmel and the structure of the tomb of the Báb.

Arriving on September 25, 1921, Curtis was met at the train station by Mr. Saichirō Fujita and Dr. Luṭfu'lláh Ḥakím, and together they rode in the Master's buckboard wagon to the old Western Pilgrim House on Haparsim Street, which was across the street from the house of 'Abdu'l-Bahá. A traditional Persian meal had been prepared, and the room was filled with the smell of sweet rice, curried lamb, and candied orange-peel.[24] Just when Dr. Ḥakím said they were waiting for the Master to come, 'Abdu'l-Bahá suddenly entered the room, took Curtis's hands in His and, after giving him a joyful welcome, said in English, "'Did you notice how easy it was to get here?'"[25]

Curtis was given a small room in the back of the Western Pilgrim House, which he shared with Mr. Fujita and Dr. Ḥakím. For eight months, the three men lived as true brothers in a tiny room with three beds, three dressers, a bookshelf, a table, and a lamp. Curtis Kelsey's biographer, Nathan Rutstein, described Curtis's first night's sleep as a restless one—not because he was sleeping on a stiff wooden board with a three-quarter-inch mattress, but because he could not stop thinking about his first meeting with 'Abdu'l-Bahá: "Being with the Master was more than he had imagined. 'Abdu'l-Bahá's nobility was obvious, but He didn't flaunt it. In His presence, Curtis didn't feel like cowering; instead he felt at ease, completely accepted—and totally loved. Before meeting 'Abdu'l-Bahá there were times when Curtis felt unworthy of being with Him. But he never experienced that feeling when he was with the Master. In fact, he was forgetful of self. Later on in life, in reflecting on why he always felt at ease with 'Abdu'l-Bahá, Curtis realized that the Master wouldn't allow you to feel unworthy, whatever your station in life."[26]

Fifteen days passed before 'Abdu'l-Bahá had Curtis begin working on the electrical lighting. During that time, Curtis settled into the rhythm of life that surrounded the Master's house. 'Abdu'l-Bahá was continually occupied with writing to the believers, with meeting travelers from near and far who sought His help and advice, and with addressing the manifold problems that continued to arise from the Covenant-breakers who sought to divide the Bahá'í community. While he waited for instructions from 'Abdu'l-Bahá, Curtis had time to get to know Mr. Fujita and Dr. Ḥakím, and with both he would develop a life-long bond of friendship.

Dr. Luṭfu'lláh Ḥakím was born in Iran and was the grandson of Ḥakím Masíh, the first Jewish convert to the Faith of Bahá'u'lláh. He was studying physiotherapy in London in 1911 when he first met 'Abdu'l-Bahá upon His visit to that city. In 1920, he made his first pilgrimage to the holy land. After his pilgrimage, 'Abdu'l-Bahá arranged for Dr. Ḥakím to return to the United Kingdom as the trusted traveling companion of Shoghi Effendi, who was to begin his studies at Oxford.[27] Later that same year, 'Abdu'l-Bahá called Dr. Ḥakím to the holy land to assist Him with the reception of pilgrims.[28] Dr. Ḥakím returned to Haifa just before Curtis Kelsey's arrival. He was only five years older than Curtis, but his quiet and calm manner made him seem much older. Dr. Ḥakím was fluent in English and was often called upon to translate when 'Abdu'l-Bahá gave talks to the English-speaking pilgrims. Dr. Ḥakím would spend most of his life serving in the holy land. After the passing of 'Abdu'l-Bahá, he served Shoghi Effendi, who appointed him to the International Bahá'í Council. When the Universal House of Justice was elected in 1963, Dr. Ḥakím was elected to that body and served until a year before his death in 1968.[29] After his passing, the Universal House of Justice sent a letter to all National Spiritual Assemblies that spoke of the full confidence reposed in him by the Master and the Guardian, his services in Persia, the British Isles, and the holy land and of how he will always be remembered in the annals of the Faith.[30]

Mr. Saichirō Fujita was thirty-four years old when he came to have the good fortune to live as a treasured member of the household of 'Abdu'l-Bahá. In 1903, at age 17, he emigrated from Japan to the United States and learned of the Bahá'í Faith in San Francisco. Upon declaring his belief in Bahá'u'lláh, he received the following Tablet (given here, in part) from 'Abdu'l-Bahá:

O thou fresh plant in the garden of the Love of God!
. . . Rest assured thy name is registered in the Book of God, and it is hoped that thou mayest enter the Paradise of the Kingdom and find stability; to reach that which is the cause of the progress of the world of humanity in the world and in the Kingdom, and with perceiving eye, attentive ear, eloquent tongue and radiant face may serve in the Vineyard of God and spread the Divine Glad Tidings. If thou art confirmed as thou oughtest to be, thou wilt certainly establish an eternal Kingdom. This Kingdom is greater than that of Mikado, for the sovereignty of the Emperor of Japan is for numbered days, but this sovereignty is lasting and will stand unto the Eternity of Eternities.

That sovereignty can be hidden under one handful of dust, that is when Mikado goes beneath the handful of dust, he is entirely effaced and erased, but this Kingdom withstands the greatest revolution of the worlds, and will stand with perfect stability unto eternity. The former kingdom is established by the power of the sword, burning fire, devouring, and the shedding of blood, while this Kingdom is built upon freedom, glory, greatness and the love of God. Consider how much difference there is between them.[31]

Later, while studying in Chicago, Fujita met 'Abdu'l-Bahá and traveled with Him during His visits to cities in America. The Master arranged for Fujita to come to Haifa in 1919, just after the end of the war. Fujita had been living in Haifa for only two years before the Master's ascension, but somehow it seemed that Fujita had lived in the house of the Master all his life. Fujita had become so akin to the pulse of life in the house of 'Abdu'l-Bahá that one might have thought that his residence in that home was ancestral. His path to the holy land is described in the following account from an audio recording of Curtis Kelsey and has been edited for clarity by the author:

Fujita was a Japanese man who had been an associate of Mr. Sessue Hayakawa, the famous Japanese silent film actor who came to the United States. They shared a house in California after their fathers had sent them to this country to go to school. Neither one of them were going to school; they were spending their money having a good time. While he was attending school in Oakland, California in 1905, he [Fujita] was taught the Faith by Mrs. Kathryn Frankland and Mrs. Helen Goodall in California. Mrs. Goodall must have written to 'Abdu'l-Bahá about Fujita because He wrote a Tablet to Fujita in California, calling attention to all of the virtues that Fujita had, and He told Fujita that the knowledge of Bahá'u'lláh was greater than ruling as the Mikado of Japan. Fujita read to me that Tablet and said, "This isn't me," but the Master kept telling him it was him. Then, two months later, Fujita received a second Tablet from 'Abdu'l-Bahá in which He again called attention to the virtues of Fujita's character. Fujita said to me, "This description of me is totally different from what I am, so I put the Tablet aside." When a third Tablet came, Fujita said, "I had better act on this because otherwise something will happen." So, without telling his house-mates, he packed up his bags secretly and went back to school to study electrical engineering in Ann Arbor, Michigan. After the war ended, 'Abdu'l-Bahá sent for Fujita and put him in charge of the Western Pilgrim House as a servant to the pilgrims there. Every morning, very early, he would cross the street to the house of 'Abdu'l-Bahá and have tea and breakfast with Him. Just the two of them. Every morning.[32]

'Abdu'l-Bahá was making plans to install electricity on Mount Carmel as early as 1913 and had identified Fujita as someone who might assist in the work, as indicated in this portion of a Tablet from 'Abdu'l-Bahá to Fujita written in May, 1913:

O thou servant of God . . .
As regard to thy profession of electricity. Endeavor from every direction that thou mayest gain perfect efficiency in it—so that I may send for thee to come with electrical machine (automobile) and lighting plant—in order that in the Holy Land thou mayest know how to run the electrical engines and dynamos, how to install electrical lights through the buildings and how to fill the batteries of the (automobile) and act (if necessary) as chauffeur. When thou shalt learn these things then I will send for thee. Thou wilt be confirmed to render a great service and this will become the cause of thine everlasting glory.[33]

Although it is unclear why Fujita did not work as an electrical engineer in Haifa, it is known that he rendered great services in the holy land. With the exception of his return to Japan from 1938–1955, Fujita lived in Haifa and served 'Abdu'l-Bahá, Shoghi Effendi, and the Universal House of Justice until his passing on May 7, 1976. The Universal House of Justice sent the following cable to the National Spiritual Assembly of Japan:

DEARLY LOVED TIRELESS STEADFAST SAICHIRO FUJITA PASSED TO ABHA KINGDOM AFTER LONG YEARS SERVICE SACRED THRESHOLD. HIS RANK IN VANGUARD FIRST JAPANESE BELIEVERS HIS LABOURS WORLD CENTER HIS DEDICATION HUMILITY SINCERITY LOVE WILL FOREVER BE REMEMBERED AND PROVIDE SHINING EXAMPLE TO RISING GENERATIONS JAPANESE BAHAIS WHO WILL VIEW WITH PRIDE DISTINCTION CONFERRED UPON HIM. PRAYING HOLY SHRINES PROGRESS HIS RADIANT SOUL UNDER LOVING GRACE HIS MASTER AND GUARDIAN BOTH OF WHOM HE SERVED SO WELL.[34]

In addition to serving in the Western Pilgrim House, Fujita was frequently the driver of the two automobiles owned by 'Abdu'l-Bahá. When Curtis Kelsey arrived in Haifa, he saw that both cars were in need of repair. One was a Ford, which Curtis knew a lot about because he had worked for a year at the Ford factory in Detroit, and the other was a seven-seater Cunningham touring automobile. It was sent by Mrs. Ella Goodall Cooper so the Master would have a car big enough to transport pilgrims to Bahjí. Curtis got both vehicles in good running condition and asked permission to drive the Ford. Curtis said, "In those days, if you went around a corner in one of the streets in Haifa, you had to back up twice to turn a corner."[35] Besides one other resident in Haifa, 'Abdu'l-Bahá was the only person who owned an automobile, but He preferred traveling by train, riding a donkey, or being pulled by a mule in His buckboard wagon.

At long last, in mid-October, 'Abdu'l-Bahá told Curtis that it was time to go to Bahjí. First, they would travel by train to 'Akká. From there, it was a two-and-a-half mile walk inland to Bahjí. At that time, Bahá'u'lláh's house in Bahjí (the Mansion of Bahjí) was occupied by certain members of His family who had broken the Covenant of Bahá'u'lláh. They refused to accept 'Abdu'l-Bahá as the one whom Bahá'u'lláh designated as the Center of His Covenant. The Bahá'ís had access to the shrine of Bahá'u'lláh and to the small house behind the shrine, but access to the Mansion and the room where Bahá'u'lláh passed away was barricaded by the Covenant-breakers. It was not until 1929 that the Guardian secured rightful authority over the mansion and evicted the malicious Covenant-breakers.[36] These circumstances did not deter Curtis from his electrical work in Bahjí, as his work was confined to the shrine itself.[37]

'Abdu'l-Bahá accompanied Curtis on this first visit to 'Akká and Bahjí. They traveled with Rúhí Afnán and Áqá Khusraw. Rúhí was one of 'Abdu'l-Bahá's grandsons, and Áqá Khusraw was a servant in the Master's household. Khusraw was of Burmese origin, and when he was six years old, he was adopted into the household by 'Abdu'l-Bahá and given the name Khusraw, which means "king" in Persian.[38]

In the passage that follows, Curtis recalls their sunset arrival to 'Akká and moonlight walk to Bahjí. Unbeknownst to Curtis, this visit would be the Master's last to the shrine of Bahá'u'lláh. The following account was transcribed from an audio recording of Curtis Kelsey; the narrative has been edited by the author for the purpose of clarity:

There was a most wonderful moon. It was one of those evenings where there was a full moon, and white clouds drifting by. The train stopped, and all the people got out and went into 'Akká. 'Abdu'l-Bahá sat down in the station and Rúhí Afnán and I stood outside waiting, and 'Abdu'l-Bahá didn't get up; He just sat there and pretty soon, coming through the desert, walking alone on the sand, was a tall Arab with his black head-dress and cape hanging down over his shoulders. He came into the station and he and 'Abdu'l-Bahá had a conversation, laughing. While they were talking, another person came toward the train station leading 'Abdu'l-Bahá's white donkey. The Arab bid 'Abdu'l-Bahá farewell and returned to the desert. Khusraw ran ahead to Bahjí to prepare our dinner while Rúhí Afnán and I walked alongside 'Abdu'l-Bahá as He rode His white donkey. It was a two-and-a-half mile walk from 'Akká to Bahjí. The sky was dark except for the moonlight. 'Abdu'l-Bahá pulled His *abá* cloak around Himself and said, in English, "Beautiful night, wonderful sky, beautiful moon!"

At that time Bahjí was not in the possession of the Bahá'ís, so we went down to the little house on the corner of the garden, we had to go up a flight of steps that took us to a room and off this room was a garden with an orange tree in it. Khusraw prepared curried lamb and saffron rice on a charcoal stove. He placed Persian melon and Damascus grapes on the table and we ate our meal.

The next morning at dawn we went to the Shrine of Bahá'u'lláh. I stood about four paces behind 'Abdu'l-Bahá as He chanted the Tablet of Visitation. Instead of going back to Haifa on the train, we returned that afternoon by riding in the buckboard wagon along the shores of the Mediterranean Sea. We were about halfway between 'Akká and Haifa when there was the most beautiful sunset over Mount Carmel. I asked the Master if I could stop and take a photograph and He said,

"Yes," and we stopped and I got one of the most wonderful shots of the sunset over Mount Carmel. Then we rode back to Haifa.[39]

Curtis alternated his stay between Haifa and 'Akká by spending two weeks working on the lighting of the shrine of Bahá'u'lláh and two weeks working on the lighting of the shrine of the Báb, so the work progressed equally on both shrines. When 'Abdu'l-Bahá asked Curtis about his plans for the electrical lighting of the shrine of Bahá'u'lláh, Curtis explained that he would wire it in such a way that the garden, the oil lamps, and the cornice of the shrine [of Bahá'u'lláh] could be illumined.[40] 'Abdu'l-Bahá was pleased and made every possible provision—including the help of an assistant electrician named Mr. Ḥasan Kahrabá'í and a service of meals consistent with an American diet—available to Curtis while he worked on the electrical project, as testified in this proviso from 'Abdu'l-Bahá to the caretaker at Bahjí:

He is God!
To Áqá Siyyid Abu'l-Qásim:
A dear guest is coming to you; he is the person who is going to arrange the lighting of the Holy Shrines with Mr. Kahrabá'í. He must have plentiful food for lunch and dinner and even breakfast. Therefore a quantity of jam, cheese and olives will be sent and Mr. Luṭfu'lláh, who knows a little about cooking, will accompany him. You must all do what you can to ensure that at lunch and dinner there will be at least one type of dish that is to his liking. Either kill a chicken or bring meat from 'Akká. There must always be some kind of meat. And in the morning, serve milk, eggs, jam and olives. It will be some

trouble for you but this service is the duty of 'Abdu'l-Bahá. I should be doing this but have no opportunity and so you must make the effort. Upon thee be the Glory of Glories.

'Abdu'l-Bahá 'Abbás[41]

Meanwhile, pilgrims who had received permission from 'Abdu'l-Bahá began to arrive in early November. John Bosch and his wife Louise arrived with Johanna Hauff, and by mid-November, Dr. Florian Krug and his wife Grace had arrived from New York City.

Curtis knew the Krugs from New York City, as they were close friends of Curtis's mother, Mrs. Valeria Kelsey. One time, when Curtis was about twenty-three years old, he became very ill with typhoid fever. While in his delirium he had a mystical experience, and Mrs. Kelsey called Grace Krug to her home to help her search the Bahá'í writings for an indication of the significance of Curtis's mystical experience and his subsequent recovery from his illness. There was no doubt in Curtis's mind that his recovery was a spiritual one. He described the experience in this way: "'The ache and pounding in my head became so acute I turned over in bed and was pushing my head into the pillow, when the pain suddenly stopped, and I heard a very beautiful orchestra playing in my room. I had never had an experience like this and I turned around quickly to see what was there. However, there were no actual instruments in the room and as I sat up the music faded away.'"[42]

As the music faded, so did Curtis's fever and illness. Later, Curtis asked 'Abdu'l-Bahá the meaning of this experience, and 'Abdu'l-Bahá told him it was a true spiritual experience and that the music he heard was the music of the Kingdom of God and was the cause of Curtis's spiritual awakening.[43] 'Abdu'l-Bahá's interpretation of Curtis Kelsey's experience is reminiscent of an address given by

'Abdu'l-Bahá in Paris, where He spoke of light and darkness: "The light of the celestial world makes war against the world of shadow and illusion. The rays of the Sun of Truth dispel the darkness of superstition and misunderstanding. You are of the Spirit! To you who seek the truth, the Revelation of Bahá'u'lláh will come as a great joy! This teaching is of the Spirit, in it is no precept which is not of the Divine Spirit."[44]

In the two months from Curtis's arrival in Haifa up until 'Abdu'l-Bahá's passing, Curtis was able to observe many important events that preceded the Master's ascension. For instance, on Friday, November 25th, three days before His passing, 'Abdu'l-Bahá said to His daughters, "The wedding of K͟husraw must take place today. If you are too much occupied, I myself will make the necessary preparations, for it must take place this day."[45] The reader may recall that it was K͟husraw who traveled with Curtis, Rúhí Afnán, and 'Abdu'l-Bahá on Curtis's first visit to Bahjí; and it was K͟husraw who prepared the special meal that night in the small house behind the shrine of Bahá'u'lláh. In one of her recollections of being in Haifa at the time of the ascension of 'Abdu'l-Bahá, Mrs. Grace Krug described the remarkable story of how K͟husraw came to live in the Master's house:

> Friends, I will digress for a moment and give you a brief history of this remarkable man, 'Abdu'l-Bahá's body servant. Many years ago while the Master was still a prisoner in 'Akká, one of the Hindu Bahá'ís on his way to visit Him, passed through the Slave Market in one of the large cities in India, and saw a forlorn child, aged six years, standing on the block to be sold. The Pilgrim's heart was so moved at this pitiful sight that he bought the poor boy and took him with him to

Palestine. 'Abdu'l-Bahá had him educated, brought him up with His own family, and he has proved to be a most faithful servant. There are no words to describe his sincere devotion to the entire family. Khusraw's bride was a daughter of one of the Persian martyrs, and she, too, was brought up in the prison with the family. Friends, I am certain, after 'Abdu'l-Bahá's ascension, Khusraw, in his agonized grief, would have killed himself had he not been married. Think of the Master's foresight![46]

Indeed, there was concern about suicide. Before the passing of 'Abdu'l-Bahá, Mírzá Abu'l Ḥasan Afnán (a member of the family of the Báb) perceiving that the Master's death was imminent, drowned himself in the sea.[47] 'Abdu'l-Bahá was deeply saddened. On the day of Mírzá Ḥasan Afnán's funeral, 'Abdu'l-Bahá helped to carry his coffin to the grave site.[48] The next day, 'Abdu'l-Bahá spoke to the friends about living for the Cause rather than resorting to suicide. According to Aḥmad Tabrizi, one of the believers present when the Master spoke to the friends, reported that 'Abdu'l-Bahá said,

> You must not injure yourselves or commit suicide . . . It is not permissible to do to yourselves what Mirza Hassan Afnan did to himself. Should anyone at any time encounter hard and perplexing times, he must say to himself, "This will soon pass." Then he will be calm and quiet. In all my calamity and difficulties I used to say to myself, "This will pass away." Then I became patient. If anyone cannot be patient and cannot endure, and if he wishes to become a martyr, then let him arise in service to the Cause of God. It will be better for him if he attains to martyrdom in this path. Arise ye in service to

the Cause of God as the Apostles arose after the departure of Christ.[49]

Curtis was also present when 'Abdu'l-Bahá spoke these words, and they had a profound effect on him. He was more of a practical person than he was a sentimental person, and 'Abdu'l-Bahá's words reflected a philosophy of life that he believed in. Before becoming a Bahá'í, Curtis's hero was Abraham Lincoln, and Curtis would have been familiar with the biblical phrase to which Lincoln famously alluded in one of his speeches: "It is said an Eastern monarch once charged his wise men to invent him a sentence, to be ever in view, and which should be true and appropriate in all times and situations. They presented him the words: 'And this, too, shall pass away.' How much it expresses! How chastening in the hour of pride! How consoling in the depths of affliction!"[50]

In the space of a few words, the adage "this, too, shall pass" expresses all of the material things associated with this life. The teachings of Bahá'u'lláh have given His followers a purpose in this life to build the Kingdom of God on earth, while never forgetting that this material world "constitutes no more than a transient, a very brief stage of their existence, that they who live it are but pilgrims and wayfarers whose goal is the Celestial City, and whose home the Country of never-failing joy and brightness."[51]

The Master's speech after Mírzá Ḥasan Afnán's funeral was not the only time He had spoken of the prohibition against suicide. On more than one occasion, He had alluded to the importance of living one's life to the fullest and of being of service to God while one is living in the physical world. The focus on a life dedicated to the service of God and His loved ones was still on the mind of 'Abdu'l-Bahá when He spoke at Áqá Khusraw's wedding. He said,

"Khusraw, you have spent your childhood and youth in the service of this house; it is my hope that you will grow old under the same roof, ever and always serving God."[52]

The weekend of Khusraw's wedding, Curtis was in Haifa working on installing the electrical generator for the shrine of the Báb. During that time, none of the houses and buildings in Haifa had electricity. Oil lamps and candles were the only source of light at night. If there was a full moon, then, one could find his way through the narrow roads of Haifa more easily. On the night 'Abdu'l-Bahá passed away, the moon was in its transition from a waning crescent phase to a new moon phase—a phase when the moon disappears from view and the sky is dark. By midnight, the candles and oil lamps were out in every house as their occupants slept, unaware of the great calamity that was about to occur. John and Louise Bosch were asleep in the Western Pilgrim House, and Johanna Hauff had been given permission to stay in the house of 'Abdu'l-Bahá that night. Dr. Florian and Grace Krug had been given the Master's bedroom, which had recently been built across the garden of the main part of the house. Curtis, Fujita, and Dr. Ḥakím were asleep in their small room at the back of the old Western Pilgrim House. 'Abdu'l-Bahá lay in a room in the main part of His house, and at His bedside sat His daughter Ruha Khánum.

Just after 1:00am, Curtis, Fujita and Dr. Ḥakím were awakened by a knock on the door of the Western Pilgrim House and a voice calling, "Get up! Get up! The Master! The Master!" Curtis described what happened next in this account taken from an audio recording and edited for clarity:

We awoke in surprise and were out of our room in no time and went over to the Master's house to find out what had happened. I walked into the Master's room and Dr. Florian Krug was just closing the Master's eyes. He had passed away. You have all heard stories about how the Master knew He was going and about how his daughter asked Him if He wanted something to drink and He said to her, "You would ask me to drink when I am passing?" The Master knew He was going. It was just as if He laid His coat aside and passed away that quickly.[53]

Curtis was not religious before he became a Bahá'í, but he came from a Westernized religious culture in which the expected response upon the death of a loved one was restraint and reserved expressions of grief. Curtis was surprised when the house of 'Abdu'l-Bahá began to fill with dozens of mourners from Haifa who began to wail aloud with an emotion that was far from the quiet reserve he expected. In the following recollection, adapted from the audio recording, Curtis described his response to the emotional chaos that ensued immediately following the passing of 'Abdu'l-Bahá:

Of course, pandemonium broke loose when the Master passed. So many people arrived at the house, wailing. There was chaos around the central hall of 'Abdu'l-Bahá's house, but I wasn't affected by this. I loved the Master very much, but it didn't affect me emotionally. I thought maybe there was something personally wrong with me, so I tried to affect this emotion and as I was trying to do so, a thought came into my mind that said, "No, this is the time to observe." So I looked around at what was going on, and I saw the Greatest Holy Leaf, the sister of the Master, going around to this one and the other one, comforting them. Then she walked over to me and said,

"Kelsey, will you take Fujita and Khusraw in the automobile and drive to 'Akká to tell the friends there of the Master's passing and then come right back?"[54]

The drive to 'Akká at 2:30am, with no moonlight to brighten the path, would take about two hours, Curtis thought. With Fujita sitting in the front seat and Khusraw in the back, Curtis drove along the route along the sea. Arriving in 'Akká, they awoke the friends to tell them of the news. Upon their return, they discovered that the high tide of the Mediterranean Sea had flooded areas of the road, and the automobile would have sunk if it had not been for the help from a group of early-morning fishermen who lifted the Ford from the water.[55]

When Curtis arrived in Haifa, he reported to the Greatest Holy Leaf that he, Fujita, and Khusraw had returned from informing the friends in 'Akká of 'Abdu'l-Bahá's passing. The Greatest Holy Leaf was tending to the plans for the funeral of 'Abdu'l-Bahá while also managing the continual flow of mourners who crowded around the house.

The funeral took place the next day, Tuesday, November 29th. By 9:00am, there were already thousands of people congregated around the Master's house, and thousands more had gathered up and down Haparsim Street. Curtis had his Graflex camera and climbed onto a rooftop, where he could get photos of the crowds. He described it in an audio recording which has been edited for clarity by the author:

'Abdu'l-Bahá's coffin was carried out the front door of His house on the shoulders of family members and other Bahá'ís, down the stairs just as if it floated on the air; and no group of people carried that coffin more than ten paces. They'd take it away from each other, each taking a turn at carrying the coffin. That's the way they carried it, all the way down the steps of the Master's house and then up Mount Carmel; and these were not just the Bahá'ís, they were the people of Haifa carrying the Master's coffin up the street. When they turned the corner up the mountain, the Boy Scouts placed a Persian shawl on the casket, and a little further along the Boy Scouts placed a wreath on it, and finally they carried the coffin up Mount Carmel.[56]

The Greatest Holy Leaf directed the events surrounding the funeral and burial of the Master, including where His holy remains were to be interred. She decided the Master would be buried in one of the empty vaults of the shrine of the Báb.[57] In *God Passes By* the Guardian described what took place after the mourners bearing the Master's coffin reached the tomb of the Báb and placed the casket on a table in front of the tomb:

Close to the eastern entrance of the Shrine, the sacred casket was placed upon a plain table, and, in the presence of that vast concourse, nine speakers, who represented the Muslim, the Jewish, and the Christian Faiths, and who included the Muftí of Haifa, delivered their several funeral orations. These concluded, the High Commissioner drew close to the casket, and, with bowed head fronting the Shrine, paid his last homage of farewell to 'Abdu'l-Bahá: the other officials of the Government followed his example. The coffin was then removed to one of the chambers of the Shrine, and there lowered, sadly and reverently, to its last resting-place in a vault adjoining that in which were laid the remains of the Báb.[58]

That night, after the funeral was complete, the Greatest Holy Leaf asked Dr. Luṭfu'lláh Ḥakím to sleep beside the tomb and guard it until it could be completely sealed the next day. The night continued in darkness as the moon had set over Haifa.

It would take Curtis Kelsey nearly eight months to complete the installation of the lights for the shrine of the Báb, the shrine of Bahá'u'lláh, and the house of 'Abdu'l-Bahá. Even though the Master did not live to see the shrines actually illuminated, His objective was soon realized. Shoghi Effendi wrote that the ". . . installment of an electric plant, the first of its kind established in the city of Haifa, flooding with illumination the Grave of One Who, in His own words, had been denied 'a lighted lamp' in His fortress-prison in Ádhirbáyján," is one of the developments which "may be regarded as the initial evidences of the marvelous expansion of the international institutions and endowments of the Faith at its world center."[59] The design to illuminate the shrines was 'Abdu'l-Bahá's final benefaction toward fulfilling His Father's desire that He construct a worthy resting place for the Prophet-Herald of the Cause of Bahá'u'lláh. It coincided with the completion of the Master's ministry on this earth.

By April, 1922, Curtis Kelsey had completed the electrical work and had installed the lighting. The official illumination of the shrines was planned for the Festival of Riḍván in 1922, when both shrines would be illuminated at the same time. Curtis's description of the achievement sounds matter-of-fact, but to the people of Haifa, the effect was miraculous:

Of course when the Master passed away, I went back and finished the work of lighting the Shrines. They were turned on at the same time: the one on Mount Carmel, I had put a search light right on the Shrine of the Báb, that shone down Mount Carmel Avenue, and I put a searchlight on the Shrine of Bahá'u'lláh. You could see these two lights from one Shrine to the other. The people of Haifa hadn't seen electric light around that time. The children were so intrigued by this light they would play in the shadows of the searchlight on Mount Carmel Avenue and run up and down the street.[60]

Shoghi Effendi was not in Haifa during the Festival of Riḍván, as he had already left for Switzerland, where he retreated to the Alps to gain the strength to assume his role as Guardian of the Cause of God. During his temporary absence, the Greatest Holy Leaf assumed the helm of the Faith.[61] How fitting that the saintly sister of 'Abdu'l-Bahá would oversee the last stages of the project to illuminate the shrine of the Prophet-Herald of the Cause of God, Who, in His imprisonment in the fortress of Máh-kú was denied even a candle to light the darkness. Now the shrine of the Báb could be bathed in light that would shine across the bay to the shrine of Bahá'u'lláh, the Qiblih of the nations of the world.

In a letter from Dr. Ziá Bagdádí, who was living in Chicago and serving on the editorial board of *Star of the West*, the news of the lighting of the shrines had reached the Spiritual Assembly of the Bahá'ís of New York City. It is important to note that the letter was written on June 9, 1922, after the ascension of 'Abdu'l-Bahá; therefore, Dr. Bagdádí refers to "three" shrines being illumined:

I beg to inform you of the joyful report this servant received from Haifa in regards to the illumined and sincere youth, Mr. Curtis Kelsey, who has been wonderfully blessed and confirmed in rendering one of the great services to the Cause of God. He has successfully illumined the Holy Shrines of Bahá'u'lláh, 'Abdu'l-Bahá and the Báb, and above all the blessed Master was very pleased with him. This is, I am sure, because of the purity of his heart, sincerity of his aim and obedience to the blessed Commands. Verily, God confirms whomsoever He wishes in whatsoever He wishes.

I will never forget how the Master acted and what He said regarding the illumination of the Blessed Shrine (of the Báb). It was on the anniversary of the martyrdom of His Holiness the Báb, while all pilgrims were at the Sacred Shrine. The beloved Master remained silent for (a) few minutes standing at the Holy Threshold. His silence broke with gushing tears and (He) cried loudly, saying: In all the years of imprisonment (in Máh-kú), the Báb spent all the night in utter darkness. Yea, not even a candle was allowed (Him) . . . Therefore, God Willing, I shall illumine His Sublime Shrine with one hundred electric lamps. . . . Now the news has come that on the last day of the Feast of Ridván (April 1922) the three Blessed Shrines were illumined with electricity and the light is flooding the Bay of 'Akká. Indeed, Mr. Kelsey deserves a thousand praises and commendations.[62]

After Ridván, Curtis prepared for his return to New York. His eight months in the holy land would mark a new beginning in his spiritual life. If anyone had been more spiritually fulfilled than Curtis, it was his mother, Valeria. Her overwhelming wish had been to meet 'Abdu'l-Bahá in the holy land, and although she was never able to meet Him in person, she knew that her son was serving Him. It was Valeria who reminded Curtis that the true Architect of the plan to illuminate the shrines was the Master. In a letter written to her son when he first arrived in Haifa, she wrote, "'I know you will have so much to do and see, and that your spirit will be constantly fed, so that you will receive good from every direction, even in your physical labors and complex situations, for you will turn always to 'Abdu'l-Bahá, and you will let 'Abdu'l-Bahá be the real builder of the lighting system.'"[63]

There were times during Curtis's stay in the holy land when he felt that 'Abdu'l-Bahá treated him in the way his mother would have treated him; that is to say, in a way characteristic of someone whose sole interest is the spiritual contentment of her child. For instance, on one occasion, 'Abdu'l-Bahá sent for Curtis to come to His room, had him sit opposite Him, and just looked into his eyes for several minutes, not saying anything.[64] Curtis felt that the Master could read his mind and know the depths of his heart. The feeling that 'Abdu'l-Bahá knew Curtis's thoughts is recalled by Curtis from an audio recording that has been edited for clarity:

On Sunday we used to go up to the shrine of the Báb and sit in the front room where the Master would talk to us about the Faith. Of course this was in Arabic, and even though I didn't understand, I enjoyed listening. There were a lot of things in the Faith that I was questioning, not that I doubted them, but that I couldn't understand them. This was the conversation that was going on in my mind during these talks at the shrine, and while I was doing this, the thought came into my mind—Look up!—and I looked up, and 'Abdu'l-Bahá was in the corner, and He was looking directly at me, and He smiled because He had caught my thought, and said, "Well, I don't have any doubts."[65]

In Shoghi Effendi's absence, the Greatest Holy Leaf made the arrangements for Curtis's departure from the holy land, and she even insisted on paying the cost of his travel.[66] Her influence upon Curtis was very profound. Shoghi Effendi said that she personified all of the attributes of Bahá'u'lláh; therefore, to be near her must have felt like being near Bahá'u'lláh Himself.[67] The accolades to the remarkable qualities of the Greatest Holy Leaf bestowed upon her by her Father, her Brother, and by the Guardian are breathtakingly noble. Bahá'u'lláh testified that "'Upon her rest the glory of My name and the fragrance of My shining robe'" and granted her "'a station such as none other woman hath surpassed'"; the Guardian praised her unique station in the Holy Family as "'the Most Exalted, the pure, the holy, the immaculate, the brightly shining Leaf, the Remnant of Bahá, and His trust, the eternal fruit and the one last remembrance of the Holy Tree.'"[68] When she passed away on July 9, 1932, the Guardian was so grieved that he cabled the Bahá'í world and wrote:

HER SACRED REMAINS WILL REPOSE VICINITY HOLY SHRINES. SO GRIEVOUS A BEREAVEMENT NECESSITATES SUSPENSION FOR NINE MONTHS THROUGHOUT BAHÁ'Í WORLD EVERY MANNER RELIGIOUS FESTIVITY.[69]

All the while that Curtis was in the holy land, his mother Valeria never stopped praying that his service would be useful to 'Abdu'l-Bahá. Curtis wrote to her, but the letters were never frequent enough. She longed to know every detail of his time with the holy family, and especially if his work met their approval. The Greatest Holy Leaf, in her thoughtful remembrance to the mother of the youthful electrician who had come to illumine the shrines, wrote:

My dear sister in this blessed Cause,

Mr. Curtis Kelsey is leaving after a sojourn of hard work recompensated by the blessing of our Lord from on high and the affection of each and every one who happened to come in contact with him; we thought that at this hour, when he is to leave us with perhaps a faint ray of hope to see us again, we would write a few words and express our idea of the sincerity and absolute devotion with which your son accomplished his allotted task and we would be in turn congratulating you for this achievement and assuring you that [each and] every time that we see those bright lights shining from those blessed Tombs we cannot but remember that sincere and diligent work which was put into it and the sacrifice of Mr. Wilhelm who supplied the necessary material.

We earnestly hope that this will be the first of the services by which Mr. Kelsey is to prove his devotion to our dear Lord, and we are sure that His grace shall ever help him in his lifetime.

Our sincerest greetings to all of the Bahá'ís there.

I remain, Your sister in His love,

The Greatest Holy Leaf[70]

Curtis Kelsey returned to the holy land two times. In 1953, he and his wife Harriet stayed in Haifa for three weeks, at the request of the Guardian. By then, Shoghi Effendi had succeeded in reclaiming the Mansion of Bahá'u'lláh in Bahjí from the Covenant-breakers, and he had designed a carpet of ornamental gardens to encircle the shrine of Bahá'u'lláh. He asked Curtis to supervise the installation of a water pump and efficient irrigation systems for these gardens at Bahjí and Mount Carmel. On Mount Carmel, the construction of an arcade around the stone edifice of the tomb of the Báb (and the temporary resting place of the Master) was underway. Upon this arcade, an octagon-shaped structure would support a drum-shaped clerestory of eighteen windows, whereupon a spectacular golden crown-like dome would mark "the spot round which the Concourse on high circle in adoration."[71] Curtis Kelsey also supervised the installation of a water pump to irrigate the rustic slope of Mount Carmel, which would one day be terraced in verdant gardens rising in concentric circles, ascending the "Pathway of the Kings and Rulers of the World" to the throne of the "Pearl of Great Price."[72]

Curtis Kelsey's last visit to the holy land was preceded by a unique commemoration held in the heart of the Mediterranean Sea. It was the first Bahá'í Oceanic Conference held August 23–25, 1968 in Palermo, Sicily. The purpose of the conference was to inspire a dramatic upsurge in the spread of the Cause of Bahá'u'lláh throughout the world. Immediately following the conference, the attendees crossed the Mediterranean, as Bahá'u'lláh had done a century before, to the prison-city of 'Akká and then to Bahjí on August 31st to commemorate the centenary of Bahá'u'lláh's prophesied arrival in the holy land.[73]

Although the prison-city of 'Akká was the most pestilential of places, and Bahá'u'lláh's suffering within its walls the greatest of all His sufferings, His arrival blessed that city beyond measure, as described by Shoghi Effendi:

'Akká, itself, flanked by the "glory of Lebanon," and lying in full view of the "splendor of Carmel," at the foot of the hills which enclose the home of Jesus Christ Himself, had been described by David as "the Strong City," designated by Hosea as "a door of hope," and alluded to by Ezekiel as "the gate that looketh towards the East," whereunto "the glory of the God of Israel came from the way of the East," His voice "like a noise of many waters." To it the Arabian Prophet had referred as "a city in Syria to which God hath shown His special mercy," situated "betwixt two mountains . . . in the middle of a meadow," "by the shore of the sea . . . suspended beneath the Throne," "white, whose whiteness is pleasing unto God." "Blessed the man," He, moreover, as confirmed by Bahá'u'lláh, had declared, "that hath visited 'Akká, and blessed he that hath visited the visitor of 'Akká." Furthermore, "He that raiseth therein the call to prayer, his voice will be lifted up unto Paradise." And again: "The poor of 'Akká are the kings of Paradise and the princes thereof. A month in 'Akká is better than a thousand years elsewhere."[74]

Bahá'u'lláh's exile to 'Akká was the last and climactic stage of His forty-year ministry; a stage which began with a miserable ten-day voyage across the Mediterranean Sea from Gallipoli to 'Akká. Shoghi Effendi wrote, "So grievous were the dangers and trials confronting Bahá'u'lláh at the hour of His departure from Gallipoli that He warned His companions that 'this journey will be unlike any of the previous journeys,' and that whoever did not feel himself 'man enough to face the future' had best 'depart to whatever place he pleaseth, and be preserved from tests, for hereafter he will find himself unable to leave'—a warning which His companions unanimously chose to disregard."[75]

Bahá'u'lláh's sea voyage from "the Land of Mystery" to "The Most Great Prison" began on August 12, 1868, with a four-day land journey from Adrianople to Gallipoli (in present-day Turkey). After a few days in Gallipoli, He sailed on a steamer ship to Smyrna, where He stayed two days. From there, He sailed across the Mediterranean Sea to Alexandria, Egypt, changed ships, and continued His voyage east to Port Said, then to Haifa, where He arrived on the morning of August 31, 1868. By midday, He was put on a sailing vessel to 'Akká, and He arrived at the gate to the prison-city in the scorching heat of the afternoon.[76]

It was fitting that the first Bahá'í Oceanic Conference was held in Sicily, an island in the very heart of that sea traversed by the Lord of Hosts, where 2,300 followers of Bahá'u'lláh—representing sixty-seven countries—gathered. In its message to the conference, the Universal House of Justice described the purpose of the conference: "The event which we commemorate at this first Bahá'í Oceanic Conference is unique. Neither the migration of Abraham from Ur of the Chaldees to the region of Aleppo, nor the journey of Moses towards the Promised Land, nor the flight into Egypt of Mary and Joseph with the infant Jesus, nor yet the Hegira of Muḥammad can compare with the voyage made by God's Supreme Manifestation one hundred years ago from Gallipoli to the Most Great Prison."[77]

Later in its message to the followers of Bahá'u'lláh at the Oceanic Conference in Palermo, the Universal House of Justice framed the history of the Mediterranean Sea by placing Bahá'u'lláh at the center of its religious legacy and the long-prophesied arrival of the King of kings on the shores of the holy land:

The great sea, on one of whose chief islands you are now gathered, within whose hinterland and islands have flourished the Jewish, the Christian and Islamic civilizations is a befitting scene for the first Oceanic Bahá'í Conference. Two millenniums ago, in this arena, the disciples of Christ performed such deeds of heroism and self-sacrifice as are remembered to this day and are forever enshrined in the annals of His Cause. A thousand years later the lands, bordering the southern and western shores of this sea witnessed the glory of Islam's Golden Age. In the day of the Promised One this same sea achieved eternal fame through its association with the Heroic and Formative Ages of His Cause. It bore upon its bosom the King of kings Himself . . ."[78]

Immediately following the Oceanic Conference, the attendees gathered in Bahjí to circumambulate the shrine of Bahá'u'lláh in commemoration of the hundredth year since His arrival in the holy land. One cannot think of Bahá'u'lláh's arrival in the holy land without calling to mind the scene of His arrival at the gate of the city of 'Akká, where He was welcomed by "banners of light" and by the "Voice of the Spirit" promising, "'Soon will all that dwell on earth be enlisted under these banners'" of light.[79] Over two thousand believers arrived in Bahjí to pay homage to Bahá'u'lláh, the Light of the World. Among them was Curtis Kelsey. How deeply significant it must have been for him to circle round the shrine that he had helped illuminate, and how much more deeply he must have felt 'Abdu'l-Bahá's presence on such an occasion.

Curtis Kelsey died two years later, at the age of seventy-six, on February 20, 1970, in Sarasota, Florida. His life had been one of continual service to the Cause. He, his wife Harriet, and their four children built a strong foundation of faith that has extended into generations of Bahá'ís. Curtis's other services to Bahá'u'lláh were numerous. He served on the Spiritual Assembly of Teaneck, New Jersey for thirty years and helped Roy Wilhelm in the expansion of Evergreen Cabin, which had been built on the spot where 'Abdu'l-

Bahá had hosted the first Unity Feast in the United States. He served on the National Teaching Committee for the Northeastern States; he was Chairman of the Maintenance Committee for the Wilhelm Trustees and the Green Acre Development Committee; and he traveled extensively throughout the United States and gave public talks on the Bahá'í Faith. He and his family also hosted weekly Bahá'í firesides in their home for over twenty-five years. Working directly under the Hand of the Cause of God Zikr'u'lláh Khádem, Curtis also served as a member of the Auxiliary Board in North America.[80] Every opportunity for service was an honor to Curtis Kelsey, but none was as great an honor as knowing and serving 'Abdu'l-Bahá, designated by Bahá'u'lláh as "the Trust of God amongst you," the "shelter for all mankind" and "a shield unto all who are in heaven and on earth."[81]

Curtis Kelsey's daughter, Mrs. Carol Rutstein, was born ten years after the passing of 'Abdu'l-Bahá, which gives her a unique proximity to the events that took place one hundred years ago. In an interview with Mrs. Rutstein, this writer asked if she would share her thoughts regarding the hundred years since the passing of 'Abdu'l-Bahá and her father's role in serving the Master. She said:

Remembering my father's experience in Haifa all those years ago brings back so many memories of how he would tell this story to us as children, and we never tired of it. Tears come to my eyes remembering my father's very personal story of his experiences with 'Abdu'l-Bahá and the Greatest Holy Leaf. It is almost like a renewal and a remembrance in my soul to recall these experiences of the early Bahá'ís who were privileged to be in the presence of the holy family and to meet the Master.

It is difficult to express adequately, but my tears are a sort of re-recognition of just how close in spirit we still are to those events one hundred years ago.

My father often thought of the time when 'Abdu'l-Bahá simply called him to His presence and just gazed at him. He often said how that experience stayed with him all his life. That wordless but exalted and ineffable feeling of complete peace and understanding would return and bring comfort to him especially in times of need or great difficulty. I am reminded of just how very trusting in divine confirmations my father was. When giving talks on the Bahá'í Faith, he would quote these words from the Bahái'í prayer, "I lay all my affairs in Thy Hand" and then he would repeat with emphasis: "ALL my affairs!"

My father's favorite subject to speak about was "Immortality and Eternal Life," and he gave that talk many times around the United States, Canada, and Hawaii. He used to quote from the writings of 'Abdu'l-Bahá about the importance of acquiring a thirst for spirituality, living a Bahá'í life, and meditating on the future life. He had a very evolved and deep understanding of the teachings, having been a student— and really a scholar—of the sacred writings from the time he became a Bahá'í. My father sometimes said that he imagined that going to the next world was just like stepping from one room into another, or just like taking your coat off, and that those souls in the next world are right here in the present and all around us.[82]

Indeed, 'Abdu'l-Bahá has written about the progress of the soul and its relationship between this world and the next world of God:

"Those souls who are pure and unsullied, upon the dissolution of their elemental frames, hasten away to the world of God, and that world is within this world. The people of this world, however, are unaware of that world, and are even as the mineral and the vegetable that know nothing of the world of the animal and the world of man."[83]

Since 1921, the resting place of 'Abdu'l-Bahá has been within the shrine of the Báb. In its Riḍván 2019 message to the Bahá'ís of the World, the Universal House of Justice, in anticipation of the centenary of the ascension of 'Abdu'l-Bahá in November of 1921, announced plans for the permanent resting place of the Servant of Bahá:

The close of the first century of the Formative Age is but two and a half years away. It will seal one hundred years of consecrated effort to consolidate and expand the foundation so sacrificially laid during the Faith's Heroic Age. At that time the Bahá'í community will also mark the centenary of the Ascension of 'Abdu'l-Bahá, that moment when the beloved Master was released from the confines of this world to rejoin His Father in the retreats of celestial glory. His funeral, which occurred the following day, was an event "the like of which Palestine had never seen." At its conclusion, His mortal remains were laid to rest within a vault of the Mausoleum of the Báb. However, it was envisaged by Shoghi Effendi that this would be a temporary arrangement. A Shrine was to be erected, of a character befitting the unique station of 'Abdu'l-Bahá, at the appropriate time.

That time has come. The Bahá'í world is being summoned to build the edifice which will forever embosom those sacred remains. It is to be constructed in the vicinity of the Riḍván Garden, on land consecrated by the footsteps of the Blessed Beauty; the Shrine of 'Abdu'l-Bahá will thus lie on the crescent traced between the Holy Shrines in 'Akká and Haifa.[84]

The location of His shrine shall be in the path the pilgrims travel from Haifa to 'Akká. The theme of His shrine is inspired by the following prayer by 'Abdu'l-Bahá.[85] In this prayer, 'Abdu'l-Bahá asks that He be "as dust in the pathway of Thy loved ones," and He has said that "Whoso reciteth this prayer with lowliness and fervor will bring gladness and joy to the heart of this Servant; it will be even as meeting Him face to face":

He is the All-Glorious!

O God, my God! Lowly and tearful, I raise my suppliant hands to Thee and cover my face in the dust of that Threshold of Thine, exalted above the knowledge of the learned, and the praise of all that glorify Thee. Graciously look upon Thy servant, humble and lowly at Thy door, with the glances of the eye of Thy mercy, and immerse him in the Ocean of Thine eternal grace.

Lord! He is a poor and lowly servant of Thine, enthralled and imploring Thee, captive in Thy hand, praying fervently to Thee, trusting in Thee, in tears before Thy face, calling to Thee and beseeching Thee, saying:

O Lord, my God! Give me Thy grace to serve Thy loved ones, strengthen me in my servitude to Thee, illumine my brow with the light of adoration in Thy court of holiness, and of prayer to Thy Kingdom of grandeur. Help me to be selfless at the heavenly entrance of Thy gate, and aid me to be detached from all things within Thy holy precincts. Lord! Give me to drink from the chalice of selflessness; with its robe clothe me, and in its ocean immerse me. Make me as dust in the pathway of Thy loved ones, and grant that I may offer up my soul for the earth ennobled by the footsteps of Thy chosen ones in Thy path, O Lord of Glory in the Highest.

With this prayer doth Thy servant call Thee, at dawntide and in the night-season. Fulfill his heart's desire, O Lord! Illumine his heart, gladden his bosom, kindle his light, that he may serve Thy Cause and Thy servants.

Thou art the Bestower, the Pitiful, the Most Bountiful, the Gracious, the Merciful, the Compassionate.[86]

# Epilogue

In the days and months following the ascension of 'Abdu'l-Bahá and the public reading of His will and testament, the house of 'Abdu'l-Bahá at 7 Haparsim Street in Haifa remained a center of activity. Designed by 'Abdu'l-Bahá and built while He had been confined to the prison-city of 'Akká, it was the house where 'Abdu'l-Bahá established His permanent residence after His release from 'Akká in 1908.[1] Architecturally, the design of the house is classic Eastern Mediterranean, yet the sandy white rough surface of the walls are contrasted with a smoother, more polished-looking masonry around the window frames and main entrance, which is an eighteenth-century European design. Especially striking are the square columns on either side of the tall, dark wooden entry doors. The shape of the columns, capitals and bases are rooted in the classical tradition of ancient Greece and Rome, but there is also something very modern about the way the columns have been simplified into bare abstract shapes, with elegant blocks instead of leafy Corinthian capitals. Above the columned entrance are thickly proportioned round windows that soften the austerity of the columns and give the entrance a welcoming appearance. The green shutters that frame the windows suggest an outward perspective to the house. The tall, wooden front doors, with ornamental wrought iron over the large windows and the iron door handles cast with the word TOURNEZ, meaning "turn" in French, suggest the Art Nouveau aesthetic of its time. Accessible just steps from the sidewalk of the street, the house is stately yet unimposing, elegant yet modest. Indeed, everything about the front of the house beckons one to come forward and enter.[2]

The simplicity of the gardens in the vicinity of the house are a reminder that even though it was a house that served as an official residence where 'Abdu'l-Bahá, and after Him Shoghi Effendi, received pilgrims from the East and West, it was also a home where the family and kindred of 'Abdu'l-Bahá lived.[3] It was in this house where Shoghi Effendi lived as a young boy, where he grew up as an adolescent, and later where he served as 'Abdu'l-Bahá's secretary.[4] Rúhíyyih Khánum wrote, "When 'Abdu'l-Bahá first moved into the new home in Haifa (which was in use by members of His family in February 1907, if not earlier) the rooms were occupied by all the members of His family . . . the house was always crowded with relatives, children, servants, pilgrims and guests."[5]

As one enters the house, there is a room to the left of the entrance where 'Abdu'l-Bahá received guests and a room to the right of the entrance where He ascended. Of further significance is the large central hall of the house, which was the venue of the public reading of the Will and Testament of 'Abdu'l-Bahá and where the delegates to the first Bahá'í International Convention in 1963 elected the Universal House of Justice.[6]

Although it seems the whole world cried out in one voice of woe when the Master took His flight from this world, the cries cannot have been more sorrowful than the grief felt by the Greatest Holy Leaf. When Bahá'u'lláh and His family were exiled to Baghdad in 1853, the Greatest Holy Leaf was a child of seven years. The whole of her life from childhood until her advanced years were dedicated to the protection of the Cause of Bahá'u'lláh from the Covenant-breakers who sought to divide the Faith of God.[7] After the passing of Bahá'u'lláh, enemies from inside and outside the family of Bahá'u'lláh tried to undermine the authority of 'Abdu'l-Bahá as the Center of the Covenant of Bahá'u'lláh. Among the members of the family of Bahá'u'lláh, the Greatest Holy Leaf stood firm in the Covenant and supported her Brother. Shoghi Effendi wrote, "She alone of the family of Bahá'u'lláh remained to cheer the heart and reinforce the efforts of the Most Great Branch, against whom were solidly arrayed the almost entire company of His faithless relatives. In her arduous task she was seconded by the diligent efforts of Munírih Khánum, the Holy Mother, and those of her daughters."[8]

After the ascension of 'Abdu'l-Bahá, Shoghi Effendi referred to the Greatest Holy Leaf as "the well-beloved and treasured Remnant of Bahá'u'lláh entrusted to our frail and unworthy hands by our departed Master."[9] As internal and external enemies of the Cause continued to undermine the authority of Shoghi Effendi as Guardian of the Cause of God, Shoghi Effendi said it was the Greatest Holy Leaf who was his "chief sustainer," his "most affectionate comforter," and the "joy and inspiration" of his life.[10] He attributed her fortitude to her having been "armed with the powers with which an intimate and long-standing companionship with Bahá'u'lláh had already equipped her, and benefiting by the magnificent example which the steadily widening range of 'Abdu'l-Bahá's activities afforded her, she was prepared to face the storm which the treacherous conduct of the Covenant-breakers had aroused and to withstand its most damaging onslaughts."[11]

Shoghi Effendi explained that, after the passing of 'Abdu'l-Bahá, he was "so stricken with grief and pain and so entangled in the troubles (created) by the enemies of the Cause of God" that he had to leave the holy land temporarily. He wrote that, in his absence "the affairs of the Cause both at home and abroad" would be "under the supervision of the Holy Family and the headship of the Greatest Holy Leaf."[12] No other woman in religious history has occupied the headship of a world religion. With the burden of the responsibilities of the Bahá'í Faith temporarily resting on the shoulders of the Greatest Holy Leaf, Shoghi Effendi retreated to the mountains of Switzerland to come to terms with his appointment as Guardian.[13]

The Greatest Holy Leaf is unrivaled by any woman in religious history, as she was elevated by Bahá'u'lláh to a "'station such as none other woman hath surpassed'" and "comparable in rank to those immortal heroines such as Sarah, Ásíyih, the Virgin Mary, Fáṭimih and Ṭáhirih, each of whom has outshone every member of her sex in previous Dispensations."[14] In his matchless tributes to the Greatest Holy Leaf after her passing in 1932, Shoghi Effendi said she personified the attributes of Bahá'u'lláh and was "the fruit of His Tree," "the lamp of His love," "the symbol of His serenity," and "the pathway of His guidance, the channel of His blessings, the sweet scent of His robe, the refuge of His loved ones and His handmaidens, the mantle of His generosity and grace."[15]

Among the family of the Master, the person who was second only to the Greatest Holy Leaf in cheering the heart and supporting the efforts of 'Abdu'l-Bahá was his wife Munírih Khánum, known as the holy mother.[16] Born in 1847, Munírih Khánum married 'Abdu'l-Bahá in 1873 when she was twenty-six years old and 'Abdu'l-Bahá was twenty-nine. At the time of their marriage, 'Abdu'l-Bahá had already distinguished Himself as an eloquent expounder of the teachings of His Father. For instance, two years after their marriage, 'Abdu'l-Bahá wrote His seminal treatise, *The Secret of Divine Civilization,* to the rulers and people of Persia. Writing anonymously, 'Abdu'l-Bahá outlined the spiritual requisites of the reformation of human society.

According to Lady Blomfield, many years later, recalling her wedding day, Munírih Khánum said, "'Oh the spiritual happiness which enfolded us! It cannot be described in earthly words . . . I was the wife of my Beloved. How wonderful and noble He was in His beauty. I adored Him. I recognized His greatness, and thanked God for bringing me to Him.'"[17] Munírih Khánum and 'Abdu'l-Bahá had eight children, four of whom survived into adulthood. Their eldest daughter, Diyá'iyyih Khánum, was the mother of Shoghi Effendi. When Shoghi Effendi was a young child, 'Abdu'l-Bahá reportedly gazed into His grandson's eyes and remarked to Munírih, "'Look at his eyes, they are like clear water.'"[18] Throughout the twenty-nine years of 'Abdu'l-Bahá's ministry as the Center of the Covenant, Munírih Khánum remained His faithful supporter despite the difficulties caused by the machinations of His faithless relatives who had broken the Covenant of God and from whom 'Abdu'l-Bahá never had a moment's rest.[19]

When the first Western pilgrims began to arrive in the holy land, it was often Munírih Khánum who welcomed them. Mrs. Corinne True, a Bahá'í from America, recalled her pilgrimage to the holy land and her close association with Munírih Khánum and the

Greatest Holy Leaf: "In the early days one of the greatest privileges of the visiting women pilgrims was this intimate association with these two divine maidservants of Bahá'u'lláh, Bahíyyih Khánum, the Greatest Holy Leaf, and Muním Khánum, the Holy Mother. We seldom saw one without the other."[20]

On the night of the passing of 'Abdu'l-Bahá, the Greatest Holy Leaf and the Holy Mother comforted the grieving friends and family who gathered in the house of 'Abdu'l-Bahá; yet, these two steadfast souls also grieved. Muním Khánum wrote that should she describe her grief fully, she would need "seventy reams of paper, and seas of blood would pour from all eyes" and in a poem to 'Abdu'l-Bahá, she asks Him to "call [her] to that other land" for "'I am caught in the talons of the eagle of sorrow.'"[21] One year after the passing of 'Abdu'l-Bahá, Muním Khánum wrote a lament for her beloved Husband and supplicated Him in that world above: "It is today one full year since You disappeared from our sight and winged your flight to the Abhá Kingdom." Further in that lament, Muním Khánum implored God to fulfill the promises of 'Abdu'l-Bahá: "I implore and supplicate at the Threshhold of Oneness that You extend the Hand of Power and raise the bright moon of the Most Excellent Branch above the horizon of Haifa . . . and I ask that the promises made by 'Abdu'l-Bahá come about, so that the eyes of all the friends may be brightened and the hearts of all the Bahá'ís may become as a rose-garden. This is not beyond the power of God."[22]

It has been noted that on the night of the passing of 'Abdu'l-Bahá, the moon had symbolically set over Haifa, in the sense that 'Abdu'l-Bahá was no longer physically present in the world. Although the Faith was left briefly without leadership, the light of God's Covenant shone brightly again with the reading of the Master's Will and

Testament. Within this document, 'Abdu'l-Bahá had outlined the steps to be taken for the establishment of the Universal House of Justice, an assemblage which, He said, "God hath ordained as the source of all good and freed from all error."[23] He further described it as the body to which "all things must be referred" and the divinely ordained institution that "enacteth all ordinances and regulations that are not to be found in the explicit Holy Text."[24] The Will and Testament of 'Abdu'l-Bahá is the charter of the Administrative Order of the Cause of Bahá'u'lláh and the inviolable safeguard of the unity and integrity of His Order.[25]

To those faithful to 'Abdu'l-Bahá, His Will and Testament was a great consolation, as it appointed Shoghi Effendi Guardian of the Cause of God. He was descended through his mother from Bahá'u'lláh's lineage and descended through his father from the Báb's lineage:

> O my loving friends! After the passing away of this wronged one, it is incumbent upon the Aghṣán (Branches), the Afnán (Twigs) of the Sacred Lote-Tree, the Hands (pillars) of the Cause of God and the loved ones of the Abhá Beauty to turn unto Shoghi Effendi—the youthful branch branched from the two hallowed and Sacred Lote-Trees and the fruit grown from the union of the two offshoots of the Tree of Holiness,—as he is the sign of God, the chosen branch, the Guardian of the Cause of God, he unto whom all the Aghṣán, the Afnán, the Hands of the Cause of God and His loved ones must turn.[26]

In the following letter, written two months after the passing of 'Abdu'l-Bahá, Shoghi Effendi addressed the believers in North

America. Penned in the earliest stages of his ministry as Guardian of the Cause of God, it is a fitting conclusion to this commemoration of the ascension of 'Abdu'l-Bahá, for it is a reminder that our task is to continue to work toward the fulfillment of God's purpose for humankind. This purpose is none other than "the unification of all the peoples of the world in one universal family."[27]

Dearly beloved brethren and sisters in 'Abdu'l-Bahá:

At this early hour when the morning light is just breaking upon the Holy Land, whilst the gloom of the dear Master's bereavement is still hanging thick upon the hearts, I feel as if my soul turns in yearning love and full of hope to that great company of His loved ones across the seas, who now share with us all the agonies of His separation.

It is idle for me to emphasize how much the sorrowful ladies of the Holy Household look forward to the work that lies before the friends in the American continent, who in the past have rendered so glorious a service to His Cause and will now, faithful to His special love for them, carry on their mission still more gloriously than ever before. True, the shock has been too terrible and sudden for us all to recover from in so short a time, but whenever we recall His Sayings and read His Writings, hope springs in our hearts and gives us the peace that no other material comfort can give.

How well I remember when, more than two years ago, the Beloved Master turning to a distinguished visitor of His, who was seated by Him in His garden, suddenly broke the silence and said:—"My work is now done upon this plane; it is time for me to pass on to the other world." Did He not in more than one occasion state clearly and emphatically:—"Were ye to know what will come to pass after me, surely would ye pray that my end be hastened?" In a Tablet sent to Persia when the storm raised years ago by that Committee of Investigation was fiercely raging around Him, when the days of His incarceration were at their blackest, He reveals the following:—"Now in this world of being, the Hand of Divine Power hath firmly laid the foundations of this all-highest Bounty and this wondrous Gift. Gradually whatsoever is latent in the innermost of this Holy Cycle shall appear and be made manifest, for now is but the beginning of its growth and the dayspring of the revelation of its Signs. Ere the close of this Century and of this Age, it shall be made clear and manifest how wondrous was that Springtide and how heavenly was that Gift!"

With such assuring Utterances and the unmistakable evidences of His sure and clear knowledge that His end was nigh, is there any reason why the followers of His Faith, the world over, should be perturbed? Are not the prayers He revealed for us sufficient source of inspiration to every worker in His Cause? Have not His instructions paved before us the broad and straight Path of Teaching? Will not His now doubly effective power of Grace sustain us, strengthen us and confirm us in our work for Him? Ours is the duty to strive by day and night to fulfill our own obligations and then trust in His Guidance and never failing Grace. Unity amongst the friends, selflessness in our labors in His Path, detachment from all worldly things, the greatest prudence and caution in every step we take, earnest endeavor to carry out only what is His Holy Will and Pleasure, the constant awareness of His Presence and of the example of

His Life, the absolute shunning of whomsoever we feel to be an enemy of the Cause . . . these, and foremost among them is the need for unity, appear to me as our most vital duties, should we dedicate our lives for His service. Should we in this spirit arise to serve Him, what surer and greater promise have we than the one His Glorious Father, Bahá'u'lláh, gives us in His Most Holy Book:—"Verily, We behold you from Our Realm of Effulgent Glory, and shall graciously aid whosoever ariseth for the triumph of Our Cause with the hosts of the Celestial Concourse and a company of Our chosen angels."

How dearly all the Holy Leaves cherish that memory of the departed Master, as He commented upon the fresh tidings that poured in from that continent, admiring the untiring activity of the friends, the complete subordination of their material interests to those of the Cause, the remarkable spread of the Movement in their midst and their staunch firmness in the Covenant of Bahá'u'lláh. It is these encouraging reflections of the Master about His loved ones in America and the tests intellectual rather than physical which He said He would send to them to purify them and make ever brighter than before— it is these comments and promises of His that make of the Movement in that land such a potential force in the world today. The Beloved Master's cable to the friends in that region is a clear indication of the presence of those counteracting forces that may usher in those storms of tests that the Master Himself has said will ultimately be for the good of the Cause in that land.

And finally, the ladies of the Sacred Household and we, the rest of His kindred and family, will pray at His Hallowed Shrine for every one of you and He will surely watch over and enhance in the course of time that noble part of His heritage that He has bequeathed to His friends in the Far West; friends from whom in return He expects so much and whom He has loved and still doth love so dearly.

Your sincere co-worker in His Cause,

SHOGHI.

Haifa, Palestine.
January 21st, 1922.[28]

# Notes

### Introduction

1. Letter written on behalf of Shoghi Effendi, quoted by the Universal House of Justice in *Messages from the Universal House of Justice, 1963–1986,* p. 161; also in the compilation *The Universal House of Justice.*

2. Shoghi Effendi, *The World Order of Bahá'u'lláh,* p. 134.

3. The Báb, *Selections from the Writings of the Báb,* 1:2:1; Bahá'u'lláh, The Kitáb-i-Aqdas, p. 253.

4. The Universal House of Justice, "The Promise of World Peace," p. 13.

5. Shoghi Effendi, *The World Order of Bahá'u'lláh,* p. 102.

6. Excerpted from *The Bahá'ís,* a publication of the Bahá'í International Community, pp. 39–40.

7. Please see "Brahman," *https://religionfacts.com/brahman.*

8. 'Abdu'l-Bahá, *Selections from the Writings of 'Abdu'l-Bahá,* no. 25.3.

9. Thomas, Römer, "Moses: The Royal Lawgiver," *https://oxford.*

*universitypressscholarship.com/view/10.1093/acprof:oso/*
*9780199664160.001.0001/acprof-9780199664160-chapter-3.*

10. "Dualism in Zoroastrianism," *https://www.bbc.co.uk/religion/*
*religions/zoroastrian/beliefs/dualism.shtml#:~:text=Moral%20*
*dualism%20refers%20to%20the,to%20misery%20and%20*
*ultimately%20Hell.*

11. "The Buddhist Core Values and Perspectives for Protection Challenges: Faith and Protection," *https://www.unhcr.org/*
*50be10cb9.pdf].*

12. 'Abdu'l-Bahá, *Some Answered Questions,* no. 27.7.

13. Bahá'u'lláh, *Gleanings from the Writings of Bahá'u'lláh,* no. 25.1.

14. Douglas Martin, "Mission of the Báb: Retrospective 1844–1944," *The Bahá'í World,* vol. 23, p. 196. Accessed online: *https://file.bahai.media/c/cb/BW_Volume23.pdf.*

15. Ibid., p. 211.

16. Ibid., pp. 220–21; "The Bahá'ís," p. 21.

17. Ṭáhirih, quoted in Hussein Ahdieh and Hillary Chapman, *The Calling,* p. 278.

18. Shoghi Effendi, *God Passes By,* p. 145.

19. Shoghi Effendi, *The World Order of Bahá'u'lláh,* p. 204.

20. 'Abdu'l-Bahá, quoted in Shoghi Effendi, *The World Order of Bahá'u'lláh,* p. 146.

21. Shoghi Effendi, *God Passes By,* p. 467.

22. Ibid., p. 324.

23. The Universal House of Justice, Riḍván Message 153, "To the Followers of Bahá'u'lláh in North America: Alaska, Canada, Greenland and the United States"; statement from the Research Department at the Bahá'í World Center on "The Epochs of the Formative Age."

24. 'Abdu'l-Bahá, *The Will and Testament of 'Abdu'l-Bahá*, p. 19.
25. Shoghi Effendi, *The World Order of Bahá'u'lláh*, p. 134.
26. Ibid., pp. 101–102.

### 1 / John and Louise Bosch

1. Western Union Telegram, Bosch papers, Box 1, U.S. National Bahá'í Archives.
2. John's handwritten account of meeting Mrs. Beckwith, John D. Bosch and Louise Bosch papers, U.S. National Bahá'í Archives.
3. Ibid.
4. Bahá'u'lláh, *Gleanings from the Writings of Bahá'u'lláh*, no. 75.1.
5. Shoghi Effendi, *Directives from the Guardian*, p. 47.
6. John D. and Louise Bosch papers, U.S. National Bahá'í Archives.
7. Letter from 'Abdu'l-Bahá to John D. Bosch, translated by Mírzá Ameen Ullah Fareed, John D. Bosch and Louise Bosch papers, U.S. National Bahá'í Archives. The translation was sent to John D. Bosch along with the original Tablet.
8. Louise Bosch, quoted in Roger White, *Occasions of Grace*, p. 49.
9. Louise Stapfer Bosch, "Bahá'í Historical Record Card," John D. Bosch and Louise Bosch papers, U.S. National Bahá'í Archives.
10. Velda Piff Metelmann, *Lua Getsinger: Herald of the Covenant*, p. 118.
11. Louise Bosch, quoted in Roger White, *Occasions of Grace*, p. 49.
12. Tablet from 'Abdu'l-Bahá to Louise Stapfer, quoted in Myrle and Irvin Somerhalder, "In Memoriam: Louise Stapfer Bosch," *The Bahá'í World*, vol. 12 (1950–1954): 707–9. Note: The

source of the translation of this Tablet is not noted in the "In Memoriam" article.

13. Louise Stapfer Bosch, quoted by Myrle and Irvin Somerhalder, "In Memoriam: Louise Stapfer Bosch," *The Bahá'í World*, vol. 12 (1950–1954): 707–9.

14. Louise Stapfer, John D. Bosch and Louise Bosch papers, U.S. National Bahá'í Archives.

15. Translated from German into English by Mrs. Louise Semple. The translation was emailed, November 2, 2013 from Mr. Jean Paul Vader on behalf of Mrs. Louise Semple to Angelina Allen.

16. Letter dated October 22, 1913 from Louise Stapfer to John D. Bosch, John D. and Louise Bosch papers, U.S. National Bahá'í Archives. (Translated by Mrs. Louise Semple.)

17. Tablet dated March 31, 1914 from 'Abdu'l-Bahá to John D. and Louise Bosch, John D. and Louise Bosch papers, U.S. National Bahá'í Archives. Note: The translation was sent to John D. Bosch and Louise Bosch along with the original Tablet.

18. John Bosch 1912 pilgrim notes, John D. and Louise Bosch papers, U.S. National Bahá'í Archives. Also, for a record of the name "Núrání" given to John Bosch, please see *Mahmúd's Diary*, "Saturday, April 20, 1912," pp. 48–49.

19. 'Abdu'l-Bahá, "The Universal Language of the Spirit," transcribed by Dr. Luṭfu'lláh Ḥakím, *Star of the West*, vol. 13, no. 7 (October 1922): 163–64.

20. John Bosch 1912 pilgrim notes, John D. and Louise Bosch papers, U.S. National Bahá'í Archives.

21. Bosch papers (copy), U.S. National Bahá'í Archives. It is important to note that 'Abdu'l-Bahá's burial in one of the vaults

of the shrine of the Báb was intended as a temporary resting place. In 2019, the Universal House of Justice announced that 'Abdu'l-Bahá's permanent resting place and shrine would be built near the Riḍván Garden, between 'Akká and Haifa.

22. Louise Bosch to Ella Cooper, "The shock of his death was indeed as an earthquake," *Star of the West*, vol. 12, no. 18 (February 7, 1922): 276–82.

23. Shoghi Effendi, *God Passes By*, p. 497.

24. Rúhíyyih Rabbání, *The Priceless Pearl*, p. 45.

25. Letter dated May 1, 1921 from 'Abdu'l-Bahá to John and Louise Bosch, translated December 14, 1922. U.S. National Bahá'í Archives. Also cited in Marzieh Gail, *Dawn Over Mount Hira*, p. 210. The translation was sent to Mr. and Mrs. John Bosch along with the original Tablet. Note: John and Louise Bosch did not actually receive this Tablet until after their return from Haifa; it was a confirmation to them that the Master wished to see them.

26. John Bosch, John D. and Louise Bosch papers, U.S. National Bahá'í Archives.

27. Ibid.

28. Louise Bosch, talk given at the California Club Building in San Francisco, November 26, 1923, p. 7, John D. and Louise Bosch papers, U.S. National Bahá'í Archives.

29. Shoghi Effendi, *The World Order of Bahá'u'lláh*, p. 134.

30. Letter dated December 5, 1921 from Louise Bosch to Ella Cooper, United States National Bahá'í Archives.

31. Universal House of Justice, letter dated November 23, 1992, addressed to the followers of Bahá'u'lláh attending the second Bahá'í World Congress; letter from the Universal House of Justice dated June 7, 1992, addressed to the Bahá'ís of the World.

32. Rúhíyyih Rabbání, *The Priceless Pearl*, p. 42.

33. Ibid., p. 42.

34. Adib Taherzadeh, *Child of the Covenant*, p. 275.

35. John D. and Louise Bosch papers, U.S. National Bahá'í Archives.

36. Ibid.

37. The Greatest Holy Leaf, quoted in Rúhíyyih Rabbání, *The Priceless Pearl*, p. 48.

38. Rúhíyyih Rabbání, *The Priceless Pearl*, p. 48.

39. Shoghi Effendi, *God Passes By*, p. 515.

40. Ibid., p. 328.

41. Shoghi Effendi, *The World Order of Bahá'u'lláh*, p. 18.

42. Ibid., pp. 21–22.

43. Ibid., p. 8.

44. Shoghi Effendi, *God Passes By*, p. 522.

45. Rúhíyyih Rabbání, *The Priceless Pearl*, p. 153.

46. John D. and Louise Bosch papers, U.S. National Bahá'í Archives.

47. Letter dated May 26, 1937, from Rúhíyyih Rabbání to John and Louise Bosch, U.S. National Bahá'í Archives, Box 6.

48. John D. and Louise Bosch papers, U.S. National Bahá'í Archives.

49. For the "In Memoriam" article on Muḥammed Taqíy-i-Isfahání, please see *The Bahá'í World*, vol. 11 (1946–1950): 500–502.

50. 'Abdu'l-Bahá, *The Promulgation of Universal Peace*, p. 430.

51. Shoghi Effendi, *This Decisive Hour*, no. 101.

52. Ḥasan Balyuzi, *'Abdu'l-Bahá: The Centre of the Covenant of Bahá'u'lláh*, pp. 97 and 111.

53. John D. and Louise Bosch papers, U.S. National Bahá'í Archives.

54. 'Abdu'l-Bahá, *Tablets of the Divine Plan,* nos. 7.14–15.
55. Ibid., nos. 7.7–7.8.
56. Shoghi Effendi, *The Light of Divine Guidance,* vol. 1, 15.
57. Mary Maxwell, "Current Bahá'í Activities," *The Bahá'í World,* vol. 7 (1936–1938): 21.
58. John D. and Louise Bosch papers, U.S. National Bahá'í Archives.
59. Rúhíyyih Rabbání, *The Priceless Pearl,* p. 57.
60. Letter dated June 30, 1922 from Soheil Afnán to John and Louise Bosch, John D. and Louise Bosch papers, U.S. National Bahá'í Archives.
61. Letter dated July 27, 1911 from John D. Bosch to Thornton Chase, John D. and Louise Bosch papers, U.S. National Bahá'í Archives; Marzieh Gail, "For John, With Love," *Bahá'í News* (July 1974): 9–21.
62. John D. and Louise Bosch papers, "John's Account," U.S. National Bahá'í Archives.
63. Letter dated July 27, 1911 from John D. Bosch to Thornton Chase, John D. and Louise Bosch papers, U.S. National Bahá'í Archives.
64. Gayle Morrison, *To Move the World,* p. 203.
65. Document Prepared Under the Supervision of the Universal House of Justice, *Century of Light,* p. 18.
66. John D. and Louise Bosch papers, "Bahá'í Historical Record," U.S. National Bahá'í Archives.
67. John D. and Louise Bosch papers, 1912 pilgrim notes, John D. and Louise Bosch papers, U.S. National Bahá'í Archives; *Mahmud's Diary,* "Saturday, April 20, 1912," pp. 48–49.
68. Shoghi Effendi, *God Passes By,* p. xxvii.
69. Shoghi Effendi, *The Advent of Divine Justice,* ¶17.

70. John Bosch 1912 pilgrim notes, John D. and Louise Bosch papers, U.S. National Bahá'í Archives.

71. Tablet dated May 1, 1921, from 'Abdu'l-Bahá to John and Louise Bosch, translated December 14, 1922, U.S. National Bahá'í Archives. The translation was sent to Mr. and Mrs. John Bosch along with the original Tablet. Note: The Tablet quoted is in part and not quoted in its entirety.

## 2 / Dr. Florian and Grace Krug

1. Helen Hoffman, *San Francisco Chronicle* (August 7, 1921): 3.

2. Ibid.

3. Ibid.

4. Coralie Franklin Cooke, "Feast of Surpassing Significance," *Star of the West,* vol. 16, no. 5, pp. 532–33, *https://bahai.works/index.php?title=File:SW_Volume16.pdf&page=157.*

5. Marzieh Gail, *Arches of the Years,* p. 112.

6. "In Memoriam: Juliet Thompson," *The Bahá'í World,* vol. 13, pp. 862–64.

7. "The Bahai Bulletin," vol. 1, no. 1, September 1908, The Bahai Publishing Society, New York, *https://file.bahai.media/ffa/Bahai_Bulletin_1.pdf.*

8. Ibid.

9. Ibid.

10. Ibid.

11. Tablet from 'Abdu'l-Bahá to Mrs. Florian Krug, through Miss Boylan, October, 1908, United States Bahá'í Archives.

12. 'Abdu'l-Bahá, quoted by Hippolyte Dreyfus in Juliet Thompson, *The Diary of Juliet Thompson,* p. 173.

13. Letter from Miss Annie Boylan to Mrs. Corinne True, September 5, 1911, United States Bahá'í Archives.

14. Ibid.
15. Letter from Miss Annie Boylan, undated, United States Bahá'í Archives.
16. Shoghi Effendi, *God Passes By*, p. 443.
17. Marzieh Gail, *Arches of the Years*, p. 113; Louise (Krug) Sayward, recorded interview by Gregory C. Dahl, April 2, 1974 in Cambridge, Massachusetts. Accessed online: See "Reminiscences of Louise Sayward" at *https://dahls.net/bahai/talks*.
18. 'Abdu'l-Bahá, *The Promulgation of Universal Peace*, p. 330.
19. Tablet from 'Abdu'l-Bahá to Grace Krug, August 7, 1912, United States Bahá'í Archives.
20. Mírzá Maḥmúd-i-Zarqání, *Maḥmud's Diary*, p. 182.
21. "In Memoriam: Grace Krug," *The Baháí World*, vol. 8, pp. 675–76, *https://bahai-library.com/pdf/bw/memoriam_bw_8.pdf*.
22. Compilation for the 2018 Counselors' Conference, passage #8, http://*www.bahai.org/r/370429213*.
23. Mírzá Maḥmúd-i-Zarqání, *Maḥmud's Diary*, p. 420.
24. 'Abdu'l-Bahá, *The Promulgation of Universal Peace*, pp. 645–46.
25. Ḥasan Balyuzi, *'Abdu'l-Bahá: The Centre of the Covenant of Bahá'u'lláh*, p. 140.
26. Tablet from 'Abdu'l-Bahá to Grace Krug, January 17, 1913, United States Bahá'í Archives; Tablet from 'Abdu'l-Bahá to Grace Krug, March 12, 1913, United States Bahá'í Archives; Tablet from 'Abdu'l-Bahá to Grace Krug, September 1, 1913 and December (nd) 1913.
27. Tablet from 'Abdu'l-Bahá to Grace Krug, January 17, 1913, United States Bahá'í Archives.
28. Shoghi Effendi, *God Passes By*, p. 456; the Universal House of Justice, letter dated November 26, 1992.

29. 'Abdu'l-Bahá, in *Bahá'í Prayers,* p. 26.

30. Letter from Grace Krug to Agnes Parsons, February 1, 1913, United States Bahá'í Archives.

31. 'Abdu'l-Bahá, *'Abdu'l-Bahá in London,* pp. 102–3.

32. Tablet from 'Abdu'l-Bahá to Grace Krug, March 12, 1913, United States Bahá'í Archives.

33. *Star of the West,* vol. 4, no. 4 (May 17, 1913): 69.

34. Shoghi Effendi, *God Passes By,* p. 448.

35. Michael Ferber, *A Dictionary of Literary Symbols,* see "Harp, lyre, and lute."

36. Tablet from 'Abdu'l-Bahá to Grace Krug, September 1, 1913, United States Bahá'í Archives.

37. Tablet from 'Abdu'l-Bahá "To the Maidservant of God Mrs. Florian Krug," December, 1913, United States Bahá'í Archives.

38. *The Daily Register,* "Baha'i Meeting Tomorrow Night," Red Bank, New Jersey (February 26, 1942): 1.

39. *The Daily Standard,* "Lectures on World Reconstruction to Start Tomorrow," Red Bank, New Jersey, July 10, 1940, *https:// www.newspapers.com/image/419242299/?terms=Charles%20 S%20Krug&match=1; The Battleboro Reformer,* March 22, 1946, *https://www.newspapers.com/image/ 547977834/?terms=Charles%20S%20Krug&match=1; The Battleboro Reformer,* August 5, 1954, *https://www.newspapers. com/image/547834658/?terms=Charles%20S%20Krug&-match=1; Portsmouth Herald,* January 26, 1944, *https://www. newspapers.com/image/56498496/?terms=Charles%20S%20 Krug%20Bahai&match=1.*

40. *Portsmouth Herald,* "Professor Glenn Shook Sees Bright Post War Years," July 12, 1943, *https://www.newspapers.*

*com/image/61058371/?terms=Charles%20S%20Krug%20 Bahai%20race&match=1.*

41. Louise (Krug) Sayward, recorded interview by Gregory C. Dahl, April 2, 1974 in Cambridge, Massachusetts. Accessed online: See "Reminiscences of Louise Sayward" at *https://dahls. net/bahai/talks.*

42. Letter from Aḥmad Sohrab to Grace Krug, January 25, 1917, with a postscript written October 12, 1918. The letter contains Aḥmad Sohrab's translation of the Tablet from 'Abdu'l-Bahá, United States Bahá'í Archives.

43. Tablet from 'Abdu'l-Bahá to Annie Boylan, October 11, 1916, United States Bahá'í Archives.

44. Tablet from 'Abdu'l-Bahá to Annie Boylan and Grace Krug, April 4, 1919, United States Bahá'í Archives.

45. *Buffalo Evening News,* New York Bureau, "New York Surgeon Convert to Bahaism" (April 8, 1921): 16.

46. U.S. passports of Dr. Florian Krug and Mrs. Grace Krug, 1920.

47. Helen Hoffman, *San Francisco Chronicle* (August 7, 1921): 3.

48. Letter from Grace Krug to Ella Cooper, March 5th, 1921, United States Bahá'í Archives.

49. *Reality Magazine,* New York: Reality Publishing Company, 1921.

50. Tablet from 'Abdu'l-Bahá to Grace Krug, May 28, 1921, United States Bahá'í Archives.

51. Cablegram from Grace Krug to 'Abdu'l-Bahá, Haifa, June 21, 1921, United States Bahá'í Archives.

52. "Account of the Passing of 'Abdu'l-Bahá by Grace Krug," talk given at West Englewood, New Jersey, November 28, 1934, United States Bahá'í Archives.

53. Shoghi Effendi, *God Passes By*, p. 491.

54. Ibid., p. 492.

55. Grace Krug, "Bahá'í Congress for Teaching and the Fourteenth Annual Convention" reported by Louis Gregory, *Star of the West*, vol. 13, no. 4. p. 69, *https://bahai.works/Star_of_the_West/Volume_13/Issue_4/Text*.

56. "Account of the Passing of 'Abdu'l-Bahá by Grace Krug," talk given at West Englewood, New Jersey, November 28, 1934, United States Bahá'í Archives.

57. Letter from Louise Bosch to Ella Cooper, December 5, 1921, cited in *Star of the West*, vol. 12, no. 18, p. 277.

58. Florian Krug, "Statement of Dr. Florian Krug written at the request of the Holy Household," United States Bahá'í Archives.

59. 'Abdu'l-Bahá, *Selections from the Writing of 'Abdu'l-Bahá*, no. 187.3.

60. 'Abdu'l-Bahá, *Will and Testament of 'Abdu'l-Bahá*, Part 1.

61. Letter from Florian Krug to Charles Krug, January 8, 1922, United States Bahá'í Archives.

62. Shoghi Effendi, *God Passes By*, p. 493.

63. Ibid., p. 493.

64. Louis Gregory quoting Grace Krug, "Bahá'í Congress for Teaching and the Fourteenth Annual Convention," *Star of the West*, vol. 13, no. 4, p. 69.

65. *The Cincinnati Enquirer*, Cincinnati, Ohio (April 9, 1921):1.

66. Florian Krug, undated, United States Bahá'í Archives. Note: This story was handwritten by Florian Krug, presumably for archival purposes.

67. Please see "Prince Molfetta" at *https://it.wikipedia.org/wiki/Tommaso_Gallarati_Scotti*.

68. Letter of Grace Krug, (nd), United States Bahá'í Archives. The Tablet to the Prince of Molfetta is held at the Bahá'í World Center.

69. Letter from Grace Krug to Agnes Parsons, October 2, 1924, United States Bahá'í Archives.

70. Letter from Grace Krug to Agnes Parsons, undated, United States Bahá'í Archives.

71. Letter from Grace Krug to Agnes Parsons, October 12, 1925, from Merano, Italy, United States Bahá'í Archives.

72. Letter from Grace Krug to Doris and Horace Holley, January 31st, 1929, from Merano, Italy, United States Bahá'í Archives.

73. Bahá'u'lláh, Epistle to the Son of the Wolf, pp. x–xii.

74. Shoghi Effendi, *God Passes By*, p. 219.

75. Letter from Grace Krug to Agnes Parsons, February 26th, 1929, from Merano, Italy, United States Bahá'í Archives.

76. *Press and Sun-Bulletin*, Binghamton, New York (September 12, 1935): 3.

77. *Bahá'í Centenary: 1844–1944*, 1944, p. 166, *https://file.bahai.media/7/7a/Centenary-1844-1944.pdf*.

78. Ibid., pp.166–67, *https://file.bahai.media/7/7a/Centenary-1844-1944.pdf*.

79. *New York Herald* (April 8, 1921): 1.

80. Letter from Carl Scheffler to Grace Krug, August 25, 1927, United States Bahá'í Archives.

81. Bahá'u'lláh, *Gleanings*, no. 153.9.

### 3 / Johanna Hauff

1. A photo of Villa Hauff and Villa Wagenburg can be found here (search for "Hier residierte der Pionier der Fotoindustrie): https://www.stuttgarter-zeitung.de/.

2. Dirk Hermann, "Villa Hauff: Märchenschloss des Fabrikanten" ("Villa Hauff: Fairytale Castle of the Manufacturer."), August 30, 2015, *https://www.stuttgarter-nachrichten.de/.*

3. Wolfgang Zedlitz, "Hauff, Friedrich Wilhelm Albert," *Deutsche Biographie,* can be found here: *https://www.deutsche-biographie.de/sfz28236.html;* "Zum 25jährigen Dienstjubiläum," Angewandte Chemie 46.52 (1933): 814 and can be found online here: *https://www.deepdyve.com/lp/wiley/zum-25j-hrigen-dienstjubil-um-IpXYjNbpLg.*

4. Hermann Ehmer, "Fritz Hauff," http://www.gaestebuecher-schloss-neubeuern.de/biografien/Hauff_Dr._Fritz.pdf.

5. A photo of both villas can be found here: (search for "Hier residierte der Pionier der Fotoindustrie): https://www.stuttgarter-zeitung.de/, *https://bahaipedia.org/Alice_Schwarz-Solivo.*

6. Alma Knobloch, "The Call to Germany," *The Bahá'í World,* vol. 7, p. 740.

7. "German Bahá'ís Celebrate 100 Years," *Bahá'í News World Service,* September 26, 2005. *https://news.bahai.org/story/390/.*

8. Robert Stockman, "The Bahá'í Faith in England and Germany, 1900–1913," p. 35, *https://bahai-library.com/pdf/s/stockman_england_germany_1900-1913.pdf.*

9. Ibid.

10. Alma Knobloch, "Call to Germany," *The Bahá'í World,* vol. 7, p. 732.

11. Ibid., p. 733.

12. Robert Stockman, "The Bahá'í Faith in England and Germany, 1900–1913," p. 35, *https://bahai-library.com/pdf/s/stockman_england_germany_1900-1913.pdf.*

13. Alma Knobloch, "The Call to Germany," *The Bahá'í World,* vol. 7, p. 735.

14. Robert Stockman, "The Bahá'í Faith in England and Germany, 1900–1913," p. 35, *https://bahai-library.com/pdf/s/stockman_england_germany_1900-1913.pdf.*

15. "The Bahai meetings in Stuttgart are held as follows . . ." *Star of the West,* vol. 2, no. 17, p. 6. Also, see Alma Knobloch, "The Call to Germany," *The Bahá'í World,* vol. 7, p. 735.

16. Bahá'í Deutschland Web Archive. Search under the tab called "Deutsche Gemeinde": *http://www.bahai.de/deutsche-gemeinde/geschichte-100-jahre/.*

17. Robert Stockman, "The Bahá'í Faith in England and Germany, 1900–1913," p. 37, *https://bahai-library.com/pdf/s/stockman_england_germany_1900-1913.pdf.*

18. Gayle Morrison, *To Move the World,* p. 315.

19. Louis Gregory, *The Heavenly Vista: The Pilgrimage of Louis G. Gregory, https://bahai-library.com/gregory_heavenly_vista.*

20. Friederich Schweizer, "Progress of the Cause in Germany," "News Notes," *Star of the West,* vol. 2, no. 17, p. 8.

21. Louis Gregory, cited in Gayle Morrison, *To Move the World,* p. 44.

22. Friederich Schweizer, "Progress of the Cause in Germany," "News Notes," *Star of the West,* vol. 2, no. 17, p. 8.

23. Bahá'u'lláh, Epistle to the Son of the Wolf, p. 179, http://www.bahai.org/r/723328892.

24. Tablet from 'Abdul'-Bahá to Margarethe Döring, August 15, 1911, cited in "Progress of the Cause in Germany," *Star of the West,* vol. 2, no. 17, January 19, 1912, p. 6, *https://bahai.works/index.php?title=File:SW_Vol2_No17.pdf&page=7.*

25. 'Abdu'l-Bahá, quoted in Louis Gregory, *The Heavenly Vista: The Pilgrimage of Louis G. Gregory, https://bahai-library.com/gregory_heavenly_vista.*

26. Ibid.

27. Arthur Cuthbert, "News of the Cause in London," *Star of the West,* vol. 2, no. 5, p. 7.

28. W. Tudor-Pole, *Star of the West,* vol. 2 no. 9, August 20, 1911, p. 3.

29. Alma Knobloch, "Call to Germany," *The Bahá'í World,* vol. 7, p. 740.

30. Ḥasan Balyuzi, *'Abdu'l-Bahá: The Centre of the Covenant of Bahá'u'lláh,* p. 378.

31. Alma Knobloch, "Call to Germany," *The Bahá'í World,* vol. 7, p. 740.

32. Wikipedia contributors, "Württemberg Central Railway," Wikipedia, The Free Encyclopedia, https://en.wikipedia.org/ (accessed April 13, 2021).

33. Ḥasan Balyuzi, *'Abdu'l-Bahá: The Centre of the Covenant of Bahá'u'lláh,* pp. 379–80.

34. Ibid.

35. Ibid., p. 380.

36. Louis Gregory, reporting the "Spirit of the Convention," in the sub-heading called "Reports from Teachers." *Bahá'í News* (84): 4–5. June 1934, *https://bahai.works/Baha%27i_News/Issue_84.* Also, Robert Stockman reports that one meeting had as many as 250 people: Robert Stockman, "The Bahá'í Faith in England and Germany, 1900–1913," *https://bahai-library.com/pdf/s/stockman_england_germany_1900-1913.pdf.*

37. Alma Knobloch, "Call to Germany," *The Bahá'í World,* vol. 7, p. 740.

38. 'Abdu'l-Bahá, quoted in "'Abdu'l-Bahá in Stuttgart," *Star of the West,* vol. 4, no. 4, p. 67.

39. Ḥasan Balyuzi, *'Abdu'l-Bahá: The Centre of the Covenant of Bahá'u'lláh,* pp. 159–397.

40. Martin Oversohl, "Gänsheide: 19th century villas," *https://second.wiki/wiki/gc3a4nsheide.* Accessed April 13, 2021.

41. "'Abdu'l-Bahá in Stuttgart," *Star of the West,* vol. 4, no. 4, May 17, 1913, p. 68.

42. Ingo Hoffman, "'Abdu'l-Bahá in Deutschland" online at *http://www.abdulbaha-in-deutschland.de/.* Accessed January 15, 2021.

43. Alma Knobloch, "The Call to Germany," *The Bahá'í World,* vol. 7, p. 741.

44. 'Abdu'l-Bahá, quoted in "'Abdu'l-Bahá in Stuttgart," *Star of the West,* vol. 4, no. 4, p. 68.

45. Susanne Pfaff-Grossmann, *Hermann Grossmann, Hand of the Cause of God: A Life for the Faith,* p. 14. Also, for more information about Alma Knobloch giving up her U.S. citizenship, please see Rosa Schwartz, "In Memoriam: Alma Knobloch," *The Bahá'í World,* vol. 9, p. 642.

46. 'Abdu'l-Bahá, *Tablets of the Divine Plan,* p. 41, http://www.bahai.org/r/733932331.

47. Charles Mason Remey, *Star of the West,* vol. 11, no. 13, "News from the Baha'is of Germany," pp. 219–26, https://bahai-library.com/pdf/sw/SW_Volume11.pdf.

48. Ibid.

49. Ibid.

50. Alice Schwartz, quoted in *Star of the West,* vol. 12, no. 8, August 1, 1921, pp. 149–50. Translated by Kate Kempner.

51. Susanne Pfaff-Grossmann, *Hermann Grossmann, Hand of the Cause of God: A Life for the Faith,* p. 22.

52. Ibid., p. 22.

53. Dr. Faramarz Abrar and Susanne Pfaff-Grossmann, "Biographie Johanna von Werthern," 2012, unpublished personal notes. Obtained from the National Bahá'í Archives of Germany.

54. Tablet from 'Abdu'l-Bahá to Johanna Hauff, August 24, 1919. Obtained from Alma Knobloch's biographer, Jennifer Redson Wiebers, who obtained it from the Washington D.C. Bahá'í Archives, "Alma Knobloch Notebook."

55. Dr. Faramarz Abrar and Susanne Pfaff-Grossmann, "Biographie Johanna von Werthern," 2012, unpublished personal notes. Obtained from the National Bahá'í Archives of Germany.

56. Ibid.

57. Ibid.

58. Ibid.

59. Alex A. Käfer, *Die Geschichte der österreichischen Bahá'í-Gemeinde,* Nationaler Geistiger Rat der Bahá'í in Österreich, 2nd edition, 2020, pp. 313–18. Reference courtesy Alexander Meinhard, Germany.

60. Tablet from 'Abdu'l-Bahá to Johanna Hauff, May 5, 1920. Copy obtained from Dr. Faramarz Abrar, Germany.

61. Dr. Faramarz Abrar and Susanne Pfaff-Grossmann, "Biographie Johanna von Werthern," 2012, unpublished personal notes. Obtained from the National Bahá'í Archives of Germany.

62. This letter, and the letter that follows, was published in the German Bahá'í magazine called *Die Sonne der Wahrheit* and translated by Mrs. Aubrey J. Kempner for publication in the *Star of the West.*

63. Johanna Hauff, "Letter telling of the passing of Abdul-Baha," *Star of the West,* vol. 12, no. 19, p. 296.
64. "Abdul Baha, Religious Leader, Dies in Persia," *New York Tribune,* Dec 1, 1921, p. 1. *https://www.newspapers.com/.*
65. Shoghi Effendi, *God Passes By, p.* 494.
66. Johanna Hauff, quoted in "Letters telling of the passing of Abdul-Baha," *Star of the West,* vol. 12, no. 19, March 2, 1922, pp. 296–99.
67. 'Abdu'l-Bahá, quoted in Lady Blomfield and Shoghi Effendi, "Passing of 'Abdu'l-Bahá," *The Bahá'í World,* vol. 1 (1925–1926). It is on page 26 of the online version: *https://bahai-library.com/shoghieffendi_blomfield_passing_abdul-baha.*
68. Rosa Schwartz, "In Memoriam: Alma Knobloch," *The Bahá'í World,* vol. 9, p. 642.
69. Alma Knobloch, "The Call to Germany," *The Bahá'í World,* vol. 7, p. 733.
70. 'Abdu'l-Bahá, quoted in "Germany, France, Italy, and Switzerland: A Compilation of Bahá'í Writings," prepared by the Research Department of the Universal House of Justice, Passage #2, *https://bahai-library.com/compilation_germany_france_italy#s1a.*
71. Cable from the Bahá'ís of Germany, quoted in Lady Blomfield and Shoghi Effendi, "Passing of 'Abdu'l-Bahá," *The Bahá'í World,* vol. 1 (1925–1926): 28, *https://bahai.works/index.php?title=File%3ABW_Volume1.pdf&page=28.*
72. 'Abdu'l-Bahá, *The Will and Testament of 'Abdu'l-Bahá, https://www.bahai.org/library/authoritative-texts/abdul-baha/will-testament-abdul-baha/2#189137811.*
73. Letter dated November 25, 2020 from the Universal House of Justice "To the Bahá'ís of the World."

74. Shoghi Effendi, *God Passes By,* p. 514.

75. Ibid., p. 523.

76. Shoghi Effendi, *Bahá'í Administration,* pp. 34–43, *https://reference.bahai.org/en/t/se/BA/ba-24.html.*

77. Ibid., p. 34.

78. Ibid., pp. 34–35.

79. Ibid., p. 37.

80. Shoghi Effendi, *God Passes By,* p. 527; Susanne Pfaff-Grossmann, *Hermann Grossmann, Hand of the Cause of God: A Life for the Faith,* p. 97.

81. Shoghi Effendi, *Bahá'í Administration,* p. 38.

82. 'Abdu'l-Bahá, *Selections from the Writings of 'Abdu'l-Bahá,* no. 31.13.

83. Ibid., no. 211.

84. 'Abdu'l-Bahá, *Tablets of the Divine Plan,* 8.16.

85. Alex A. Käfer, *Die Geschichte der österreichischen Bahá'í-Gemeinde,* Nationaler Geistiger Rat der Bahá'í in Österreich, 2nd edition, 2020, pp. 313–18. Reference courtesy Alexander Meinhard, Germany.

86. Susanne Pfaff-Grossmann, *Hermann Grossmann, Hand of the Cause of God: A Life for the Faith,* p. 95.

87. Ibid., p. 125.

88. Ibid., p. 143.

89. Bahá'u'lláh, *Tablets of Bahá'u'lláh,* p. 173.

90. Shoghi Effendi, *The Light of Divine Guidance,* vol. 1, p. 18.

91. Letter dated June 27, 1933 from Shoghi Effendi to Dr. Mühlschlegel, in Shoghi Effendi, *The Light of Divine Guidance,* p. 49.

92. Shoghi Effendi, *God Passes By,* pp. 573–74.

93. Letter written on behalf of Shoghi Effendi to Hermann Grossmann, in *The Light of Divine Guidance,* December 30, 1945, pp. 99–100.

94. Dr. Faramarz Abrar and Susanne Pfaff-Grossmann, "Biographie Johanna von Werthern," 2012, unpublished personal notes. Obtained from the National Bahá'í Archives of Germany.

95. Alex A. Käfer, *Die Geschichte der österreichischen Bahá'í-Gemeinde,* Nationaler Geistiger Rat der Bahá'í in Österreich, 2nd edition, 2020, pp. 313–18. Reference courtesy Alexander Meinhard, Germany.

96. The letter written on behalf of the Guardian is cited in German in Dr. Faramarz Abrar and Susanne Pfaff-Grossmann, "Biographie Johanna von Werthern," 2012, unpublished personal notes. Obtained from the National Bahá'í Archives of Germany.

97. Ibid.

98. Ibid.

99. Bahá'u'lláh, *Tablets of Bahá'u'lláh,* p. 173.

100. Dr. Faramarz Abrar and Susanne Pfaff-Grossmann, "Biographie Johanna von Werthern," 2012, unpublished personal notes. Obtained from the National Bahá'í Archives of Germany.

101. Jürgen Brand, "Hier residierte der Pionier der Fotoindustrie," Stuttgarter Zeitung, *https://www.stuttgarter-zeitung.de/inhalt.30-jahre-werkstatthaus-hier-residierte-der-pionier-der-fotoindustrie.acf83c72-ab8e-46c6-a2d7-8754be764314.html.* Accessed April 14, 2021.

102. "Das Wekstatthaus," *http://werkstatthaus.net.*

103. 'Abdu'l-Bahá, quoted in "Germany, France, Italy, and Switzerland: A Compilation of Bahá'í Writings," prepared by the Research Department of the Universal House of Justice, no. 3.

## 4 / Curtis Kelsey

1. 'Abdu'l-Bahá, quoted in John Esslemont, *Bahá'u'lláh and the New Era*, p. 274. Also see The Universal House of Justice, *Bahá'í Holy Places at the World Centre*, p. 44.

2. Ḥasan Balyuzi, *'Abdu'l-Bahá: The Centre of the Covenant of Bahá'u'lláh*, p. 132.

3. Shoghi Effendi, *God Passes By*, p. 373.

4. Bahá'u'lláh, The Kitáb-i-Aqdas, notes 7, 8.

5. Shoghi Effendi, *God Passes By*, pp. 438, 437–38.

6. Adib Taherzadeh, *The Revelation of Bahá'u'lláh*, Vol. 4, p. 351.

7. Bahá'u'lláh, *Tablets of Bahá'u'lláh*, pp. 4–5.

8. Shoghi Effendi, *Directives from the Guardian*, *https://reference. bahai.org/en/t/se/DG/dg-2.html*.

9. Shoghi Effendi, *God Passes By*, p. 432.

10. 'Abdu'l-Bahá, quoted in Shoghi Effendi, *God Passes By*, p. 437.

11. Shoghi Effendi, *God Passes By*, p. 436.

12. Ibid., pp. 436–37.

13. Ibid., pp. 548–49.

14. Ibid., pp. 23–25.

15. Ibid., *God Passes By*, p. 40.

16. The Báb, quoted in Shoghi Effendi, *God Passes By*, p. 41.

17. The Báb, *Selections from the Writings of the Báb*, no. 3:13.1.

18. 'Abdu'l-Bahá, *Selections from the Writings of 'Abdu'l-Bahá*, no. 227.22.

19. Carol Rutstein, June Remignanti, Mary Louise Suhm, "In Memoriam: Curtis DeMude Kelsey," *The Bahá'í World*, vol. 15, p. 470, *https://bahai.works/index.php?title=File:BW_Volume15.pdf&page=494*.

20. Ibid.

21. Nathan Rutstein, *He Loved and Served: The Story of Curtis Kelsey*, p. 42.

22. The Nautical Gazette, Volume 101, September 10, 1921, p. 335, *https://www.google.com/books/edition/The_Nautical_Gazette/*.

23. Nathan Rutstein, *He Loved and Served: The Story of Curtis Kelsey*, p. 43.

24. Ibid., p. 49.

25. 'Abdu'l-Bahá, quoted in Rutstein, *He Loved and Served: The Story of Curtis Kelsey*, p. 50.

26. Ibid., p. 51.

27. Rúhíyyih Rabbání, *The Priceless Pearl*, p. 31.

28. Ḥasan Balyuzi, *'Abdu'l-Bahá: The Centre of the Covenant of Bahá'u'lláh*, p. 448.

29. The Universal House of Justice, *Messages from the Universal House of Justice, 1963–1986*, p. 115.

30. Ibid., p. 139.

31. Tablet from 'Abdu'l-Bahá to Mr. Saichirō Fujita, translated by Ameen Fareed, November 10, 1906, Bahá'í Reference Library, *https://reference.bahai.org/en/t/c/JWTA/jwta-28.html*.

32. Curtis Kelsey, audio recording, "Stories of 'Abdu'l-Bahá and the Guardian," minute 40.44, *https://bahai-library.com/audio/k/kelsey_stories_abdulbaha_guardian.mp3*.

33. 'Abdu'l-Bahá, quoted in Barbara Sims, *Japan Will Turn Ablaze!*, p. 27, *https://bahai-library.com/compilation_japan_turn_ablaze&chapter=4*.

34. The Universal House of Justice, *Bahá'í News*, June 1976, p. 2.

35. Curtis Kelsey, audio recording, "Stories of 'Abdu'l-Bahá and the Guardian," minute 18.17, *https://bahai-library.com/audio/k/kelsey_stories_abdulbaha_guardian.mp3*.

36. Rúhíyyih Rabbání, *The Priceless Pearl*, pp. 228–33.

37. Nathan Rutstein, *He Loved and Served: The Story of Curtis Kelsey*, p. 57.
38. Ḥasan Balyuzi, *'Abdu'l-Bahá: The Centre of the Covenant of Bahá'u'lláh*, p. 171. It may be of interest to the reader to know that when 'Abdu'l-Bahá began his journey to the West, it was K͟husraw who, along with Shoghi Effendi and one of 'Abdu'l-Bahá's secretaries, Mizrá Munír, were ordered by the port physician in Naples to return to Alexandria. There were strong reasons to doubt the physician's claim that the three young men had eye infections; nevertheless, his dubious impartiality deemed that Shoghi Effendi, Mirzá Munír and Áqá K͟husraw were medically disqualified from the voyage to the United States. This was reportedly one of the biggest disappointments in the life of Shoghi Effendi. (See Balyuzi, p. 171.)
39. Curtis Kelsey, audio recording, "Stories of 'Abdu'l-Bahá and the Guardian," minute 21.43, *https://bahai-library.com/audio/k/kelsey_stories_abdulbaha_guardian.mp3*.
40. Nathan Rutstein, *He Loved and Served: The Story of Curtis Kelsey*, p. 62.
41. Ibid., p. 72.
42. Curtis Kelsey, quoted in Carol Rutstein, June Remignanti, and Mary Louise Suhm, "In Memoriam: Curtis DeMude Kelsey," *The Bahá'í World*, vol. 15, p. 493, *https://bahai.works/index.php?title=File:BW_Volume15.pdf&page=493*.
43. Nathan Rutstein, *He Loved and Served: The Story of Curtis Kelsey*, p. 60.
44. 'Abdu'l-Bahá, *Paris Talks*, no. 28.11–12.
45. Shoghi Effendi and Lady Blomfield, "The Passing of 'Abdu'l-Bahá," p. 4, https://bahai-library.com/shoghieffendi_blomfield_passing_abdul-baha.

46. "Account of the Passing of 'Abdu'l-Bahá by Grace Krug," talk given at West Englewood, New Jersey, November 28, 1934, United States Bahá'í Archives.

47. Aḥmad Tabrizi, "Letter from Ahmad Tabrizi to Dr. Ziá Bagdádí," *Star of the West*, vol. 12, no. 18 (February 7, 1922): 280–81.

48. Nathan Rutstein, *He Loved and Served: The Story of Curtis Kelsey*, p. 81.

49. 'Abdu'l-Bahá quoted in Aḥmad Tabrizi, "Letter from Ahmad Tabrizi to Dr. Ziá Bagdádí, *Star of the West*, vol. 12, no. 18 (February 7, 1922): 280–81.

50. Abraham Lincoln, "Address before the Wisconsin State Agricultural Society," September 30, 1859, *http://www.abraham-lincolnonline.org/lincoln/speeches/fair.htm*.

51. Shoghi Effendi, *The World Order of Bahá'u'lláh*, p. 198.

52. Shoghi Effendi and Lady Blomfield, "The Passing of 'Abdu'l-Bahá," p. 5, https://bahai-library.com/shoghieffendi_blomfield_passing_abdul-baha.

53. Curtis Kelsey, audio recording. "Stories of 'Abdu'l-Bahá and the Guardian," minute 27.43, *https://bahai-library.com/audio/k/kelsey_stories_abdulbaha_guardian.mp3*.

54. Ibid., minute 28.27, *https://bahai-library.com/audio/k/kelsey_stories_abdulbaha_guardian.mp3*. Also, see Rutstein, *He Loved and Served: The Story of Curtis Kelsey*, p. 95.

55. Nathan Rutstein, *He Loved and Served: The Story of Curtis Kelsey*, p. 96.

56. Curtis Kelsey, audio recording, "Stories of 'Abdu'l-Bahá and the Guardian," minute 30.47, *https://bahai-library.com/audio/k/kelsey_stories_abdulbaha_guardian.mp3*.

57. Ḥasan Balyuzi, *'Abdu'l-Bahá: The Centre of the Covenant of Bahá'u'lláh*, p. 464.

58. Shoghi Effendi, *God Passes By,* p. 496.

59. Ibid., pp. 548–49.

60. Curtis Kelsey, audio recording, "Stories of ʻAbduʼl-Bahá and the Guardian," minute 38.32, *https://bahai-library.com/audio/k/kelsey_stories_abdulbaha_guardian.mp3.*

61. Janet Khan, *Prophet's Daughter,* pp. 78–86, 131–73.

62. Dr. Ziá Bagdádí, quoted in Carol Rutstein, June Remignanti, Mary Louise Suhm, "In Memoriam: Curtis DeMude Kelsey," *The Baháʼí World,* vol. 15, p. 469.

63. Valeria Kelsey, quoted in Carol Rutstein, June Remignanti, and Mary Louise Suhm, "In Memoriam: Curtis DeMude Kelsey," *The Baháʼí World,* vol. 15, p. 496.

64. Nathan Rutstein, *He Loved and Served: The Story of Curtis Kelsey,* p. 52.

65. Curtis Kelsey, audio recording, "Stories of ʻAbduʼl-Bahá and the Guardian," minute 37.52, *https://bahai-library.com/audio/k/kelsey_stories_abdulbaha_guardian.mp3.*

66. Nathan Rutstein, *He Loved and Served: The Story of Curtis Kelsey,* p. 108.

67. Shoghi Effendi, in *Baháíyyih K͟hánum: The Greatest Holy Leaf,* p. 56

68. Baháʼuʼlláh, quoted in *Baháíyyih K͟hánum: The Greatest Holy Leaf,* p. 1; Baháʼuʼlláh, quoted in *Baháíyyih K͟hánum: The Greatest Holy Leaf,* p. 3; Shoghi Effendi, quoted in *Baháíyyih K͟hánum: The Greatest Holy Leaf,* p. 23.

69. Shoghi Effendi, *This Decisive Hour,* p. 3, no. 3.1, http://www.bahai.org/r/885773159.

70. The Greatest Holy Leaf, quoted in Nathan Rutstein, *He Loved and Served: The Story of Curtis Kelsey,* p. 111.

71. Shoghi Effendi, *Citadel of Faith,* p. 96.

72. Letter from the Universal House of Justice dated January 4, 1994, http://*www.bahai.org/r/340712001*; Shoghi Effendi, *Citadel of Faith*, p. 96.

73. See "The First Oceanic Conference," *The Bahá'í World*, vol. 25, pp. 73–79, and "The Commemoration at the World Centre of the Centenary of the Arrival of Bahá'u'lláh in the Holy Land," pp. 81–86.

74. Ibid., p. 291.

75. Bahá'u'lláh, quoted in Shoghi Effendi, *God Passes By*, pp. 289, 287.

76. Map, "Voyage of Bahá'u'lláh from the Land of Mystery to the Most Great Prison in the Holy Land, August 1868," *The Bahá'í World*, vol. 25, p. 72.

77. Universal House of Justice, "To the Hands of the Cause of God and the Bahá'í Friends assembled in Palermo, Sicily, at the First Bahá'í Oceanic Conference," August, 1968.

78. Ibid.

79. Bahá'u'lláh, quoted in Shoghi Effendi, *God Passes By*, p. 292.

80. Carol Rutstein, June Remignanti, Mary Louise Suhm, "In Memoriam: Curtis DeMude Kelsey," *The Bahá'í World*, vol. 15, p. 470.

81. Shoghi Effendi, *The World Order of Bahá'u'lláh*, p. 135.

82. Carol Rutstein, email correspondence between Carol Rutstein and Angelina Diliberto Allen, February 5, 2021 and March 19, 2021.

83. 'Abdu'l-Bahá, *Selections from the Writings of 'Abdu'l-Bahá*, no. 163.6.

84. The Universal House of Justice, Riḍván message, 2019.

85. Bahá'í World News Service, "Design Concept for the Shrine of 'Abdu'l-Bahá Unveiled," September 20, 2019, *https://news.bahai.org/story/1353/*.

86. 'Abdu'l-Bahá, in *Bahá'í Prayers,* pp. 332–33.

### Epilogue

1. Ḥasan Balyuzi, *'Abdu'l-Bahá: The Centre of the Covenant of Bahá'u'lláh,* p. 132.

2. For assistance in describing the architectural design of the House of the Master, the writer consulted Dr. Shirin Fozi. She specializes in Medieval European Art and Architecture and currently holds the position of Associate Professor of the History of Art and Architecture at the University of Pittsburg.

3. The Universal House of Justice, *Bahá'í Holy Places at the World Centre,* p. 55.

4. Ibid.

5. Rúhíyyih Rabbání, *The Priceless Pearl,* p. 13.

6. The Universal House of Justice, *Bahá'í Holy Places at the World Centre,* pp. 54–57.

7. See Shoghi Effendi, *God Passes By,* Chapter XV: "The Rebellion of Mírzá Muḥammad-'Alí"; see also Rúhíyyih Rabbání, *The Priceless Pearl,* p. 118; see also Janet A. Khan, *Prophet's Daughter,* p. 5.

8. Shoghi Effendi, *Bahá'í Administration,* p. 191.

9. Ibid., p. 187.

10. Ibid.

11. Ibid., p. 190.

12. Ibid., p. 25.

13. Rúhíyyih Rabbání, *The Priceless Pearl,* pp. 58–61.

14. Bahá'u'lláh, quoted in Shoghi Effendi in *God Passes By,* p. 551.

15. Shoghi Effendi, in *Baḥíyyih Khánum: The Greatest Holy Leaf,* p. 56.

16. Shoghi Effendi, *Bahá'í Administration,* pp. 187–96.

17. Munírih <u>Kh</u>ánum, quoted by Lady Blomfield, *The Chosen Highway*, p. 89.

18. 'Abdu'l-Bahá, quoted in Rúhíyyih Rabbání, *The Priceless Pearl*, p. 14.

19. Shoghi Effendi, letter dated July 17, 1932, in "The Passing of the Bahíyyih <u>Kh</u>ánum, The Most Exalted Leaf," *The Bahá'í World*, vol. 5, pp. 169–180.

20. Corinne True, "In Memory of Munírih <u>Kh</u>ánum," *The Bahá'í World*, vol. 8, p. 266.

21. Munírih <u>Kh</u>ánum, in *Munírih <u>Kh</u>ánum: Memoirs and Letters*, p. 58; Munírih <u>Kh</u>ánum, cited in Baharieh Rouhani Ma'ani, *Leaves of the Twin Divine Trees*, p. 352.

22. Munírih <u>Kh</u>ánum, in *Munírih <u>Kh</u>ánum: Memoirs and Letters*, pp. 57–61.

23. 'Abdu'l-Bahá, *The Will and Testament of 'Abdu'l-Bahá*, Part One.

24. Ibid.

25. See *The Universal House of Justice: A Compilation Prepared by the Research Department of the Universal House of Justice*, no. 71.9; see Shoghi Effendi, *The World Order of Bahá'u'lláh*, p. 144.

26. 'Abdu'l-Bahá, *Will and Testament of 'Abdu'l-Bahá*, Part One.

27. The Universal House of Justice, "The Promise of World Peace."

28. Shoghi Effendi, *Bahá'í Administration*, pp. 15–17.

# Bibliography

### Works of Bahá'u'lláh

*Gleanings from the Writings of Bahá'u'lláh.* Wilmette, IL: Bahá'í
  Publishing, 2005.
*Days of Remembrance.* Haifa: Bahá'í World Center, 2016.
*The Hidden Words of Bahá'u'lláh.* Translated by Shoghi Effendi.
  Wilmette, IL: Bahá'í Publishing, 2002.
*The Kitáb-i-Aqdas.* Wilmette, IL: Bahá'í Publishing Trust, 1993.
*The Kitáb-i-Íqán.* Wilmette, IL: Bahá'í Publishing, 2019.
*Tablets of Bahá'u'lláh.* Wilmette, IL: Bahá'í Publishing Trust, 1993.
*Epistle to the Son of the Wolf.* Wilmette, IL: Bahá'í Publishing Trust,
  1988.

### Works of the Báb

*Selections of the Writings of the Báb.* Compiled by the Research De-
  partment of the Universal House of Justice and translated by
  Habib Taherzadeh with the assistance of a Committee at the
  Bahá'í World Center. Haifa: Bahá'í World Center, 2006.

### Works of 'Abdu'l-Bahá

'Abdu'l-Bahá in London. London: Bahá'í Publishing Trust, 1987.

Paris Talks. Wilmette, IL: Bahá'í Publishing, 2006.

The Promulgation of Universal Peace. Wilmette, IL: Bahá'í Publishing Trust, 2007.

Selections from the Writings of 'Abdu'l-Bahá. Translated by a committee at the Bahá'í World Center and by Marzieh Gail. Wilmette, IL: Bahá'í Publishing, 2010.

Some Answered Questions. Wilmette, IL: Bahá'í Publishing Trust, 2014.

Tablets of the Divine Plan. Wilmette, IL: Bahá'í Publishing Trust, 1993.

"The Universal Language of the Spirit." Transcribed by Dr. Lutfu'lláh Ḥakím. Star of the West, vol. 13, no. 7 (October 1922): 163–64.

The Will and Testament of 'Abdu'l-Bahá. Wilmette, IL: Bahá'í Publishing Trust, 1971.

### Works of Shoghi Effendi

The Advent of Divine Justice. Wilmette, IL: Bahá'í Publishing Trust, 2006.

Bahá'í Administration. Wilmette, IL: Bahá'í Publishing Trust, 1968.

Citadel of Faith. Wilmette, IL: Bahá'í Publishing Trust, 2014.

This Decisive Hour: Messages from Shoghi Effendi to the North American Bahá'ís, 1932–1946. Wilmette, IL: Bahá'í Publishing Trust, 2002.

Directives from the Guardian. New Delhi: Bahá'í Publishing Trust, 1973.

*God Passes By.* Wilmette, IL: Bahá'í Publishing Trust, 2010.

*The Light of Divine Guidance, vol. 1.* Germany: Bahá'í Verlag, 1982.

*The World Order of Bahá'u'lláh.* Wilmette, IL: Bahá'í Publishing Trust, 2012.

### Works of the Universal House of Justice

*Messages from the Universal House of Justice, 1963–1986.* Wilmette, IL: Bahá'í Publishing Trust, 1996.

"The Promise of World Peace: A Statement of the Universal House of Justice." October, 1985. https://www.bahai. org/documents/the-universal-house-of-justice/promise-world-peace.

### Compilations

Bahá'u'lláh, the Báb, 'Abdu'l-Bahá. *Bahá'í Prayers.* Wilmette, IL: Bahá'í Publishing Trust, 2002.

*Bahíyyih Khánum, the Greatest Holy Leaf: A Compilation from Bahá'í Sacred Texts and Writings of the Guardian of the Faith and Bahíyyih Khánum's Own Letters.* Compiled by the Research Department at the Bahá'í World Center. Haifa: Bahá'í World Center, 1982.

*Holy Places at the Bahá'í World Centre.* Compiled by the Research Department at the Bahá'í World Center. Haifa: Bahá'í World Center, 1968.

*The Universal House of Justice. A Compilation Prepared by the Research Department of the Universal House of Justice.* Wilmette, IL: Bahá'í Publishing Trust, 2021. Accessed online: *https://www.bahai.org/library/authoritative-texts/compilations/universal-house-of-justice-compilation/1#207001270.*

## Other works

Abrar, Dr. Faramarz and Susanne Pfaff-Grossmann. "Biographie Johanna von Werthern." 2012. Unpublished. Obtained from the National Bahá'í Archive and Library Committee of Germany.

Ahdieh, Hussein and Hillary Chapman. *The Calling: Tahirih of Persia and Her American Contemporaries.* Bethesda, MD: Ibex Publishers, 2017.

*Bahá'í Centenary.* Bahá'í Publishing Committee, Wilmette, IL: Bahá'í Publishing Committee, 1944. Accessed online: *https://file.bahai.media/7/7a/Centenary-1844-1944.pdf.*

*Bahá'í News, The.* U.S. National Bahá'í Archives. Issue numbers 84, 520.

*Bahá'í World, The.* Volumes 1, 5, 7, 8, 9, 11, 12, 13, 15 and 23.

*Bahá'ís, The.* A publication of the Bahá'í International Community. Wilmette, IL: Bahá'í Publishing, 2017.

Balyuzi, Ḥasan. *'Abdu'l-Bahá: The Centre of the Covenant of Bahá'u'lláh.* Oxford: George Ronald, 1971.

Blomfield, Lady Sara. *The Chosen Highway.* Oxford: George Ronald, 1975.

*Century of Light.* Document prepared under the supervision of the Universal House of Justice. Haifa: Bahá'í World Center, 2001.

Chapman, Anita. *Leroy Ioas, Hand of the Cause of God.* Oxford: George Ronald, 1998.

Compilation for the 2018 Counsellors' Conference. Accessed online: http://www.bahai.org/r/370429213.

Esslemont, John E. *Bahá'u'lláh and the New Era.* Wilmette, IL: Bahá'í Publishing Trust, 2006.

Ferber, Michael. *A Dictionary of Literary Symbols.* Third Edition. New York: Cambridge University Press, 2017.

Gail, Marzieh. *Arches of the Years*. Oxford: George Ronald, 1991.

———. *Dawn Over Mount Hira*. Oxford: George Ronald, 1976.

Gregory, Louis. *The Heavenly Vista*. Washington: R.L. Pendleton, 1911. Accessed online: *https://bahai-library.com/gregory_heavenly_vista*.

Khádem, Javidukht. *Zikr'u'lláh Khádem: The Itinerant Hand of the Cause*. Wilmette, IL: Bahá'í Publishing Trust, 1990.

Khan, Janet A. *Prophet's Daughter*. Wilmette, IL: Bahá'í Publishing, 2005.

Krug, Grace. "Account of the Passing of 'Abdu'l-Bahá by Grace Krug," talk given at West Englewood, New Jersey, November 28, 1934, United States Bahá'í Archives.

Ma'ani, Baharieh Rouhani. *Leaves of the Twin Divine Trees*. Oxford: George Ronald, 2009.

Maḥmúd-i-Zarqání. *Maḥmúd's Diary*. Oxford: George Ronald, 1998.

Morrison, Gayle. *To Move the World*. Wilmette, IL: Bahá'í Publishing Trust, 1982.

Munírih Khánum. *Munírih Khánum: Memoirs and Letters*. Los Angeles: Kalimát Press, 1986.

Pfaff-Grossmann, Susanne. *Hermann Grossmann, Hand of the Cause of God: A Life for the Faith*. Oxford: George Ronald, 2009.

Piff Metelmann, Velda. *Lua Getsinger: Herald of the Covenant*. Oxford: George Ronald, 1997.

Rabbání, Rúhíyyih. *The Priceless Pearl*. London: Bahá'í Publishing Trust, 1969.

Rutstein, Nathan. *He Loved and Served: The Story of Curtis Kelsey*. Oxford: George Ronald, 1982.

Sims, Barbara, ed. *Japan Will Turn Ablaze!* Tokyo: Bahá'í Publishing Trust of Japan, 1992.

*Star of the West.* Volumes 2, 4, 11, 12, 13, 16.

Stockman, Robert. "The Bahá'í Faith in England and Germany, 1900–1913." *World Order Magazine,* vol. 27, no. 3. The National Spiritual Assembly of the Bahá'ís of the United States, 1996. Accessed online: *https://bahai-library.com/pdfs/stockman_england_germany 1900–1913.pdf.*

Taherzadeh, Adib. *The Child of the Covenant.* Oxford: George Ronald, 2000.

———. *The Revelation of Bahá'u'lláh, Vol. 4.* Oxford: George Ronald, 1992.

Thompson, Juliet. *The Diary of Juliet Thompson.* Los Angeles: Kalimát Press, 1983.

White, Roger. *Occasions of Grace.* Oxford: George Ronald, 1992.

*World Order Magazine.* Volumes 12, 27.

# Photos

The Master on the steps of His house at 7 Haparsim Street, Haifa, May, 1921.
© Bahá'í International Community.

John and Louise Bosch at their home in
Geyserville, California. © U.S. Bahá'í Archives.

Louise Stapfer Bosch, passport photo, 1920.

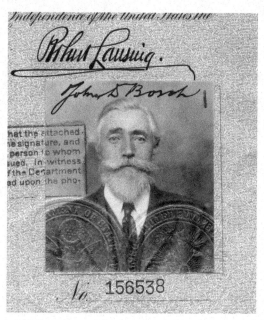

John David Bosch, passport photo, 1920.

Photo of 'Abdu'l-Bahá taken in Dublin, New Hampshire on July 24, 1912. On that same day, 'Abdu'l-Bahá told Mirzá Maḥmúd-i-Zarqání to write this in his diary: "The time will come when her whole family will be proud of Mrs. Krug and her faith. Her husband is still distant and heedless; the time will come when he will feel himself exalted on account of Mrs. Krug's faith. I see what they do not see. Ere long the whole of her family will consider the faith of that lady as the crown of honor on their heads." Photo © Baháʾí International Community.

Grace Krug, photo from her first
pilgrimage to Haifa, 1920.
© U.S. Bahá'í Archives.

Florian Krug, c. 1910, New York.
© U.S. Bahá'í Archives.

The first National Spiritual Assembly of the Bahá'ís of Austria, formed at Riḍván, 1959. Front row: Johanna (Hauff) von Werthern, Franz Pollïnger, Bertha Matthisen, and Leopoldine Heilinger. Back row: Dr. Mehdi Varqá, Gunther Hang, Ursula Kohler, Dr. Masoud Berdjis, and Dr. Aminolláh Ahmedzadeh. Photo from Bahá'í News, Issue 342.

Villa Hauff (center-left of photo), Stuttgart, circa 1920. The roof of Villa Wagenburg can be seen to the right of Villa Hauff. © City of Stuttgart.

'Abdu'l-Bahá with a group of friends gathered in the garden of Villa Wagenburg, Stuttgart, Germany, 1913. © Bahá'í International Community.

Curtis DeMude Kelsey, passport photo, 1921.
Photo courtesy of Carol Kelsey Rutstein.

Curtis DeMude Kelsey, c. 1921. © U.S. Bahá'í Archives.

Lights on path below the shrine of the Báb, 1922.
© Bahá'í International Community.

Shrine of the Báb before the superstructure was built, early 1900s.
© Bahá'í International Community.

Shrine of the Báb after completion of the superstructure, 1954,
(Bay of Haifa in background).
© Bahá'í International Community.

Entrance to the shrine of Bahá'u'lláh c. 1940.
© Bahá'í International Community.

'Abdu'l-Bahá walking up Haparsim Street; the three children are eating sweets that 'Abdu'l-Bahá gave to them, c. 1920. © Bahá'í International Community.

Ten thousand mourners from numerous religious backgrounds attend the
funeral of 'Abdu'l-Bahá in Haifa, November 29, 1921.
© Bahá'í International Community.

The Western Pilgrim House, 4 Haparsim Street, Haifa, c. 1920s.
© Bahá'í International Community.

Múnirih Khánum, wife of 'Abdu'l-Bahá.
© Bahá'í International Community.

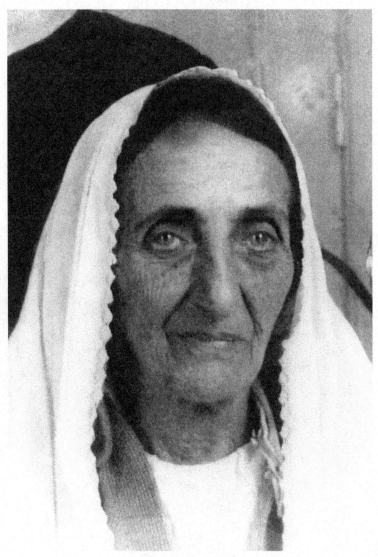

Bahíyyih <u>Kh</u>ánum, the Greatest Holy Leaf.
© Bahá'í International Community.

Photograph of Shoghi Effendi taken in 1919.
© Bahá'í International Community.

Last photograph, taken in September 1957 by Amatu'l-Bahá
Rúhíyyih Khánum, of Shoghi Effendi. © Bahá'í International Community.